INTERNATIONAL
SCOUT
Gold Portfolio
<u>1961-1980</u>

Compiled by
R.M.Clarke

ISBN 1 85520 305 7

BROOKLANDS BOOKS LTD.
P.O. BOX 146, COBHAM,
SURREY, KT11 1LG. UK

Printed in Hong Kong

Brooklands Books

MOTORING

B.B. ROAD TEST SERIES

Abarth Gold Portfolio 1950-1971
AC Ace & Aceca 1953-1983
Alfa Romeo Giulietta Gold Portfolio 1954-1965
Alfa Romeo Giulia Coupés 1963-1976
Alfa Romeo Giulia Coupés Gold Port. 1963-1976
Alfa Romeo Spider 1966-1990
Alfa Romeo Spider Gold Portfolio 1966-1991
Alfa Romeo Alfasud 1972-1984
Alfa Romeo Alfetta Gold Portfolio 1972-1987
Alfa Romeo Alfetta GTV6 1980-1986
Allard Gold Portfolio 1937-1959
Alvis Gold Portfolio 1919-1967
AMX & Javelin Muscle Portfolio 1968-1974
Armstrong Siddeley Gold Portfolio 1945-1960
Aston Martin Gold Portfolio 1948-1971
Aston Martin Gold Portfolio 1972-1985
Aston Martin Gold Portfolio 1985-1995
Audi Quattro Gold Portfolio 1980-1991
Austin A30 & A35 1951-1962
Austin-Healey 100 & 100/6 Gold Port. 1952-1959
Austin-Healey 3000 Ultimate Portfolio 1959-1967
Austin-Healey Sprite Gold Portfolio 1958-1971
Berkeley Sportscars Limited Edition
BMW 6 & 8 Cyl. Cars Limited Edition 1935-1960
BMW 1600 Collection No. 1 1966-1981
BMW 2002 Gold Portfolio 1968-1976
BMW 6 Cylinder Coupés & Saloons Gold P. 1969-1976
BMW 316, 318, 320 (4 cyl.) Gold Port. 1975-1990
BMW 320, 323, 325 (6 cyl.) Gold Port. 1977-1990
BMW 3 Series Gold Portfolio 1991-1997
BMW 5 Series Gold Portfolio 1981-1987
BMW 5 Series Gold Portfolio 1988-1995
BMW 6 Series Gold Portfolio 1976-1989
BMW 7 Series Performance Portfolio 1977-1986
BMW Alpina Performance Portfolio 1967-1987
BMW Alpina Performance Portfolio 1988-1998
BMW M Series Gold Portfolio 1976-1997
BMW Z3 & Z3M Limited Edition
Borgward Isabella Limited Edition
Bricklin Gold Portfolio 1974-1975
Bristol Cars Gold Portfolio 1946-1992
Buick Automobiles 1947-1960
Buick Muscle Cars 1965-1970
Cadillac Allanté 1986-1993
Cadillac Automobiles 1949-1959
Cadillac Automobiles 1960-1969
Checker Limited Edition
Chevrolet 1955-1957
Impala & SS Muscle Portfolio 1958-1972
Corvair Performance Portfolio 1959-1969
El Camino & SS Muscle Portfolio 1959-1987
Chevy II & Nova SS Muscle Portfolio 1962-1974
Chevelle & SS Muscle Portfolio 1964-1972
Caprice Limited Edition 1965-1976
Chevrolet Muscle Cars 1966-1971
Chevy Blazer 1969-1981
Camaro Muscle Portfolio 1967-1973
Chevrolet Camaro & Z-28 1973-1981
High Performance Camaros 1982-1988
Chevrolet Corvette Gold Portfolio 1953-1962
Chevrolet Corvette Sting Ray Gold Port. 1963-1967
Chevrolet Corvette Gold Portfolio 1968-1977
High Performance Corvettes 1983-1989
Chrysler 300 Gold Portfolio 1955-1970
Imperial Limited Edition 1955-1970
Valiant 1960-1962
Citroen Traction Avant Gold Portfolio 1934-1957
Citroen 2CV Ultimate Portfolio 1948-1990
Citroen DS & ID 1955-1975
Citroen DS & ID Gold Portfolio 1955-1975
Citroen SM 1970-1975
Cobras & Replicas 1962-1983
Shelby Cobra Gold Portfolio 1962-1969
Cobras & Cobra Replicas Gold Portfolio 1962-1989
Crosley & Crosley Specials Limited Edition
Cunningham Automobiles 1951-1955
Datsun Roadsters 1962-1971
Datsun 240Z & 260Z Gold Portfolio 1970-1978
Datsun 280Z & ZX 1975-1983
DeLorean Gold Portfolio 1977-1995
De Soto Limited Edition 1952-1960
Charger Muscle Portfolio 1966-1974
Dodge Viper Performance Portfolio 1990-1998
ERA Gold Portfolio 1934-1994
Excalibur Collection No.1 1952-1981
Facel Vega 1954-1964
Ferrari Limited Edition 1947-1957
Ferrari Limited Edition 1958-1963
Ferrari Dino 1965-1974
Ferrari Dino 308 & Mondial Gold Portfolio 1974-1985
Ferrari 328 348 Mondial Ultimate Portfolio 1986-94
Fiat 500 Gold Portfolio 1936-1972
Fiat 600 & 850 Gold Portfolio 1955-1972
Fiat Pininfarina 124 & 2000 Spider 1968-1985
Fiat X1/9 Gold Portfolio 1973-1989
Fiat Abarth Performance Portfolio 1972-1987
Ford Consul, Zephyr, Zodiac Mk. I & II 1950-1962
Ford Zephyr, Zodiac, Executive Mk. III & IV 1962-1971
Ford Cortina 1600E & GT 1967-1970
High Performance Capris Gold Portfolio 1969-1987
Capri Muscle Portfolio 1974-1987
High Performance Fiestas 1979-1991
Ford Escort RS & Mexico Limited Edition 1970-1979
High Performance Escorts Mk. I 1968-1974
High Performance Escorts Mk. II 1975-1980
High Performance Escorts 1980-1985
High Performance Escorts 1985-1990
High Perf. Sierras & Merkurs Gold Port. 1983-1990
Ford Automobiles 1949-1959
Ford Fairlane Performance Portfolio 1955-1970
Ford Ranchero Muscle Portfolio 1957-1979
Edsel Limited Edition 1957-1960
Falcon Performance Portfolio 1960-1970
Ford Galaxie & LTD Limited Edition 1960-1973
Ford Thunderbird 1955-1957
Ford Thunderbird 1958-1963
Ford GT40 Gold Portfolio 1964-1987
Ford Torino Limited Edition 1968-1974
Ford Bronco 4x4 Performance Portfolio 1966-1977
Ford Bronco 1978-1988
Goggomobil Limited Edition
Holden 1948-1962
Honda S500 • S600 • S800 Limited Edition 1962-1970
Honda CRX 1983-1987
Hudson Limited Edition 1946-1957
International Scout Gold Portfolio 1961-1980
Isetta Gold Portfolio 1953-1964
ISO & Bizzarrini Gold Portfolio 1962-1974
Jaguar and SS Gold Portfolio 1931-1951
Jaguar C-Type & D-Type Gold Portfolio 1951-1960
Jaguar XK120, 140, 150 Gold Portfolio 1948-1960
Jaguar Mk. VII, VIII, IX, X, 420 Gold Port. 1950-1970
Jaguar Mk. 1 & Mk. 2 Gold Portfolio 1959-1969
Jaguar E-Type Gold Portfolio 1961-1971
Jaguar E-Type V-12 1971-1975
Jaguar S-Type & 420 Limited Edition 1963-1968
Jaguar XJ12, XJ5.3, V12 Gold Portfolio 1972-1990
Jaguar XJ6 Series I & II Gold Portfolio 1968-1979
Jaguar XJ6 Series III Perf. Portfolio 1979-1986
Jaguar XJ6 Gold Portfolio 1986-1994
Jaguar XJS Gold Portfolio 1975-1988
Jaguar XJ-S V12 Ultimate Portfolio 1988-1996
Jaguar XK8 Limited Edition
Jeep CJ-5 & CJ-6 1960-1976
Jeep CJ-5 & CJ-7 4x4 Perf. Portfolio 1976-1986
Jeep Wagoneer Performance Portfolio 1963-1991
Jeep J-Series Pickups 1970-1982
Jeepster & Commando Limited Edition 1967-1973
Jeep Cherokee & Comanche Pickups
Performance Portfolio 1984-1991
Jeep Wrangler 4x4 Performance Portfolio 1987-1999
Jeep Cherokee & Grand Cherokee 4x4
Performance Portfolio 1992-1998
Jensen Interceptor Gold Portfolio 1966-1986
Jensen - Healey Limited Edition 1972-1976
Kaiser - Frazer Limited Edition 1946-1955
Lagonda Gold Portfolio 1919-1964
Lancia Aurelia & Flaminia Gold Portfolio 1950-1970
Lancia Fulvia Gold Portfolio 1963-1976
Lancia Beta Gold Portfolio 1972-1984
Lancia Delta Gold Portfolio 1979-1994
Lancia Stratos 1972-1985
Land Rover Series I 1948-1958
Land Rover Series II & IIa 1958-1971
Land Rover Series III 4x4 Perf. Portfolio 1971-1985
Land Rover 90 110 Defender Gold Portfolio 1983-1994
Land Rover Discovery 1989-1994
Land Rover Story Part One 1948-1971
Fifty Years of Selling Land Rover
Lincoln Gold Portfolio 1949-1960
Lincoln Continental 1961-1969
Lincoln Continental 1969-1976
Lotus Sports Racers Gold Portfolio 1953-1965
Lotus Seven Gold Portfolio 1957-1973
Lotus Caterham Seven Gold Portfolio 1974-1995
Lotus Elan Gold Portfolio 1962-1974
Lotus Elan & SE 1989-1992
Lotus Europa Gold Portfolio 1966-1975
Lotus Elite & Eclat 1974-1982
Lotus Elise Limited Edition
Marcos Coupés & Spyders Gold Portfolio 1960-1997
Matra Limited Edition 1965-1983
Mazda Miata MX-5 Performance Portfolio 1989-1997
Mazda Miata MX-5 Takes On The Competition
Mazda RX-7 Gold Portfolio 1978-1991
McLaren F1 Sportscar Limited Edition
Mercedes 190 & 300 SL 1954-1963
Mercedes G-Wagen 1981-1994
Mercedes S & 600 1965-1972
Mercedes S Class 1972-1979
Mercedes 230 • 250 • 280SL Gold Portfolio 1963-1971
Mercedes SLs & SLCs Gold Portfolio 1971-1989
Mercedes SLs Performance Portfolio 1989-1994
Mercury Limited Edition 1947-1959
Mercury Comet & Cyclone Limited Edition 1960-1970
Mercury Muscle Cars 1966-1971
Cougar Limited Edition 1967-1973
Messerschmitt Gold Portfolio 1954-1964
MG Gold Portfolio 1929-1939
MG TA & TC Gold Portfolio 1936-1949
MG TD & TF Gold Portfolio 1949-1955
MGA & Twin Cam Gold Portfolio 1955-1962
MG Midget Gold Portfolio 1961-1979
MGB Roadsters 1962-1980
MGB MGC & V8 Gold Portfolio 1962-1980
MGB GT 1965-1980
MGC & MGB GT V8 Limited Edition
MG Y-Type & Magnette ZA/ZB Limited Edition
MGF Limited Edition
Mini Gold Portfolio 1959-1969
Mini Gold Portfolio 1969-1980
Mini Gold Portfolio 1981-1997
High Performance Minis Gold Portfolio 1960-1973
Mini Cooper Gold Portfolio 1961-1971
Mini Moke Gold Portfolio 1964-1994
Morgan Three-Wheeler Gold Portfolio 1910-1952
Morgan Plus 4 & Four 4 Gold Portfolio 1936-1967
Morris Minor Collection No. 1 1948-1980
Shelby Mustang Muscle Portfolio 1965-1970
High Performance Mustang IIs 1974-1978
Mustang 5.0L Muscle Portfolio 1982-1993
Nash & Nash-Healey Limited Edition 1949-1957
Nash-Austin Metropolitan Gold Portfolio 1954-1962
NSU Ro80 Limited Edition
NSX Performance Portfolio 1989-1999
Oldsmobile Automobiles 1955-1963
Oldsmobile Muscle Portfolio 1964-1971
Cutlass & 4-4-2 Muscle Portfolio 1964-1974
Oldsmobile Toronado 1966-1978
Opel GT Gold Portfolio 1968-1973
Opel Manta Limited Edition 1970-1975
Packard Gold Portfolio 1946-1958
Pantera Gold Portfolio 1970-1989
Panther Gold Portfolio 1972-1990
Barracuda Muscle Portfolio 1964-1974
Pontiac Limited Edition 1949-1960
Pontiac Tempest & GTO 1961-1965
GTO Muscle Portfolio 1964-1974
Firebird & Trans-Am Muscle Portfolio 1967-1972
Firebird & Trans-Am Muscle Portfolio 1973-1981
High Performance Firebirds 1982-1988
Pontiac Fiero 1984-1988
Porsche 356 Gold Portfolio 1953-1965
Porsche 912 Limited Edition
Porsche 911 1965-1969
Porsche 911 1970-1972
Porsche 911 1973-1977
Porsche 911 SC & Turbo Gold Portfolio 1978-1983
Porsche 911 Carrera & Turbo Gold Port. 1984-1989
Porsche 911 Gold Portfolio 1990-1997
Porsche 914 Ultimate Portploio
Porsche 924 Gold Portfolio 1975-1988
Porsche 928 Performance Portfolio 1977-1994
Porsche 928 Takes On The Competition
Porsche 944 Gold Portfolio 1981-1991
Porsche 968 Limited Edition
Porsche Boxster Limited Edition
Railton & Brough Superior Gold Portfolio 1933-1950
Range Rover Gold Portfolio 1970-1985
Range Rover Gold Portfolio 1986-1995
Reliant Scimitar 1964-1986
Renault Alpine Gold Portfolio 1958-1994
Riley Gold Portfolio 1924-1939
R. R. Silver Cloud & Bentley 'S' Series Gold P. 1955-65
Rolls Royce Silver Shadow Ultimate Portfolio 1965-80
Rolls Royce & Bentley Gold Portfolio 1980-1989
Rolls Royce & Bentley Limited Edition 1990-1997
Rover P4 1949-1959
Rover 3 & 3.5 Litre Gold Portfolio 1958-1973
Rover 2000 & 2200 1963-1977
Rover 3500 & Vitesse 1976-1986
Saab Sonett Collection No.1 1966-1974
Saab Turbo 1976-1983
Studebaker Gold Portfolio 1947-1966
Studebaker Hawks & Larks 1956-1963
Avanti 1962-1990
Suzuki SJ Gold Portfolio 1971-1997
Vitara, Sidekick & Geo Tracker Perf. Port. 1988-1997
Sunbeam Tiger & Alpine Gold Portfolio 1959-1967
Toyota Land Cruiser Gold Portfolio 1956-1987
Toyota Land Cruiser 1988-1997
Toyota MR2 Gold Portfolio 1984-1997
Triumph TR2 & TR3 Gold Portfolio 1952-1961
Triumph TR4, TR5, TR250 1961-1968
Triumph TR6 Gold Portfolio 1969-1976
Triumph TR7 & TR8 Gold Portfolio 1975-1982
Triumph Herald 1959-1971
Triumph Vitesse 1962-1971
Triumph Spitfire Gold Portfolio 1962-1980
Triumph 2000, 2.5, 2500 1963-1977
Triumph GT6 Gold Portfolio 1966-1974
Triumph Stag Gold Portfolio 1970-1977
Triumph Dolomite Sprint Limited Edition
TVR Gold Portfolio 1959-1986
TVR Performance Portfolio 1986-1994
VW Beetle Gold Portfolio 1935-1967
VW Beetle Gold Portfolio 1968-1991
VW Beetle Collection No.1 1970-1982
VW Karmann Ghia 1955-1982
VW Bus, Camper, Van 1954-1967
VW Bus, Camper, Van 1968-1979
VW Bus, Camper, Van 1979-1989
VW Scirocco 1974-1981
VW Golf GTI 1976-1986
Volvo PV444 & PV544 1945-1965
Volvo 120 Amazon Ultimate Portfolio
Volvo 1800 Gold Portfolio 1960-1973
Volvo 140 & 160 Series Gold Portfolio 1966-1975
Forty Years of Selling Volvo
Westfield Limited Edition

B.B. ROAD & TRACK SERIES

Road & Track on Alfa Romeo 1964-1970
Road & Track on Alfa Romeo 1971-1976
Road & Track on Aston Martin 1962-1990
R & T on Auburn Cord and Duesenburg 1952-84
Road & Track on Audi & Auto Union 1952-1980
Road & Track on Audi & Auto Union 1980-1986
Road & Track on Austin Healey 1953-1970
Road & Track on BMW Cars 1966-1974
Road & Track on BMW Cars 1975-1978
Road & Track on BMW Cars 1979-1983
R & T on Cobra, Shelby & Ford GT40 1962-1992
Road & Track on Corvette 1953-1967
Road & Track on Corvette 1968-1982
Road & Track on Corvette 1982-1986
Road & Track on Corvette 1986-1990
Road & Track on Ferrari 1975-1981
Road & Track on Ferrari 1981-1984
Road & Track on Ferrari 1984-1988
Road & Track on Fiat Sports Cars 1968-1987
Road & Track on Jaguar 1950-1960
Road & Track on Jaguar 1961-1968
Road & Track on Jaguar 1968-1974
Road & Track on Jaguar 1974-1982
Road & Track on Jaguar 1983-1989
Road & Track on Lamborghini 1964-1985
Road & Track on Lotus 1972-1983
R & T on Mazda RX-7 & MX-5 Miata 1986-1991
Road & Track on Mercedes 1952-1962
Road & Track on Mercedes 1963-1970
Road & Track on Mercedes 1971-1979
Road & Track on Mercedes 1980-1987
Road & Track on MG Sports Cars 1949-1961
Road & Track on MG Sports Cars 1962-1980
R & T on Nissan 300-ZX & Turbo 1984-1989
Road & Track on Pontiac 1960-1983
Road & Track on Porsche 1951-1967
Road & Track on Porsche 1968-1971
Road & Track on Porsche 1972-1975
Road & Track on Porsche 1975-1978
Road & Track on Porsche 1979-1982
Road & Track on Porsche 1985-1988
R & T on Rolls Royce & Bentley 1950-1965
R & T on Rolls Royce & Bentley 1966-1984
Road & Track on Saab 1972-1992
R & T on Toyota Sports & GT Cars 1966-1984
R & T on Triumph Sports Cars 1953-1967
R & T on Triumph Sports Cars 1967-1974
R & T on Triumph Sports Cars 1974-1982
Road & Track on Volkswagen 1951-1968
Road & Track on Volkswagen 1968-1978
Road & Track on Volkswagen 1978-1985
Road & Track on Volvo 1957-1974
Road & Track on Volvo 1977-1994
Road & Track - Henry Manney at Large & Abroad
Road & Track - Peter Egan "At Large"
Road & Track - Best of PS

B.B. PRACTICAL CLASSICS SERIES

PC on Austin A40 Restoration
PC on Land Rover Restoration
PC on Midget/Sprite Restoration
PC on MGB Restoration
PC on Sunbeam Rapier Restoration
PC on Triumph Herald/Vitesse

RACING & THE LAND SPEED RECORD

The Land Speed Record 1930-1939
The Land Speed Record 1940-1962
The Carrera Panamericana Mexico - 1950-1954
Le Mans - The Bentley & Alfa Years - 1923-1939
Le Mans - The Jaguar Years - 1949-1957
Le Mans - The Ferrari Years - 1958-1965
Le Mans - The Ford & Matra Years - 1966-1974
Le Mans - The Porsche Years - 1975-1982
Le Mans - The Porsche & Jaguar Years - 1983-91
Le Mans - The Peugeot & Porsche Years - 1992-99
Mille Miglia - The Alfa & Ferrari Years - 1927-1951
Mille Miglia - The Ferrari & Mercedes Years - 1952-57
Targa Florio - The Post War Years - 1948-1973
Targa Florio - The Porsche & Ferrari Years - 1955-1964
Targa Florio - The Porsche Years - 1965-1973

B.B. CAR AND DRIVER SERIES

Car and Driver on BMW 1955-1977
Car and Driver on Corvette 1978-1982
Car and Driver on Corvette 1983-1988
C and D on Datsun Z 1600 & 2000 1966-1984
Car and Driver on Ferrari 1955-1962
Car and Driver on Ferrari 1963-1975
Car and Driver on Ferrari 1976-1983
Car and Driver on Mopar 1956-1967
Car and Driver on Mustang 1964-1972
Car and Driver on Pontiac 1961-1975
Car and Driver on Porsche 1955-1962
Car and Driver on Porsche 1963-1970
Car and Driver on Porsche 1970-1976
Car and Driver on Porsche 1977-1981
Car and Driver on Porsche 1982-1986
Car and Driver on Volvo 1955-1986

B.B. HOT ROD 'ENGINE' SERIES

Chevy 265 & 283
Chevy 302 & 327
Chevy 348 & 409
Chevy 350 & 400
Chevy 396 & 427
Chevy 454 thru 512
Chrysler Hemi
Chrysler 273, 318, 340 & 360
Chrysler 361, 383, 400, 413, 426 & 440
Ford 289, 302, Boss 302 & 351W
Ford 351C & Boss 351
Ford Big Block

B.B. RESTORATION & GUIDE SERIES

Auto Restoration Tips & Techniques
Basic Bodywork Tips & Techniques
BMW 2002 - A Comprehensive Guide
BMW '02 Restoration Guide
Classic Camaro Restoration
Chevrolet High Performance Tips & Techniques
Chevy Engine Swapping Tips & Techniques
Chevy-GMC Pickup Repair
Chrysler Engine Swapping Tips & Techniques
Engine Swapping Tips & Techniques
Land Rover Restoration Tips & Techniques
MG 'T' Series Restoration Guide
MGA Restoration Guide
Mustang Restoration Tips & Techniques

MOTORCYCLING

B.B. ROAD TEST SERIES

AJS & Matchless Gold Portfolio 1945-1966
BMW Motorcycles Gold Portfolio 1950-1971
BMW Motorcycles Gold Portfolio 1971-1976
BSA Singles Gold Portfolio 1945-1963
BSA Singles Gold Portfolio 1964-1974
BSA Twins A7 & A10 Gold Portfolio 1946-1962
BSA Twins A50 & A65 Gold Portfolio 1962-1973
BSA & Triumph Triples Gold Portfolio 1968-1976
Ducati Gold Portfolio 1960-1973
Ducati Gold Portfolio 1974-1978
Ducati Gold Portfolio 1978-1982
Harley-Davidson Sportsters Perf. Port. 1965-1976
Harley-Davidson Super Glide Perf. Port. 1971-1981
Harley-Davidson FXR Series Perf. Port. 1982-1992
Honda CB750 Gold Portfolio 1969-1978
Honda CB500 & 550 Fours Perf. Port. 1971-1977
Honda CB350 & 400 Fours Perf. Port. 1972-1978
Honda Gold Wing Gold Portfolio 1975-1995
Honda CBX 1000 Gold Portfolio 1978-1982
Kawasaki Z1 900 Performance Portfolio 1972-1977
Laverda Gold Portfolio 1967-1977
Moto Guzzi Gold Portfolio 1949-1973
Norton Commando Gold Portfolio 1968-1977
Suzuki GT750 Performance Portfolio 1971-1977
Triumph Bonneville Gold Portfolio 1959-1983
Vincent Gold Portfolio 1945-1980
Yamaha RD350/400 Performance Portfolio 1972-79

B.B. CYCLE WORLD SERIES

Cycle World on BMW 1974-1980
Cycle World on BMW 1981-1986
Cycle World on Ducati 1982-1991
Cycle World on Harley-Davidson 1962-1968
Cycle World on Harley-Davidson 1978-1983
Cycle World on Harley-Davidson 1983-1987
Cycle World on Harley-Davidson 1987-1990
Cycle World on Harley-Davidson 1990-1992
Cycle World on Honda 1962-1967
Cycle World on Honda 1968-1971
Cycle World on Honda 1971-1974
Cycle World on Husqvarna 1966-1976
Cycle World on Husqvarna 1977-1984
Cycle World on Kawasaki 1966-1971
Cycle World on Kawasaki Off-Road Bikes 1972-1979
Cycle World on Kawasaki Street Bikes 1972-1976
Cycle World on Norton 1962-1971
Cycle World on Suzuki 1962-1970
Cycle World on Suzuki Off-Road Bikes 1971-1976
Cycle World on Suzuki Street Bikes 1971-1976
Cycle World on Triumph 1967-1972
Cycle World on Yamaha 1962-1969
Cycle World on Yamaha Off-Road Bikes 1970-1974
Cycle World on Yamaha Street Bikes 1970-1974

MILITARY

B.B. MILITARY VEHICLES SERIES

Complete WW2 Military Jeep Manual
Dodge Military Vehicles No. 1 1940-1945
Hail To The Jeep
Military & Civilian Amphibians 1940-1990
Off Road Jeeps: Civilian & Military 1944-1971
US Military Vehicles 1941-1945
US Army Military Vehicles WW2-TM9-2800
VW Kubelwagen Military Portfolio 1940-1990
WW2 Jeep Military Portfolio 1941-1945

20/21099

Brooklands
Books

CONTENTS

ACKNOWLEDGEMENTS

At Brooklands Books, we are always guided in our choice of new titles by popular demand. Interest in the International Scout has grown considerably in recent years as enthusiasts everywhere come to recognise what an important and yet practical vehicle it was - so here is our contribution to their hobby.

Like the other Brooklands Books titles, this one depends for its existence on the generous co-operation of the world's leading publishers of motoring magazines. Our sincere thanks on this occasion go to *Bushdriver, Car and Driver, Car Life, Four Wheeler, Mechanix Illustrated, Motor, Motor Life, Motor Trend, Off Road Fun Cars, ORV, Overlander, Popular Mechanics, PV4, 4 Wheel and Off Road* and *4x4*. We are also grateful to motoring writer James Taylor for agreeing to write a brief introduction to this book.

R.M. Clarke

The International Harvester Company of Chicago was best known for its trucks before 1961. In that year, however, it introduced a new type of vehicle - a light cross-country machine with optional four-wheel drive which it called the Scout. This was the first serious challenge to the established Jeep range, and it quickly caught on: more than 35,000 examples of the new vehicle were sold in 1961 to make it International's biggest-selling line!

Over the next decade, the Scout did not change fundamentally, but its success inspired others to enter the sport-utility market which had grown up in its wake. Ford introduced the Bronco, Chevrolet came up with the Blazer ..... and even on the other side of the Atlantic, the British Rover Company picked up on the concept and came up with the Range Rover in 1970.

The Scout, then, was a pioneering vehicle in many ways. It was also very able as a cross-country machine, and its ruggedness and durability have ensured that many examples have survived for enthusiasts to enjoy today. There is a wide variety of models to choose from, ranging from the capacious Traveler to rugged pick-ups, and embracing deliberately more sporty models such as the Scout II which was introduced in 1977. There should have been a Scout III - and such a vehicle had been designed - but International decided to drop its 4x4 at the end of the 1970s and to concentrate on its other interests. If the company could only have foreseen the worldwide boom in sport-utility vehicles during the 1980s, the Scout would be with us still.....

James Taylor

PASSING IN REVIEW on Fort Wayne assembly line: four-wheel-drive chassis, featuring box frame, four-cylinder engine.

THE SCOUT

A new kind of compact has Fort Wayne agog. Here's why.

AT PATTERSON FLETCHER, one of Fort Wayne's largest department stores, people stopped to peer at a canvas-shrouded shape in the lobby. "Here it is!" announced a sign. "The new International Harvester Scout. First retail delivery in the United States."

With the Scout's unveiling just days away, curiosity was mounting all over Fort Wayne. So was optimism. Local orders for the all-purpose compact were already sizable. Early returns from some of the Scout's 5,000 dealers also were heartening. In La Moure, North Dakota, Farmer Albert Smith watched a movie showing the Scout in action, promptly picked up his telephone, canceled his order for a Chevrolet pickup, then signed up for the Scout. In Dallas, Dairyman Jacob Metzger and his wife dropped in on their IH dealer, saw a series of Scout pictures, were so impressed they bought one on the spot. Meanwhile, in Fort Wayne, assembly lines shifted into high gear. TODAY was there, too, to give its readers this first look at the Scout.

ON PARADE. Scout rides smartly over gravel test area. Exhaust pipe, muffler, wiring are tucked into frame, safe from stumps and rocks.

THE SCOUT

A tester's testimonial: "She's

tough as a hickory nut."

THE FIRST SCOUT — a trim, metallic-blue model — rolled off the assembly line on a Friday afternoon. The next day, Works Manager Henry Torgerson whipped it through a vigorous 200-mile workout, bounced it over rut-filled back roads, roared up and down steep hills, slogged through muddy fields. His delighted verdict: "She's tough as a hickory nut."

All in all, it was a busy weekend for Torgerson. When he wasn't behind the wheel, he was eagerly showing off the Scout to friends, neighbors, "just about everybody who wanted to listen." Torgerson had plenty to brag about: the Scout's engine — 90 horsepower, four cylinders (actually one half of a Harvester V-8 truck engine); the Scout's versatility — removable steel top, removable windows and doors, fold-down windshield, attachments that enable it to do everything from plowing snow to digging postholes; the Scout's price — two-wheel-drive $1,598, four-wheel-drive $1,948 (plus local and federal taxes, f.o.b. Fort Wayne).

When it came to performance, however, Torgerson didn't waste words. His standard invitation was "Hop in. Try her yourself." "I'd just sit next to 'em real quiet," Togerson beams. "After a few minutes, they'd do their own talking."

WHEN A CHASSIS meets a body. Assemblies consist of two 220-foot parallel lines flowing in opposite directions.

NEXT STEP: men fasten chassis bolts. Pickup body is five feet long; overall Scout length is less than 13 feet. Wheelbase measures 100 inches.

SCOUT MOVES UP body assembly line. Passenger compartment seats three, pickup body can seat six more on wheel housing benches. Other Scout features: removable windows, doors and steel top, fold-down windshield.

"SCOUTSTANDING" was test engineers' performance rating for all-purpose compact. Five experimental Scout models operated under rugged conditions for combined total of 200,000 miles, suffered no breakdowns.

MOUNTAIN-CLIMBING SCOUT scoots over 90 percent grade. Powerful four-cylinder engine is actually one half of performance-proved V-8 t...

THE SCOUT / *"Darned right I'm buying one. I've seen what goes into her."*

SPRAY FOR A SCOUT in new Fort Wayne plant's two-stage paint booth. Scout is available in six colors: white, red, green, blue, yellow and tan.

...e. Scout will be sold and serviced through nationwide network of International dealers and truck branches.

FITTINGLY ENOUGH, the place where the Scout is built is every bit as impressive as the Scout itself. Airy, glistening, masterfully laid out (a newspaper called it "an automobile manufacturer's dream"), the 60-acre factory is a former U.S. Rubber Plant purchased only last April. Converted in a whirlwind operation, it was turning out Scouts by December.

Just as appropriately, the men who work in the plant are among the Scout's most fervent boosters. And their enthusiasm is more than talk. They're buying Scouts, lots of them. "I'm getting one. Darned right I am," says Foreman Phil Ware. "I've seen what goes into this baby. It's got everything —power, economy, design. I've been in this business more than 20 years and I've never seen anything like it."

PEERING ENGINEERS study Scout's body-chassis assembly techniques.

END OF THE LINE Completed Scouts get final once-over. Plant is turning out more than 100 Scouts a day.

THE SCOUT

OPEN AIR ASSEMBLY LINE. Road Test Engineers
Ray Miller (left) and Ralph Spaw
convert Scout from open model without top,
windows or doors to enclosed passenger
runabout. At left, they put on outside-hinged
40-pound doors. Then they raise folddown
windshield, add window frames and sliding glass.
Finally, they replace cab roof (below).
To do the job, they pushed in four pins,
tightened 22 capscrews; it took less than
10 minutes. Snowplows, winches and other
auxiliary equipment can be driven from either
end of the four-wheel-drive model.
Shown on ground in picture at right:
an optional, full-length Travel-Top that
encloses both driver compartment and body.

SCOUT PERFORMS same jobs as four competitors combined. Left to right: Corvair, Falcon Ranchero, Volkswagen panel truck, Willys Jeep.

"The market's got to be there. This baby does everything!"

THE MOST SIGNIFICANT THING about the Scout's pre-production tests was that nothing significant went wrong. For months, test engineers pummeled and probed, unleashed every conceivable punishment on five hand-built experimental models. Between them, the five Scouts racked up 200,000 miles. They all held up. "A remarkable machine," said Test Supervisor Jack Lineberry. "We ran one around our two-mile testing oval 1,000 times. That oval includes a half mile of Belgian blocks — rough, jagged cobblestones. The Scout didn't have a single major mishap. Now, any engineer will tell you, that's phenomenal performance. We test engineers don't

often get carried away. We've usually got our reservations. But not on the Scout. I've never seen the guys so enthusiastic. And talk about a market, say, it's just *got* to be there. I don't see how it can miss."

Market appeal should, indeed, be widespread, company sales officials agree. One of the Scout's greatest assets, they say, is its versatility — a car for family, business or the sportsman; for the farm and for the city. "An important milestone for International Harvester," one calls it. "For the first time in our history, we're selling a vehicle that almost everyone can use."

11

The Scout

New Rival for the Jeep, Land-Rover and Gipsy Introduced by International Harvester

NEAT in appearance but strictly practical, the Scout is shown here in four-wheel-drive form and with the three-seat cab. A two-wheel-driven version is also offered, and the body can be used open or fitted with a full-length steel top.

HALVING their V-8 engine in the manner pioneered on the Pontiac Tempest, International Harvester have produced this 2½-litre "four" which leans to the right at 45°.

POWERED by what is virtually the right-hand half of their own 5-litre V-8 lorry engine, the Scout is a new model from the Fort Wayne, Indiana factory of International Harvester Co. which will compete against Willys Jeeps, Land-Rovers, Austin Gipsies and similar models in world markets.

Over-square, the 2½-litre engine is a modern pushrod o.h.v. design, with the exhaust valves at an angle to the inlet valves. Heavy at 542 lb. complete with accessories, this engine gives 86 b.h.p. net at 4,400 r.p.m., and with its 5-bearing crankshaft is said easily to have passed a 1,000-hour full-power endurance test. A compression ratio of 8.2/1 is designed for American regular-grade petrol of 93 (Research Method) octane rating.

Alternative versions of the Scout have either 4-wheel drive or rear-wheel drive only, the same 4.27 top gear being used in either case: 2-wheel-drive examples, with an I-beam front axle and optionally a spin-limiting differential, are lighter by about 200 lb., more softly sprung, and have a rather more compact turning circle. When 4-wheel drive is specified, a transfer-box behind the 3-speed synchromesh gearbox can provide an extra reduction-ratio of 2.46/1 when required.

One basic body style (in any of six colours) is used for the Scout, an open pick-up with the wheel-arches extended forward to form inward-facing benches, beneath one or both of which a fuel tank of 11 U.S. gallons capacity is accommodated. The tail gate can be lowered completely or held horizontally as an extension of the 60-inch body floor. Either a three-seat all-steel cab or a full-length roof can be added to the body, or for rough service the windscreen can be folded flat and the sliding glass side-windows removed from the front doors.

To suit the very varied jobs which a vehicle of this type may be required to do, International Harvester list a big variety of optional extras. Models with 4-wheel drive can have front and rear power take-offs, or a front winch, and will operate a snow plough. Other options include interior heating, arm rests and radio for the passengers: flashing turn signals, a rear bumper, a towing attachment, an oversize battery, a second fuel tank, and special tyres are available to order.

Specification

Engine

Cylinders...	4 in line, inclined at 45° to right, with forged 5-bearing crankshaft.
Bore and stroke	98.4 mm. × 81.76 mm. (3.875 in. × 3.22 in.).
Cubic capacity ...	2,489 c.c. (151.84 cu. in.).
Piston area	47.1 sq. in.
Compression ratio	8.2/1.
Valvegear	Overhead valves operated by self-adjusting hydraulic tappets, pushrods and rockers from gear-driven camshaft.
Carburation	Holley single-choke downdraught carburetter, fed by mechanical pump, from 9-gallon tank on left of body.
Ignition ...	12-volt coil, centrifugal and vacuum timing control.
Lubrication	Floating oil pump intake, and full-flow filter.
Cooling ...	Water cooling with pump, fan and thermostat.
Electrical system	12-volt 40 amp. hr. battery charged by 25-amp. generator.
Maximum power (net)	86 b.h.p. (93.4 gross b.h.p.) at 4,400 r.p.m., equivalent to 102 lb./sq. in. b.m.e.p. at 2,140 ft./min. piston speed and 1.82 b.h.p. per sq. in. of piston area.
Maximum torque (net)	137.3 lb. ft. (142.7 gross) at 2,400 r.p.m., equivalent to 137 lb./sq. in. b.m.e.p. at 1,285 ft./min. piston speed.

Transmission

Clutch ...	10-in. single dry plate.
Gearbox ...	3-speed synchromesh with direct drive on top gear; transfer gearbox giving lower range of ratios used only with optional 4-wheel drive.
Overall ratios ...	4.27, 7.90 and 14.23 (low range: 10.50, 19.44 and 35.0).
Propeller shaft ...	Open tubular (two on 4-wheel-drive version).
Final drive ...	11/47 hypoid bevel and optional Powr-Lok differential.

Chassis

Brakes ...	Hydraulic; mechanical parking brake on rear wheels.
Front suspension	40 in. × 1¾ in. semi-elliptic springs and rigid axle (beam type on 2-wheel driven version) with telescopic dampers.
Rear suspension...	46 in. × 1¾ in. semi-elliptic springs, rigid axle and telescopic dampers.
Wheels and tyres	Bolt-on disc wheels: 6.50-15 tubeless tyres with 2-wheel drive, or 6.00-16 tubed tyres with 4-wheel drive.
Steering ...	Cam and roller gear ahead of front axle.

Dimensions

Length ...	Overall 12 ft. 10 in.; wheelbase 8 ft. 4 in.
Width ...	Overall 5 ft. 8⅝ in.
Height ...	5 ft. 7 in.; ground clearance 9 in.
Turning circle	38 ft. (over bumpers) with 2-wheel drive or 43 ft. with 4-wheel drive.
Kerb weight ...	24¼ cwt. with 2-wheel drive or 26¼ cwt. with 4-wheel drive (without fuel but with oil, water, tools, spare wheel, etc.).

Effective Gearing

Top gear ratio ...	18.4 m.p.h. at 1,000 r.p.m. and 34.3 m.p.h. at 1,000 ft./min. piston speed.
Maximum torque	2,400 r.p.m. corresponds to approx. 44 m.p.h. in top gear.
Maximum power	4,400 r.p.m. corresponds to approx. 81 m.p.h. in top gear.
Probable top gear	280 lb./ton approx. for 2-wheel drive model or 240 lb./ton approx. for 4-wheel drive model (computed by The Motor from manufacturer's figures for torque, gear ratio and kerb weight, with allowances for 3½ cwt. load, 10% losses and 60 lb./ton drag).

CAR LIFE ROAD TEST
INTERNATIONAL HARVESTER SCOUT

International Harvester hopes that this specialized vehicle will have general appeal—with that in mind, we set out to discover if the company was backing a loser. The results were surprising.

We discovered that the Scout is not what it first appeared to be—merely a re-hash of the old WW II "jeep." There's much more to this 100-inch wheelbase goatmobile than at first meets the eye.

To start with, it doesn't ride as harshly as its short, high and narrow exterior dimensions might lead you to expect. Sure enough, the semi-elliptic leaf springs are designed with stiff enough rates to keep the Scout from bottoming out on even the most emphatic "thank you, ma'm," but even with the driver as the only occupant, the ride was still more than just acceptable for a vehicle of this type. Direct acting shocks damp rebound so that, at least, you feel each bump only once!

Cruising ability was the next surprise the Scout had to offer us. Although the rear axle ratio of 4.27:1 is about 25% greater (more engine revs per mile) than the average passenger car carries nowadays, we found no difficulty in keeping up with the fast-moving traffic that abounds in Southern California. On our way out to the desert (that's how far you have to go to find bad roads out here) we had ample opportunity to find out what speeds seemed to keep the Scout's 4-cylinder powerplant the happiest. Although a top of 80 honest mph would no doubt be possible from a completely broken-in example of this make, ours was still a little stiff, and didn't quite make it, although the speedo had just enough error that we could hit an *indicated* 80 at will. That, however, is *not* a happy speed in a Scout. Neither, for that matter, is 75, but we found an indicated 70 (approximately 65 actual) to be quite acceptable, and since that rate of travel precisely coincides with the California basic speed law, that's the pace the Scout was run during most of its highway travel while in our possession.

While running the little devil at varying rates of speed during our initial "get acquainted" period, we had a chance to put its handling ability to an unusually severe test. We encountered a local phenomenon known as a "Santa Ana Wind," wherein the normal from-the-sea-toward-the-land direction of the prevailing breeze is not only reversed, but substantially intensified. At 70 mph under these conditions, tooling the Scout was reminiscent of approximately twice that velocity in a hot-rod roadster —in other words, far from a "hands off" proposition, but not dangerous, just spooky. In calm air, the Scout should exhibit handling qualities at its highest cruising speeds to satisfy almost anyone.

Not wishing to be responsible for this brand new vehicle having its paint and glass sandblasted by the desert wind mentioned earlier, we cut our run to the Mojave short, testing the Scout's ability to rough it by several extemporaneous short-cuts over to another main highway leading back toward our starting point. During these excursions down roads that only qualify as such under the loosest terminology, we found that none of IHC's claims for roadability for the Scout are exaggerated—indeed, only a 4-wheel drive model could have exhibited any greater "go-anywhere" ability.

But even more surprises were in store for us—both from the Scout and from the weatherman. As it often does in this neck of the woods, a reversal of wind direction is followed by a rain squall and, as recorded by our alert

photographer, this gave us an unexpected opportunity to check out the Scout for weather-tightness. At this point, we discovered the first (and only major) flaw in the Scout. Frankly, with the short-top cab installed, it leaks like a sieve. After one fast pass through a flooded section of road for the photographer's benefit, the driver was sharing the cab with several sloshing pints of water and was

Yet we're compelled by honesty to state that the Scout does leak, albeit under pressure. Whether or not the full-length top offered as an option (it extends over the bed, making a sedan out of a truck) will also leak we don't know, but suspect it would be little, if any, dryer.

On the plus side of the ledger, the Scout had another surprise for us—its fuel economy. In spite of bucking winds, making high speed runs, acceleration tests, etc., our first fill-up showed a consumption of 22.5 miles per gallon. We therefore rate it as having 18-22 habits, since slogging along in the lower gears (as would be required in really rough country) would increase the fuel flow. As we see it, that's mighty economical.

This focused our attention on the source of this economical power. Admittedly half a V-8 (à la Tempest), the powerplant of the Scout is a 152-cubic-inch slant four of undisputably International Harvester parentage, as the V-8 they "carved up" to make it is one of their most popular models. Of ohv design, it is smoother than you might expect from a "4-barrel," and delivers great gobs of torque at ridiculously low rpm, yet doesn't object (at least not *too* strenuously) to being momentarily wound up to 4500 rpm, as we did to get our best acceleration figures. This type of versatility, coupled with the aforementioned economy, makes this a highly desirable powerplant in our book. Add the built-in dependability handed down from this little four's parent V-8, and you've got trouble-free power throughout a broad rpm range.

A 10-inch clutch and a super-sturdy 3-speed floorshift gearbox take the torque back to the conventional rear axle. If your No. 1 car is equipped with power steering and your hobby isn't weight lifting, you're in for a surprise the first time you pry a Scout out of low and head for second. What Charles Atlas says he'll do for you in just 15 minutes a day is nothing compared with what a little gearbox drill in a Scout will do for your right deltoid.

thoroughly soaked himself. When asked if he could provide "just one more" (when didn't a photographer ask that?) he replied, "Why not, I'm already in the pool!"

In all fairness, it should be pointed out that we've yet to see a removable top on any car that didn't leak, and that the blast we took through the water for the photographer was equivalent to parking under a small waterfall.

This, plus the heavy-for-a-car-of-this-weight (2800 lb) steering makes this a real man's car. The ladies may think it's cute, but they aren't going to think it's fun after they've grunted it around the block a few times.

Which brings us to an interesting subject—just what *is* the Scout's place in the general automotive market? Aside from its obvious appeal to farmers, ranchers and fleet operators whose vehicles must rough it, such as to far-flung outposts of the telephone companies, who is going to buy the Scout?

Well, we thought perhaps *you* might—and don't look so surprised. Outdoors is big business in America today. Aside from the big boom in boating, camping equipment sales are up like never before. Why? Because living in such close proximity to each other seems to be giving some of us sort of an unclassified (as yet) type of claustro-

SPECIFICATIONS

List price	$1751
Price, as tested	1879
Curb weight, lb	2800
Test weight	3100
distribution, %	55/45
Tire size	6.50-15
Tire capacity, lb	4000
Brake lining area	139
Engine type	4 cyl, ohv
Bore & stroke	3.88 x 3.219
Displacement, cc	2492
cu in	152
Compression ratio	8.19
Bhp @ rpm	87 @ 4000
equivalent mph	74.5
Torque, lb-ft	135 @ 2400
equivalent mph	44.6

GEAR RATIOS

4th ( ), overall	n.a.
3rd (1.00)	4.27
2nd (1.85)	7.90
1st (3.33)	14.2

DIMENSIONS

Wheelbase, in	100
Tread, f and r	55.1
Over-all length, in	154
width	68.6
height	67.0
equivalent vol, cu ft	410
Frontal area, sq ft	25.6
Ground clearance, in	9.0
Steering ratio, o/a	n.a.
turns, lock to lock	4.6
turning circle, ft	38.0
Hip room, front	59.0
Hip room, rear	n.a.
Pedal to seat back	39.0
Floor to ground	15.0
Luggage vol, cu ft	n.a.

PERFORMANCE

Top speed (est), mph	80.0
best timed run	78.3
3rd ( )	
2nd (4500)	45
1st (4500)	25

FUEL CONSUMPTION

Normal range, mpg	18/22

ACCELERATION

0-30 mph, sec	5.5
0-40	9.0
0-50	14.0
0-60	20.1
0-70	28.7
0-80	
0-100	
Standing ¼ mile	21.7
speed at end	62

PULLING POWER

3rd, lb/ton @ mph	220 @ 39
2nd	380 @ 32
1st	480 @ 19
Total drag at 60 mph, lb	250

SPEEDOMETER ERROR

30 mph, actual	27.3
60 mph	55.0
80 mph	76.9

CALCULATED DATA

Lb/hp (test wt)	35.6
Cu ft/ton mile	91.5
Mph/1000 rpm	18.6
Engine revs/mile	3220
Piston travel, ft/mile	1725
Car Life wear index	55.5

ACCELERATION & COASTING

SS¼

3rd

2nd

1st

MPH

5   10   15   20   25   30   35   40   45

ELAPSED TIME IN SECONDS

phobia, and only getting out in the boondocks occasionally is going to cure it. For this, the Scout is literally made to order—its extra ground clearance and rough-and-ready nature are perfect for those back-country roads.

Picture yourself as the head of a two-car family, a conventional family hauler (station wagon?) and a Scout. You leave the wagon with your wife, who needs its capacity for shopping and ferrying your offspring to and from school, the piano lessons, etc. *You,* feeling every inch the man in the Marlboro ad, wend your way to work in your rugged, he-man Scout. Comes the week-end, and with wife riding shotgun and the nippers in the back, you're off to the only kind of togetherness that really makes sense—that is, the kind where you and yours are the only humans for umpteen miles around.

If you fear for your moppets' health riding back there in a 65-mph breeze, then be a big man and spend a little extra for the full-length top we mentioned. At Scout's under-two-grand base price, the serious outdoorsman should be able to afford it—and look at the mileage you'll get during the week that your full-sized wagon won't give you!

Seriously, there's just one more thing we'd like to mention about the Scout, and that's its rugged styling. As sturdy looking as it is, nobody, but nobody, cuts you off in this one. For some reason, it packs more "bluffsmanship" in traffic than cars twice its weight. Try one on your own regular route and see if we aren't right. ∎

the all-new SCOUT

"It's a helluva buy," says Uncle Tom after a rugged wring-out of International Harvester's unusual "all purpose" vehicle.

By Tom McCahill

UNCLE TOM poses with two models of Scout. White-bodied job in rear with a standard steel top is 4x4 rig. One in front with whitewall tires has a two-wheel drive.

L EWIS and Clark would have given at least 87 beaver pelts and their last axe for one of International Harvester's new "all-purpose" Scouts. The 100-inch wheelbase Scout comes in either a two- or four-wheel-drive package, offers several body combinations and, unlike most light-duty vehicles of its kind, can be had in any one of five standard colors (red, metallic green, metallic blue, yellow or tan).

The Scout has more innovations than a Chinese New Year's punch and lots of little features never seen before in this type vehicle. The standard steel cab top can be removed by taking off ten easy-to-reach bolts. The full-length steel Travel-Top, which encloses both the driver's compartment and the payload space and which can be bought for an

extra $128.52, requires the unwrenching of a mere 21 bolts to remove the whole thing including the rear door and window. Both side doors on the Scout can also be removed easily by taking out the specially-designed hinge pins. In addition, the windshield can be folded forward, making the Scout an excellent hunting or reconnaissance car. Also available as an extra on the four-wheel-drive job are two species of snow plows and an "Angledozer" in case you have the urge to push earth around with your Scout.

I've been a four-wheel-drive nut for years, as I do a lot of hunting and back-woods exploring whenever I get the chance. For this work the Scout has an added feature rarely found in other 4x4 rigs. For an extra 35 bucks it (as

TRAVEL-TOP has side and rear windows. It can be purchased for additional $128.52.

SCOUT equipped with Travel-Top has cargo space five feet long, 54 inches wide at top.

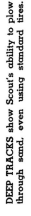

DEEP TRACKS show Scout's ability to plow through sand, even using standard tires.

TUG-OF-WAR between Scout and Jeep (chained back to back) ended up in a tie.

est, which uses half of a Pontiac V8, many Scout parts are interchangeable with the International Harvester V8's, making service from coast to coast fairly simple.

My particular interest was in the four-wheel-drive job which lists at $2,128.84 F.O.B. Fort Wayne, Ind. (Factory price of the two-wheel-drive model is $1,750.84.) Unfortunately, the Scout they sent me wasn't equipped with Powr-Lok—and the tire size of 6.00 x 16 was not too good a choice; a 7.00 or a 7.50 tire would have given a lot more traction. Now, we had been experiencing a dry spell in Florida and there were no mucklands wet enough for a good traction test, so I headed up the beach from Daytona until we started hitting what they call locally a "coquina" surface. Unlike the anvil-hard sands of Daytona Beach, just a few miles north at certain times a coquina covering four to six inches thick seems to make a pocket over the hard sand underneath—and there is usually water in between. Coquina consists of coral, shells and various other little nasty things. It doesn't pack like sand and when you get close to the water it bears a certain resemblance to thickened quicksand. In other words, you can stand still with both feet planted on this stuff and without moving a muscle you'll be in water up to your shins in a matter of minutes.

It was toward this stretch of coquina that we headed. I took the Land Rover along as a rescue car. As long as we kept up a head of speed, meaning 25-30 mph, we glided over it, only making tracks an inch or two deep. The slower we went, the deeper we sank—and this was my undoing. As the coquina started to get worse, I made a slow loop toward the ocean in order to turn back. This brought me to a narrow sluice where water was running off. To avoid bathing the brand-new Scout chassis in a spray of salt water, I slowed down to about four to five [Continued on page 52]

[Continued on page 52]

FOUR-WHEEL-drive job reveled plenty of boff in a rugged climb over sand dunes.

FITTINGS are "pleasant but not posh," Tom says. He suggests shorter steering post.

---

well as the 4x2) can be ordered with a Powr-Lok rear axle, which is known to many as a "limited slip." I asked why this couldn't also be available for the front axle which would then make the car a true four-wheel drive. They told me that the front-axle manufacturer thought the stress might be too much and wouldn't guarantee it.

Anyway, in a four-wheel-drive Scout equipped with Powr-Lok you do have positive three-wheel drive, which is one more than I get with my Jeep or Land Rover. On several occasions I've been mired in bottomless goo with both my Jeep and Land Rover when the left wheels, front and rear, were spinning while the right wheels remained motionless. For our six readers in Kasavubuland who aren't hip to such things, let me explain what this is all about. My Land Rover, when traveling in a

straight line on a dry road in four-wheel drive, has drive force at all four wheels. Thus, the only time I have real four-wheel drive is when I don't have it! This seems pretty silly but those are the facts, ma'am. When the going gets gooey, icy and rough, the only assurance I have is that one wheel in the front and one in the rear will turn, and not in any particular order. The 4x4 Scout with Powr-Lok can guarantee you three-wheel traction forward, which is a 50 per cent improvement.

Two Scouts were sent to me in Florida: one a four-wheel drive with the standard steel cab top, the other a two-wheel twirler with the full-length Travel-Top and whitewall tires. These jobs, à la Pontiac Tempest, are powered by a 152-cubic-inch, four-cylinder mill, actually the right bank of the big International Harvester V8. Like the Temp-

19

Even though standard highway tires were used here, Scout had necessary traction to back over steep hill that was strewn with large rocks, stumps and loose dirt.

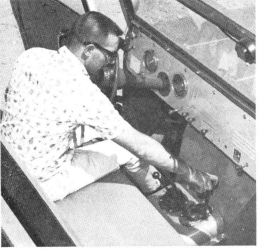

Two-range selector engages the driving front axle, which provides extra bite in rough terrain. Transmission is a three-speed synchromesh with 4.27 axle ratio.

Hydraulic clutch employs Girling master cylinder made in England. Clutch has a heavy-duty, coil-spring vibration damper.

Optional, locking hubs help prevent wear on front axle by disengaging the front wheels from drive parts on smooth roads.

I-H SCOUT

INTERNATIONAL HARVESTER'S venture into the all-purpose vehicle market came at the beginning of the year with the official unveiling of the new IH Scout. As might be expected from a concern with the background and know-how of IH (which has for years been one of the leaders in trucks and work vehicles), a great deal of planning and engineering went into the Scout before it reached the public.

The Scout was designed, basically, to serve as an all-purpose unit capable of withstanding rugged use in off-the-highway travel. But its designers went several steps further and made the Scout both functional and attractive so that it fits in well with city driving also. And what's more, they were able to keep the cost at a reasonable level, all of which adds up to a pretty attractive package for the guy who likes to combine work and pleasure driving with a bit of off-beat travel into the wilderness.

Offered in two-wheel- and four-wheel-drive models, the new Scout is a workhorse with plenty of muscle in its 152-cubic-inch, four-cylinder engine. In just a few minutes, it can be converted from pickup or panel truck for business use to a stripped-down bundle of energy capable of pulling its way over rough and rutty back trails, through streams or over steep inclines. In short, wherever you care to go (on land, that is), the Scout will do the job.

During the development period of

the Scout, practically every existing four-cylinder automotive engine available was considered, but Scout designers and engineers were not quite satisfied. In view of the popular acceptance of their International six- and eight-cylinder powerplants, they decided to design an all-new four-banger, using similar principles and many interchangeable parts.

The result is the Comanche engine, an economical little bomb that resembles the popular International V-304 eight-cylinder engine with a single bank (instead of two) of four cylinders. High-quality units common to both engines give the Comanche good efficiency and wear-resistance plus performance. Unlike many vehicles of its kind, the Scout cruises down the highway at 65 mph without a great deal of strain, and on regular grades of gasoline.

Although the IH Scout was intended for rugged service, it rides and handles suprisingly well for a vehicle of this type. Not so smooth and comfortable as a passenger car, of course, it does nevertheless take the corners with comparative ease, and its 100-inch wheelbase makes it easy to maneuver under most conditions.

For off-the-highway travel, the driving front axle of the four-wheel-drive model will handle almost any rugged chore. Working through a transfer case which controls the four-wheel-drive the front axle can be operated in either low or high range, depending on the amount of traction needed to do the job.

In full dress, the Scout can be made into a pickup truck with an open body, or it can become a panel truck with an optional full cab with full body protection. In either case, both tops are removable in a matter of minutes, and the Scout becomes an open-air vehicle for the highway or back trails. Further stripping, for the most rugged use, is made possible by removable doors, windows and windshield. Such options as a winch, snow plow, special tires and power take-off help make it one of the most versatile vehicles in operation today.

Both models are equipped with 10-inch clutches and three-speed synchromesh transmissions. Axle gear ratio is 4.27:1. The axles have a capacity of 2000 pounds in front and 2300 pounds at the rear. Semi-elliptic springs and direct-acting shocks are employed at both front and rear. Ground clearance – important on a vehicle intended for off-highway use – is slightly more than nine inches.

Suggested retail price of the Scout with two-wheel drive and standard equipment is $1598, plus local and federal taxes. The four-wheel-drive model carries a suggested retail tag of $1948.

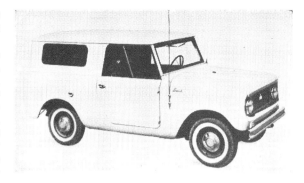

Travel-Top (above) converts Scout to a panel truck, giving full body protection. Standard top is easily removed (in lower photo) for open-air driving.

All-steel body is built for rugged use and the roughest conditions. The top, doors and windshield may be removed.

Four-cylinder Comanche engine was developed especially for the Scout. It has a displacement of 152 cubic inches, down-draft carburetor and 8.19:1 compression. Horsepower rating is 86.9.

Stripped for action, the Scout displays plenty of muscle for off-the-highway travel. Fully clothed, its functional style is not unbecoming to use in the city or out on the highways.

SCOUT SCARES TROUT as it churns merrily upstream
through a foot of water on soft gravel creek bottom

SPOTLIGHT ON THE
International Scout

By Jim Whipple

Ex-GI's who drove the Army's famed Jeep, (Truck, ¼-ton 4x4, to you soldier!) may go into shock when they get behind the wheel of the Scout, International Harvester's stylish new utility vehicle.

Try to imagine yourself on winter maneuvers snugly buttoned up in a three-passenger steel cab looking out through clear glass windows, warmed by the soft breezes from the fresh-air heater, while the Scout's four-wheel drive pulls you through creekbeds and up muddy hillsides.

And that's not all, you've got a five-foot pickup box hauling a 500-lb. load tacked on behind you! All this on a mere 100-inch wheelbase and measuring less than 13 feet from bumper to bumper.

But the Scout's real trump card is riding comfort. We can still recall the creeping paralysis of the posterior that set in during one three-day period when we drove a WWII Jeep some 1300 miles. We wound up sitting on two folded GI blankets.

No such problem with a Scout. Its riding qualities are comparable to that of a modern pickup truck — quite firm but never harsh or jouncy on the road. Crossing a plowed field will bounce you around some but no more than with any other vehicle capable of traversing rough terrain.

But, in spite of Scout's sinful comforts and civilized ways, it's ready, willing and able to slog across country with the best of

FROM THE DEEP TO THE STEEP was next move for Scout equipped with the optional Travel Top enclosure

the "off-the-roaders." It has low-range gearing in the transfer case permitting a power ratio of 2.46 to 1 to be applied to front and rear axles when in four-wheel drive. Total reduction; low gear (3.33 to 1) x transfer gears (2.46 to 1) x axle ratio (4.27 to 1) or 35.07 to 1 over-all.

When you couple this compound gearing to Scout's beefy, 93 horsepower four-cylinder engine, you've got real stump-pulling power to work with. As an option you can have a limited-slip differential on the rear axle which means that three out of four wheels **must** turn. If you don't think that you can make it with this setup, add the optional power takeoff and Ramsey winch and haul yourself up a cliff.

The Scout's sleek, enclosed bodywork may lead you to believe that it isn't suited for deep-rutted forest roads (or no roads at all), but its angles of approach and departure (47 and 35 degrees), which govern how steep a ditch side it can climb, are competitive with the Jeep's. Ground clearance, at 9.3 inches front and rear, is superior to Jeep's by an inch. Tires are 6:00 x 16.

After you tire of fording streams or climbing stone walls, you may wonder what Scout's like out on the pavement. Well, it's no Thunderbird, but after you disconnect the optional locking front hubs to deactivate the front drive, you find that you can roll along at 50, 60 or up to 70 with no trouble, although with more noise and vibration than you might expect from, say, a Falcon Ranchero. The transmission is synchromesh, clutch and brake pedals require more than passenger car pressures but work well and the engine is surprisingly smooth. Incidentally, Scout's power plant is the righthand bank of International's 304-cubic-inch V-8 truck engine.

Steering is fairly easy and most women won't find driving the Scout in traffic too troublesome. Its high cab, compact dimensions and good glass area make for excellent vision and aid parking in close quarters.

For those who don't do too much off-the-road work, Scout is available with two-wheel drive and I-beam front axle. This model costs $1750.84 at the Fort Wayne, Ind., factory, which is $378 less than the four-wheel-drive job.

Adding Powr-Lok limited-slip differential at $38 would give you some of the mud and snow traction of the four-wheel-drive job.

Although Scout looks like a permanently enclosed vehicle, cab top, windows and doors can be unbolted and windshield folded down in minutes to make a hunter's field car.

As an option to the standard cab you can get the Travel-Top enclosure, for the entire body, which turns it into a small station wagon at an extra cost of $128.

If the Scout's many abilities fit your transportation needs, by all means get one —it's a lot of fun for a reasonable cost.
★★★

NEWS

FROM:

CONSUMER RELATIONS DEPARTMENT
INTERNATIONAL HARVESTER COMPANY
180 NORTH MICHIGAN AVE. • CHICAGO I, ILLINOIS
ANDOVER 3-4200

CHICAGO -- The Scout, a new, small all-purpose vehicle designed for low cost transportation of passengers and cargo, has been introduced by the motor truck division of International Harvester Company, it was announced by D. F. Kuntz, divisional sales manager.

Functional design of the Scout, which is offered in two-wheel or four-wheel drive models, includes a three-person passenger compartment with removable steel top, five-foot long pickup body, fold-down windshield, removable door glass, removable doors and a new International Comanche four-cylinder economy engine as standard equipment. A full-length one-piece steel Travel-Top, that encloses both driver compartment and body, is optional.

Suggested retail price of the Scout with two-wheel drive and standard equipment is $1,598, plus local and federal taxes, FOB, Fort Wayne, Ind., Kuntz said. The four-wheel drive model carries a suggested FOB retail price of $1,948. Both models will be sold and serviced through a nationwide network of 5,000 International dealers and branches.

"The Scout represents a new concept in automotive versatility," Kuntz said. "It can quickly and easily be converted from a completely enclosed passenger runabout, small pickup or panel truck to an open model without top, windows or doors.

"Because of its unique and versatile design the Scout can provide efficient and economical transportation for a wide variety of family, commercial, sporting and agricultural uses," Kuntz said. "It has been subjected to severe testing, both in the field and engineering laboratory, to assure long operating life and maximum durability."

Styling of the Scout features a low silhouette with loaded overall height of 67 inches for the two-wheel drive model. The four-wheel drive model is 68 inches high, loaded. Heights are the same with either Travel-Top or standard passenger compartment top. The Travel-Top has windows on both sides and rear for maximum visibility, and top and bottom hinged station-wagon type tailgates.

Overall length of both models is 12 feet, ten inches. Wheelbase is 100 inches.

A full-width 52-inch front seat provides three-person passenger comfort. Additional seating is available on two full-length wheel housings in the five-foot integral pickup body.

Outstanding performance for the Scout is delivered by the IH-built Comanche engine, a 152-cubic inch, four-cylinder valve-in-head powerplant. It develops approximately 90 horsepower at 4,400 revolutions-per-minute.

The Comanche incorporates many components of International's performance-proved V-304 eight-cylinder truck engine. It features the same basic block, including five main bearings, water pump, fuel pump, oil filter, combustion chamber and valve rotators as the V-304 engine. It is a heavy-duty powerplant built for extremely long service life as well as economical operation.

Further strength and durability are built into the Scout as a result of a three by four-inch welded box frame, with two box crossmembers and two channel crossmembers.

Both models are equipped with ten-inch clutches, 4.27 gear ratio rear axles, three-speed synchromesh transmissions, 11-gallon fuel tanks and 12-volt electrical systems with 25-ampere generators.

Front axle capacity at the ground is 2,000 pounds. Rear axles are rated at 2,300 pounds. Front springs on both models are one and three-quarter inches by 40 inches. Rear springs are one and three-quarter by 46 inches. The 4x2 model is equipped with 15-inch disc wheels while 16-inch wheels are standard on the 4x4.

Optional equipment available for the 4x2 Scout includes a Powr-Lok differential, dual 11-gallon fuel tanks, radio, heater and defroster, rear bumper, rear tow loop and increased capacity battery and cooling system.

The 4x4 Scout is offered with all 4x2 optional equipment, plus front wheel locking hubs, front-mounted winch, power takeoff and snow plow.

All models are available with choice of white, red, metallic green, metallic blue, yellow or tan colors. The cab top and Travel-Top are painted white, for two-tone styling in combination with standard body colors.

New all-purpose Scout has a five-foot-long integral pickup body. Wheel housings are designed from front to back of the pickup body to allow additional seating. Optional one-piece Travel-Top provides weather tight protection for both passenger compartment and pickup body.

Passenger compartment of the new Scout seats three persons in comfort. Seat is 52 inches wide. Shift lever for the low-cost Scout is floor-mounted while brake and clutch pedals are suspended. Compartment has a removable steel top, door glass and doors and fold-down windshield. Radio and heater are optional.

New International Comanche four-cylinder engine, with approximately 90 horsepower, furnishes power for the 100-inch wheel base Scout. Suggested retail prices begin at $1598, plus federal and local Taxes, FOB, Fort Wayne, Ind.

Windows on sides and rear provide effective all-round visibility. Both Travel-Top and standard top are removable.

INTERNATIONAL'S

4wd SCOUT

International Harvester's Scout is the newest four-wheel drive rig available from the standpoint of design and engineering. It is also the "wonder boy" of the industry. In slightly more than a year since its introduction it has become the largest selling model in the International line. Last year alone the firm produced 35,000 units.

To be so popular there must be a reason and the thorough road test the FOUR WHEELER staff has just completed and is reporting here, turned-up several excellent features which could be responsible. But if I personally had to be pinned down to a single reason, I would not hesitate in

answering — versatility. For the Scout is equally at home in big city traffic or on the back trail. Naturally there are several other advantages and these will be pointed out as we go along.

Actually the Scout was no stranger to the staff of the FOUR WHEELER. When I took delivery of the test car it was almost precisely a year since I drove one of the first IH Scouts at International's Arizona proving grounds.

But this road test was the first time a regular test in depth was possible. The car was driven over 2500 miles through all types of terrain — and loaded with all

types of camping gear. Part of the test included the classic Hemet Cavalcade and another section consisted of a 1000 mile trip through the desert and mountains near the Colorado River.

The Scout is powered by International's Comanche engine, which displaces 152-cubic-inches and develops 90 hp at 4400 rpm while producing 135 lbs.-ft. of torque at 2400 rpm. As most four wheelers are already aware this engine is virtually identical to International's 304-cubic-inch V-8 with one bank of cylinders sliced off. Among the identical parts are the pistons, rings, piston pins and connecting rods;

A four-wheel drive newcomer that is already carving a solid niche for itself

cylinder head assembly, including valve springs and spring dampners; valves and valve rotators; five main bearings; water jacketed aluminum intake manifold; water pump, fuel pump, oil filter and starter.

For all practical purposes this means that the Scout has a Four that is as rugged as the heavy duty V-8 that has been standard equipment in IH trucks for years.

Before discussing the performance of the Four it might be well to clear up one question that is frequently asked about the Scout. Since its Four is half the V-8, what about the conversion possibilities? The answer is yes, the 304, V-8 would go in and probably would be a bolt-on job. The extra weight, 617.6 lbs. for the V-304 as opposed to 414.5 lbs. for the Four would not present too much of a problem. The difficulties would lie in the physical dimensions and the re-cutting of the fire

wall, etc., that would be necessary to make it fit.

The answer to whether it *should be converted* would be no, unless you are an out-and-out performance enthusiast who won't have anything but a V-8 under the hood.

The biggest reason for this answer is that the Four is excellent for its purpose. It will tool the car along at a comfortable highway speed — well over 60 mph — and it takes an exceptionally long hill, plus a heavy payload to slow down the outfit at all. Along with its good top end, the engine also lugs well in the low range for off-trail maneuvers.

Another advantage of the Four is that it gives reasonably good fuel consumption. The 11-to-21 mpg range given here is an overall, inclusive range and should cover almost anybody's driving. Actually during

the test the overall change in various tankfuls varied from 14 mpg to 18 mpg depending on the type of driving being done. When the car was driven slowly, around 50 mph, the mileage improved considerably. When we tooled across the road at California's legal 65 mph limit and then switched to 4wd for a long stretch of back country driving it dropped off sharply.

The Scout has an option which the FOUR WHEELER wholeheartedly recommends to anyone purchasing the car. This is the extra gas tank mounted on the passenger's side. Virtually every car being sold in the west now has this option and it is well worth the extra cost. It holds an additional 11 gallons and when paired with a couple of separate spare gas cans gives the four wheeler over 30 gallons of gas — more than enough for the longest off-trail runs.

There is no manual switching from tank to tank, but the "T" that connects them is small. This means that the two tanks must be filled individually. It also creates a sort of mental hazard for the driver. The gas gauge registers through one tank and sometimes gives a false reading. On one camp-out the gauge was reading full — the next morning it registered almost empty. The trouble was that we parked the Scout on a side hill where the gas ran into the tank that did not register. Luckily before we accused our fellow four wheelers of having a rubber hose we parked on even ground for a few minutes where the tanks leveled themselves and the gauge gave us a true reading.

This is not a particularly bad disadvantage but can cause some annoyance. Just remember before turning off on a long back trail to have your car on the level a few minutes first.

Incidentally the filler pipe on the passenger's side is almost directly over the exhaust pipe. This also presents somewhat of a problem since it is conceivable, although not too probable, that some gas might spill on the hot exhaust pipe and flare up. It can be corrected by putting an extension on the pipe or watching carefully whenever the tank is filled.

The Comanche Four is coupled with a three-speed transmission with a floor-mounted shift. This also drives through a transfer case. The rear axle ratio is 4.27-to-1 and the transfer case ratio 2.46-to-1. With a low gear of 3.333 this gives the Scout an overall compound low ratio of 35-to-1, which is a practical gear for most back country situations.

The transmission is International-built and is an excellent piece of enginering. Those four wheelers accustomed to a synchromesh second gear might find second a little hard to get used to. But a simple double-clutch when shifting makes it slide in as smooth as any transmission. Double clutching when going d o w n through the gears with this transmission is the easiest of any I have found in driving dozens of 4wd outfits. It is exceptionally good for the fellow who has trouble with double shifting. With only a few minutes practice he will be master not only of the transmission, but of the transfer case as well. Within a dozen miles of off trail driving. I was shifting from two-wheel drive, high range, second gear, to four-wheel drive, low range, second gear without stopping. But the biggest advantage is the ease with which the transfer case goes in and out of the low range while r.oving. This means you can slow down for difficult driving and speed up when the trail smooths out without stopping — and not for the expert only either, nearly anyone can master double clutching on the Scout in a few minutes.

It might be well to give the shifting procedures for the Scout since it will be of value to the new owner and may remind the experienced driver of something he has forgotten.

First of all the Scout's controls are all mechanical and manually operated. They are mounted on the transmission hump with the gear shift on the left, the front axle control in the center and the transfer case lever on the right.

Scout's cargo compartment is one of it's best features — actually a five-foot pick-up bed. Spare tire fits inside, and tailgate doubles as camp table. Lower picture shows optional rear seat plus full camping load.

Scout is powered by International's Comanche engine. Conversion is possible, but actually unnecessary. For minor repairs, hood can be latched in halfway position.

Major repairs — pulling engine, working on head and valves, etc. — call for this full-open position of hood, when it fits into lock that holds windshield down for bobtailing.

The gear shift is a simple H-pattern, common to all domestic three-speed transmissions. The throws are exceptionally short and make for fast shifting. The transfer case has three positions: high, neutral and low. It cannot be put in the low range unless the front axle is engaged, conversely the front axle cannot be disengaged if the transfer case is in low.

It is actually easier to put the Scout in four-wheel drive if the outfit is in motion. It is not necessary to disengage the clutch, just pull the control lever to its back position.

If difficulty is encountered in engaging the front axle when the car is not moving, it means the splines on the engaging clutch are not matched. Forcing the lever will not make it engage but stands a good chance of damaging the linkage. Simply put the outfit in low gear, inch ahead, and when the splines are matched, it will engage.

The torque build-up between the front and rear axles usually makes it difficult to put the car in two-wheel drive when it is in motion. In order to disengage the front axle when moving it is necessary to relieve this torque build-up between the front and rear axles by one of two things. Take your foot off the accelerator abruptly or release the clutch while the car is in motion. If this doesn't work try both of them at the same time. While doing this keep a steady pressure on the front axle lever. If this procedure doesn't work, it might be necessary to stop, put the outfit in reverse and back up a short distance. This doesn't happen very often and usually only when the car is new.

More than any other operation, four wheelers will want to shift the transfer case from low to high and back while using four wheel drive. In the Scout it is a snap.

Going from low to high is easiest. Just ease off on the accelerator and push in the clutch. Then shift the transfer control from low to neutral. Next let the clutch

Well just over wheel in right side of the Scout's engine compartment serves as an excellent storage space for tools or for building in a compressor, generator, tool box or you-name-it.

pedal out and depress it again, then shift into high. Now let the clutch pedal out and speed up the engine.

The shift from high to low is a little more complicated, but not very difficult. Disengage the clutch and move the lever to neutral. Now engage the clutch by taking your foot off the pedal. At the same time speed the engine up until the engine speed and transfer case gear speed are nearly equalized. Now push the clutch pedal down and quickly push the transfer case control to low. The first few times this is tried the gears will probably grind,

but after a little practice it becomes second nature and is one of the most valuable skills a back country driver can master. The Scout's transmission is one of the easiest for newcomers to learn how to master.

The test Scout had one other option that the staff of the FOUR WHEELER can be entirely enthusiastic about recommending. This is the limited slip differential for which International's trade name is Powr-Lok. While this option is a substantial extra-cost item, it is in our opinion well worth the money.

No test of the Scout would be complete without mentioning its excellent use of inside space. The front seat — or cab depending on which top is used—is excellent for two, adequate for three, and four small persons could be huddled in. Of course, the shift levers cut out a lot of usable leg space, but it can be done. The seats are firm, but comfortable.

The test car was equipped with safety belts, and after a trip over the back trails I think they are also a good option. I'm a little tall and they kept me from bumping my head on the ceiling time after time. Safety belts also keep you down in the seat and make a rough ride a lot more acceptable. Of course, they are intended to protect the driver and passengers in case of accident, but in off trail driving they have a few other advantages.

The cargo compartment is one of the Scout's best features — and one of the best that has ever been offered on production 4wd rigs. For all practical purposes it is a five-foot pick-up bed. In back the tailgate is level-folding, and flush with the bed, which makes loading or unloading a push-in, pull-out arrangement. This gate also has another advantage. It is fairly flat, and just the right height to make a table with campstools putting the average person at precisely the right height. Or, it can be used for the icebox, water jug and camp stove.

The test car was equipped with the full-length metal top with windows. This is the best arrangement for sleeping in the back, (with the tailgate down), or for protecting a large load of camping gear. It is fully lockable with a single key. The only real disadvantage to the full metal top is that it is a little warm in summer. This is no real problem, however, since

A limited slip differential has separate clutches which automatically transfer all the power to the opposite wheel should one begin slipping. For instance, when driving in muddy terrain one wheel might get into a slick spot and start spinning. Without a limited slip differential the car would probably be stuck. But if the other wheel is on firm ground, the limited slip differential arrangement immediately transfers the power to the wheel on firm ground, and the car pulls out of the slick spot — usually without even slowing down.

While the mud and water section of this road test consisted of only a few miles down Coyote Canyon, another section of different terrain proved the worth of the International Powr-Lok option.

This area was covered with the soft surface sand dunes, which are found everywhere in southern California's desert. Although all four wheels were invariably on the unfirm surface of the sand, it was possible to feel the shift of power occasionally. This meant that the test rig kept moving in a dozen situations where it would ordinarily have meant at the least, slowing down, if not stopping to dig out.

Driving the Scout is effortless and may be too easy to some persons. The steering ratio is geared quite slow and this means that the wheel must be twisted around considerably when turning a corner. While this makes driving around town a little more work, it does take a lot of effort out of some off-trail maneuvers. It requires little strain to pull the front wheel out of a rut or over a small rock.

Exhaust pipe shown here is located directly below the gas filler pipe for the extra gas tank. A place to be careful of when filling up at a service station.

Rear window on the long metal cab has two tabs which will lock it in up position. During the test these proved to be exceptionally sturdy, even on the roughest roads.

After its first year the Scout has proven itself as more han just an adequate back country car

this top, or any of the others for that matter, can be removed completely. In fact the windows can also be removed and the windshield folded down for open air travel. If desired, even the doors come off.

In top selection, the Scout has a wide choice of various styles. Besides the full metal top there is a short metal top which converts the rig into a compact pickup truck. Three more canvas tops, both short and long, are available.

Besides the normal factory options the test car was equipped at various times with two other accessories that are available from most International dealers. One was a rock skid plate for the front steering knuckle. This was installed to protect this vulnerable component on the Hemet run, which is famous for its many rock gardens. The second accessory was a rear seat,

which is a slip-in deal. Both were judged excellent. The first is made by Nelson Machinery, and the second by Con-Ferr Mfg. Co.

Overall the Scout is an excellent 4wd machine that is already assured of a sturdy place among back country driving enthusiasts. One encouraging note is the evidence that International is making a series of gradual improvements instead of offering a new model each year. This is tradition in four-wheel drive cars and one of the biggest assets a buyer can have.

To show how this works at International, here are a few examples. The steel in the rear axle was recently changed and is now a tougher, more durable material. Another example, an optional axle ratio, 4.38-to-1, is now available for persons who need even more power in the low end.

Since much of the test was scheduled over rocky country, the test Scout had an optional skid plate to protect the steering box, a good investment for this type of country.

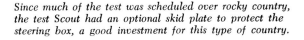

Specifications

ENGINE
Four cylinder, overhead valve
Bore and stroke: 3.875x3.219
Displacement: 152 cubic inches
Compression ratio: 8.19-to-1
Horsepower: 90 @ 4,400 rpm
Torque: 130 lbs.-ft. @ 2400 rpm
Fuel consumption: 11-21 mpg

SPECIFICATIONS:
Wheelbase: 100 inches
Length: 154 inches
Width: 68.6 inches
Height: 68 inches
Ground clearance: 9.3 inches
Turning radius: 21.5 feet
Curb weight: 3000 lbs.
Payload: 900 lbs.
Base price: $1951

GEARING
Rear axle: 4:27-to-1
Transfer case: 2.46-to-1
Transmission: 3.333, 1.851, 1
Overall ratios:
   Normal: 14.23, 7.9, 4.27
   Compound: 35, 19.45, 10.5

A Scout is power to discover the past

There is no paved road to the past. Go straight over the mountain and take a hard left through the rocks at the old landslide scar. The trip is no picnic, but the INTERNATIONAL® SCOUT,® with its new V-8 power and with all-wheel drive, will carve you a road where there is none.

The SCOUT is built to feel at home on the smooth highways of the present or the rugged paths of the past. Big new V-8 engine or sturdy, economical 4-cylinder size, try one at your INTERNATIONAL Dealer's. Get the feel of it. Open it up and cross over into a man's world of driving. The world's finest full-powered sports and hunting car costs less than most second cars. And our Dealers are ready to make it easy for you to buy!

International Harvester Company, Chicago, Illinois 60611.

IH. INTERNATIONAL HARVESTER COMPANY

The new top-powered V-8 SCOUT!

"FORM FOLLOWS FUNCTION" has long been International Harvester's operating theory in their Scout, but the 180 changes made on the new '66 Scout 800 show that the function has been broadened considerably.

Among refinements are a completely new dash layout (replacement of idiot lights with full instrumentation), a new transfer case that eliminates the noise that used to come from their 4-wheel drive, a new fixed windshield with an improved weather seal, and a single release tailgate latch — which means no more hooks and chains.

Basic body style remains the same. There's a choice of 6 different tops, from canvas to metal and from half-cab to full. Bucket seats, metallic and 2-tone paint jobs, vinyl-coated canvas tops, and a new grille remove all chance of the adjective "plain" being applied.

The Travelall station wagon, with a whopping 124-cubic-feet payload capacity, has been dolled up, too, but it still keeps all its utility. Roomier seats and a soundproof interior are examples of new creature-comfort improvements.

New turbocharger, 8 on the floor, 4-wheel drive give '66 Scout 880 more versatility than most cars. Redesigned grille, new dashboard, and bucket seats are among changes.

The D-1000 Travelall comes with a torsion-bar front suspension. Other models use I-beam front axles. A 141-hp 6 is the standard engine, with 2 V-8s rated at 155 and 193 hp as options. Four-wheel drive, standard on the 1200 series, makes the Travelall a real hauler — even after the road ends.   /MT

✳ Scout & Travelall

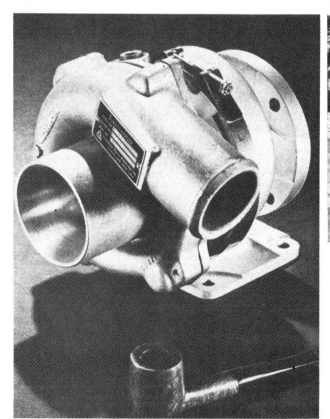

(ABOVE) International Travelall is one of few cars you step up into. D-1000 model has independent front suspension, but others come with solid I-beam axles for back-road travel. A huge selection of rear-axle ratios, 2- and 4wd, automatic or standard transmission are part of buyer's choice. Counterbalanced tailgate with a power window is standard equipment.

(LEFT) Turbocharger (optional) boosts Scout's 4-banger from 92.5 hp to 111. Exhaust-driven blower cuts in only above a limit of 2000 rpm. Nine-inch road clearance puts Scout well above ruts. Windshield now stands in upright, fixed position.

SPECIAL ORDER SCOUT

by JOHN RUCKER

Four wheelers are a special breed of people. They love to get off the beaten path and make it across the most forbidding roads in search of something new and different. Though they are in pursuit of the same things collectively, their means of getting there, via four wheels, is ofttimes an expression of pure individuality. Take, for example, the 1965 Scout shown here. Built to fill special needs, this machine is the culmination of more than two years work by J.V. Dickson of Anaheim, California. Given a few hours attention here, and a few there, the drab little four-banger was finally transposed into a dual-purpose machine that would function as well on the road as off.

Dickson ordered his International Scout with 3500-pound heavy-duty rear axles but with standard springs. His intention was to replace the four-cylinder engine with a Chevy V-8, thus beefy axles, but since he wasn't going to be hauling big loads, he wanted softer ride characteristics, so standard springs. No sooner did he get his four wheeler home than the engine came out. A 1963 Chevy truck engine, 283-incher of 160 hp, was installed with the aid of a Chuchua bell housing adapter and engine mounts. These engine mounts join the engine at block side to the stock Scout body mounts. If a front saddle mount was used, he would have had to run an electric fuel pump and build new frame engine mounts.

Because the adapter plate spaced the engine forward of the transmission, a 9 1/2 inch Jeep input shaft and cluster gear had to be installed in the Scout transmission. A small notch had to be cut in the left firewall, also, to accommodate the Chevy. Inside the cab, Dickson lined the flooring about the bell housing with sheet asbestos, household carpet and padding; mainly to keep out engine heat (throttle is close to bell housing), sec-

ondly for looks. Carpet cuts transfer case noise, too.

Like many other four-wheelers, his Scout was being designed to his needs while keeping a close eye on the budget. So, he found a '62 Corvette cross-flow radiator with a pair of tiny holes in it at a local wrecking yard. Cost; $20.00. He built his own surge tank because the 'Vette unit would be hard to mount. He had to cut the right side frame member slightly to allow room for the radiator

outlet pipe, otherwise the unit would ride too high.

While towing a 3000-pound, 16-foot house trailer into the mountains last summer, the Scout rolled merrily along, an Eaz-Lift trailer hitch doing its job. Engine overheating was encountered, though, and after discovering the radiator wasn't pulling enough air, J.V. installed an air shroud about the fan, solving the problem. To do this, though, the body front crossmember under the radiator

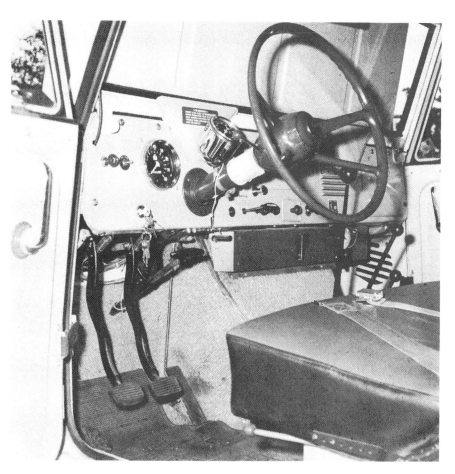

had to be cut away and lowered two inches to offer room for the shroud. Likewise, the body mount directly below the radiator, on the crossmember, had to be lowered.

The next alteration came in the form of a Rancho overdrive unit to reduce engine speed, thus saving on gasoline costs, and cut down noise and vibration at highway speeds. Installing the overdrive according to instructions, a minute oil leak was discovered between one of the steel shims. A thin film of Goodyear Plio-Bond "super glue" between each shim halted all leaks. Because the overdrive mounts on back of the transfer case, the drive shaft had to be shortened. Following this operation, J.V. had the shaft rebalanced to prevent vibrations and ruined U-joints. Another, and perhaps the most important, reason for installing an overdrive unit in the Scout, was to reduce transfer case gear speed. 1966 and earlier Scouts and Jeeps drive directly through the transfer case in two-wheel drive.

Along with this worthwhile addition came a set of Warn hubs for the front end. A simple twist of the wrist lets you disengage your front drive unit for highway driving thereby saving tires, gas, gears and general wear and tear on front drive components.

At the time Dickson ordered his Scout, he specified 16-inch diameter wheels. His motive; to use the centers when he later came up with five, 15-inch wide-based Chrysler rims. Two years ago it cost him $48.00 for the five custom rims. Goodyear 9.00 x 15-inch Double Eagles haul the Scout in style.

To date the Dickson Scout was all he could ask for when it came to street driving, but how about the off-the-road side of this dual-purpose vehicle? Well, still with an eye on the budget and a yen to "do-it-himself," J.V. bought a surplus Jack & Heintz aircraft starter motor from Airborne Sales Company in Culver City, Calif. With a gear reduction ratio of 225 to 1, this unit, popular with four-wheelers, would soon be in use as a power winch. Approximately 13 inches by seven inches in size, the motor turns around 45 rpm on 12 volts DC. Cost; only $21.50. To install the winch motor, the front bumper was moved forward 2 3/4 inches for clearance. A piece of 2 1/2 inch x 1/4 inch wall tubing 9 1/2 inches long with side plates was made to hold 150 feet of 5/16 inch steel cable that cost an additional $22.00. The starter motor comes with a dog clutch and a second half which was welded to the cable spool. The motor was wired up so it can be operated from either the cab or along side the front bumper, which is ideal for a one-man operation.

One outstanding feature of Dickson's

power winch is that it features a built-in brake that will allow him to back down a hill safely. The motor came with a small drive cup on the side opposite the power take-off. J.V. replaced it with a small wheel, wrapped with a steel friction band, which in turn is fitted with a cable leading into the cab. This cable-controlled friction brake thus operates through the motor. If you are using the winch to pull yourself up a steep incline, then discover you must back down any distance at all, but can't do so safely with the standard brakes, then the friction brake on the motor will do it safely.

Another neat trick he employed in this dual-purpose craft is an air compressor. Out in the desert with lowered air pressure in the tires is just the ticket, but can be damaging on pavement. With a Hadley air compressor pump mounted on the firewall working off manifold vacuum, a surplus aircraft oxygen tank mounted behind the right rear tire (cost, $12.00) will store pressure to 100 pounds p.s.i. before automatically shutting off. A used service station hose stored under the seat is used to pump tires back to normal pressure upon returning to paved roads.

To dampen road shock, Dickson installed a Heco Flex-all steering stabilizer between axle and tie rod. He explained that where a person is pulling large rubber up front, should a tire blow at speed, this device can well save your life by preventing the wheel from being pulled from your grip.

Possessing a complete library of FOUR WHEELER magazines, J.V. referred to a back issue when it came to modifying his front seat so it would tip forward for easy entrance to the rear cab. He did, however, perform this job a little differently, to suit his needs.

Other minor alterations included moving the hand operated parking brake handle to the left so it can be used with the left hand, rather than right. In hill country, where it might be required at the same time as shifting, this is a smart move. Then a dome light was installed, with door switches, too, and another battery was installed in the left fender well, in a '59 Chevy carrier, and is wired in parallel. A custom rear bumper of 6 inch channel, notched to form-fit the body, and solidly braced, caps everything off.

Surprisingly enough, what with all of these alterations, one would never know Dickson's Scout is anything but stock. It handles well, hauls his trailer, takes him around town in comfort, and can get to the hill country and over it with ease. Yep, this is one neat little Scout that fills the bill for this owner.

UTILITY WITH A FLAIR

New Scout Sportop offers off-road family fun

IN THIS DAY of the special-purpose vehicle, one wonders why it took so long to revive what is essentially the theme first set by the late and lamented Jeepster in 1948. Now International has done it with the Scout Sportop, and we know that they are approximately six months ahead of similar competitive efforts.

The reason for the introduction of this civilized Scout lies in the sales record of the original short-wheelbase model which unlike the Jeep comes standard with doors, windows and a 2-man steel top. Over 140,000 have been sold since its introduction in 1961, and about 80% of these were to persons who planned to use them for pleasure rather than business.

Certainly just as much if not more pleasure may be derived from 4wd mounted underneath comfortable seating for four, wind-up windows and a choice of collapsible or removable top. About the only problem introduced with such a vehicle is that the owner might worry about his pretty sheetmetal while charging through cactus country.

Where some volume producers go to considerable initial expense to tool up for a simplified, idiot-lighted instrument panel, IHC takes the other and more satisfactory (to us) route of buying from a supplier a cheap but adequate gauge and switch for every function. They stretch impressively across the whole driver's half of the panel. There is even a switch for each windshield wiper, keeping them out of sequence and thus

the driver awake. Both a hand throttle and a choke are provided.

The heater controls, though, require a little study. We kept getting heat when we didn't want it with all visible controls in the OFF position until we learned that you were supposed to shut off the water supply to the heater by turning a valve under the hood.

Another thing you soon learn is the reason why you seem to run out of gas so quickly. There are two small tanks in the rear fenders in lieu of one big one, and these have to be switched manually, as does the gauge.

The high tunnel has one virtue besides restricting the guest list. Both the transmission and transfer-case levers have a short gate and are still right at hand. The 4-speed box is a worthwhile option, and one wishes that IHC as well as the other utility vehicle makers would invest in the design of a synchromesh low. This may be just a convenience in a passenger car, but with an off-road vehicle, if you have to stop to shift into low, you might be stopped, period.

Temporarily, at least, another valid reason for choosing the 4-speed option is the relatively low (93) horsepower of the standard 4-cylinder engine. Just a year ago, nobody seemed to expect more, but then the Jeep people came along with their V-6 hot rod rated at 155 hp. In retaliation, Ford is known to be planning a V-8 for its Bronco, and since the IHC unit is simply half of a V-8 already in production, this company could easily put the two halves

2wd hardtop (foreground) ground to stand-still, while 4wd sailed to top of 40% grade.

PHOTOS BY HERB MCLAUGHLIN

Fiberglass top and rear windows are removable, chromed bumpers are standard on Sportop. Two side-filling tanks are optional.

53.1-inch track stabilizes Scout while cornering. Steering is quick and precise, even on models equipped with 4-wheel drive.

back together again. To be sure, IHC has an optional supercharger that increases output by 20%, but it doesn't cut in until 2000 rpm. Most off-road usage is at an rpm lower than that figure.

However, if more power is not wanted, the little 4, slanted 40 degrees to the driver's right, makes servicing a delight. If it didn't get a little hot there, you could easily carry some luggage in the space left over under the hood. A convenient feature is an arrangement whereby the points may be set externally with the engine running.

The Sportop comes in two forms. The cheaper one has a removable hard top constructed of double-walled fiberglass. This sells for $2389.59 without 4wd. A hand-folded rag top costs only $33.58 more, and as it is equally weatherproof with its wind-up windows, it would seem to be the biggest bargain since the 15-cent Staten Island ferry ride. What do

you do with the bulky, heavy fiberglass top once you get it off? The rag top is a little bulky when folded, but at least you carry it around with you, making it handy in case it rains.

On the highway, both the 2- and 4wd Scout feel more at home than the Jeep. The springing is softer, and you don't get any of that almost harmonic, choppy reaction to the sections in a concrete road. Although you sit about 25 inches off the ground in both, perhaps it is the security of the Scout's metal doors that dispels the illusion of towering over other traffic. These doors, incidentally, are easily removable by punching out the hinge pins in case you want to hunt jack rabbits or lasso cattle.

Another measure of security comes from the 53-inch track of the Scout, which is 4.5 inches wider than the Jeep even though the Scout is about five inches thinner overall. The Jeep penal-

izes itself with its step plates and side-mounted spare.

Off-road, the 4wd Scout is no match for the V-6 Jeep, and the 2wd Scout doesn't belong here at all. The picture on top of page 68 shows a 4wd Scout successfully puffing up a 40% grade with a rather soft surface. The 2wd Scout (bottom) quit at the position shown, with its rear wheels helplessly excavating the equipage into even deeper trouble.

At a time when teams of copywriters work long into the evening dreaming up such color descriptions as "nightwatch" blue, "montero" red and "candlelite" cream, it was refreshing to receive the official IHC handout on the Scout. This simply states that the car is available in "automotive" yellow, red, green, white, gold, beige and blue. If you don't like an off-white top, *you* can paint it some other color. —*Don MacDonald*

Four bags occupy only a portion of available luggage area. One hand releases gate.

The complete, functional instrument panel carries a gauge or switch for everything.

Wheel wells narrow rear seat to two adults, but they have plenty of leg room. Front bucket seats are both adjustable. The top can be folded manually with no difficulty.

INTERNATIONAL SCOUT SPORTOP

2-door, 4-passenger, 4-wheel-drive utility vehicle

SPECIFICATIONS FROM MANUFACTURER

ENGINE IN TEST CAR: Ohv 4
  Bore and stroke: 3⅞ x 3 7/32 ins.
  Displacement: 152 cu. ins.
  Advertised horsepower: 93.4 @ 4400 rpm
  Max. torque: 142.7 lbs.-ft. @ 2400 rpm
  Compression ratio: 8.19:1
  Carburetion: 1 1-bbl.
TRANSMISSION TYPE & FINAL DRIVE RATIO: 3-speed manual, floor-mounted lever. 4.27:1 rear-axle ratio (front also when transfer case is ordered)
SUSPENSION: Semi-elliptic springs front and rear, with direct-acting shocks at each wheel
STEERING: Cam and roller-mounted single-lever gear
  Turning diameter: 40.2 ft., curb to curb
  Turns lock to lock: 4.5
WHEELS: Steel disc, 16-in. dia. on 4-wheel drive; 15-in. on 2-wheel drive
TIRES: 6.00 x 16 rayon, or 7.35 x 15 4-ply rated
BRAKES: Hydraulic duo-servo
  Diameter of drum: front, 10 ins.; rear, 9 ins.
SERVICE:
  Type of fuel recommended: Regular
  Fuel capacity: 11 gals.
  Oil capacity: 4 qts.; with filter, 5 qts.
  Shortest lubrication interval: 2000 mi.
  Oil- and filter-change interval: 4000 mi.

BODY & FRAME: Box-section perimeter frame, all-steel body
  Wheelbase: 100.0 ins.
  Track: front, 53.1 ins.; rear, 53.1 ins.
  Overall: length, 154.0 ins.; width, 68.6 ins.; height, 68.0 ins.
  Min. ground clearance: 9.3 ins.
  Usable trunk capacity: not applicable
  Curb weight: 3000 lbs.

ACCESSORY PRICE LIST

Engine options: 111.3-hp, turbocharged	$279.00
*4-speed close-ratio transmission	86.00
Overdrive (Borg-Warner)	240.00
Heavy-duty clutch	2.15
Limited-slip differential (either axle)	35.75
Progressive-rate springs	11.00
Heavy-duty front spring	2.80
Heavy-duty rear spring	6.00
*Warn hubs	64.00
Skid plates	45.00
*Tire carrier (external)	11.00
*Auxiliary gas tank (11 gals.)	25.00
*AM radio	58.00
*Heater and defroster	66.50
*Whitewall tires	63.00
*Bucket seats	std.

*On test car

MANUFACTURER'S SUGGESTED PRICE: $2650 (incl. taxes, safety equip't & PCV device)

PRICE OF CAR TESTED: $3023.50 (incl. excise tax, delivery & get-ready charges, but not local tax & license)

MANUFACTURER'S WARRANTY: 12,000 miles and/or 12 months

NEWS

from:

INTERNATIONAL HARVESTER COMPANY
PRODUCT PUBLICITY
401 North Michigan Avenue
Chicago, Illinois 60611 • (312) 527-0200
FOR MORE INFORMATION CONTACT:

David E. Hartman

FOR RELEASE: FEBRUARY 20, 1967

NEW V8 SCOUT MODEL MAKES ITS BOW

CHICAGO, Ill. -- A new high-performance Scout model, featuring V8 power matched with all-wheel drive, is being announced by International, according to E. P. O'Connor, manager of marketing for International Harvester Company's motor truck division.

In addition to its smooth V8 engine, the new Scout model has higher capacity components throughout---front and rear axles included---a dual brake system and a wide variety of other safety features that are standard equipment.

For a sporty flavor, the V8 Scout can be equipped with a four-speed transmission with floor-mounted shift, fast-back top, bucket seats and dozens of convenience items including a stereo tape player.

The new Scout V-266 V8 engine develops 155 hp. and 227 lb./ft. of torque. It is IH-built and has a cubic displacement of 266 inches. Compression ratio is 8.40 to 1.

"This is the second improvement in Scout engine power announced within six months' time," O'Connor noted. In October of last year, a 111-hp. 4-cyl. engine was placed in production to augment the original Scout powerplant, a 4-cyl. model with 93 hp. Both 4-cyl. models, incidentally, remain available.

"Essentially," O'Connor continued, "the Scout's V8 is a high performance engine we have been building for other vehicles in the International line for more than seven years, so it is a thoroughly-proven power source

"Scout fans have been eagerly awaiting a V8 model," he noted, "and we expect sales to increase measurably in the coming months as a result. We believe that the model will attract many new customers too. This is an exciting vehicle to drive.

"As another product improvement stemming from high owner demand, we have made the 3,500 lb. Scout rear axle standard equipment. In the past, this was an optional item."

A new front axle for the V8 Scout also has increased capacity--- 2,500 lbs., up from 2,000 lbs. Still other items of increased capacity are radiator frontal area, cooling system, battery and rear springs.

Headed by the dual brake system, the safety features that are standard equipment on the V8 Scout include a padded dash, padded sun visors, inside and outside rear view mirrors, seat belts, windshield washers, glare-reduction wiper arms, backup lights, hazard switch, 7.75x15 PR PC tubeless tires and 5.50K rims.

A choice of six steel, fiberglass and fabric tops is offered. Two of these tops cover the front seat only; the other four fully-enclose the vehicle. Two full-length tops are convertibles and one is a fast-back. Most tops are removable and several are interchangeable.

The 100-inch wheelbase Scout is the sales leader among all-purpose compacts and International's largest selling model. Approximately 25,000 were built last year. It was introduced in 1961 and it retains the same basic body lines today that it had then.

The Scout is sold and serviced by a nationwide network of more than 3,900 International dealers, branches and stores.

#####

International engineers check out the high-performance 266-cu. in. 155-hp. V-8 engine, powerplant for the newly-introduced Scout V8 model (background). This is the second improvement in Scout engine power within the last several months --- an 111-hp. four cyl. engine was introduced in October, 1966 to augment the original 93-hp. four-cyl. Scout engine. The 100-in. wheelbase Scout is the industry sales leader in the all-purpose compact class and is the largest selling model in the broad International line.

Better Than The Best

SCOUT 800A

Two years ago when FOUR WHEELER road tested the first V-8 model of International's Scout, our test crew stated flatly that it was the best Scout ever built. We haven't changed our minds about that statement but now the 800A has to be reported as even better than "the best Scout ever built."

It has more power with equal economy; it has improved engineering and ride with no sacrifice in back country ability; and there are more comfort and luxury items available for those who want them.

Actually, this road test is a little unusual because elsewhere in this issue we are presenting the announcement story of the 800A. Ordinarily, a vehicle is not available for testing until several weeks after it has been introduced. On this occasion, however, we were fortunate to have a vehicle in our hands even before the press was aware of the announcement.

Our test Scout was equipped with the four-speed manual transmission and in our earlier experience (coupled to the old Four) we were quite unhappy with the gear box. We had our mind changed in the parking lot and this experience was the first clue to how the bigger engine was going to operate.

With the Four it was necessary to start in low gear and go through all four gears to get started even on the level. The V-304 engine has enough guts that we amused ourself by starting in second and third with no difficulty, unloaded and on the level, of course.

The 800A's powerplant is named for its displacement: 304 cubic inches. Horsepower rating is 193.1 at 4400 rpm while maximum torque of 272 lbs.-ft. is produced at 2800 rpm. The increases over the previous V-8 are: 38 cid, 38 horsepower and 45 lbs.-ft. torque.

Just looking at the figures makes the increase seem moderate but the gain is actually about 25 percent. A touch on the throttle proves it even more dramatically.

The 800A is gutty in all gears and most of the rpm range. Hills are no problem and there is ample power for pulling a travel trailer. Normal loads for back country trips aren't going to strain the Scout in the least.

In our opinion, this engine gives the Scout enough margin to be a serious competitor in off road racing and there is no doubt that it will soon be on the entry lists.

Along with the bigger power International engineers have beefed up many of the running gear components. In a short duration test it was impossible to thoroughly evaluate them but they are worthy of mention. The suspension, motor mounts and front axles have all been beefed up. The rear suspension has been completely redesigned and driving tests indicated that the ride and handling have been improved.

While we are discussing the possibility of competition for the Scout an evaluation of the four-speed manual transmission with shich it was equipped is in order. Our original introduction to this transmission several years ago was not exactly

42

what you would call a meeting of the minds. Its performance with the Four was less than ideal (the Four has since been beefed up) and we felt that the spacing of the gears was too close to be optimum for off road driving.

The new V-8 virtually eliminates the criticism of close spacing since it has the power to operate efficiently in every gear. A lower, low would be a big advantage but it is not the necessity it once was. What is important is that the T-45 is probably one of the best arranged four-speed manual for off road racing. With its close spacing, acceleration out of slow situations is going to be more rapid and better use of maximum torque will always be available. It should be a dandy for cross country enduros and should really shine on the closed circuit obstacle.

Both the four-speed transmission and the transfer case are International-built and both are heavy duty. The transfer case has a 2.03-to-1 low range and is a little faster than we would prefer for most back country maneuvers. Once again, the bigger engine makes the difference and this complaint can only be termed one of personal preference. In tests the rig performed very well at walking speeds.

What is new about the transfer case is the shift lever. This year Scout has a one-lever control and has done away with the old two-lever arrangement. Positions are 2wd high, 4wd high, 4wd low and neutral. Shifting can be done while moving and all the operations were firm and precise.

One area where we are always amazed is in the recapitu-

lation of the mileage figures. The 800A, with its bigger V-8, recorded only about a half-mile less per gallon than its predecessor. The figures ranged between 12 and 14 miles and an average was struck at approximately 13.5 mpg. The earlier version was just slightly over 14 mpg for an equivalent amount and type of driving.

Inside, except for the controls, little has changed. Another exception would be the luxury items which are now available. While not as ornate as could be, the test rig had bucket seats, padded dash and a host of accessories. We had the rig during California's rainy season so we can vouch for the body's tightness and resistance to leaking. During the storms the interior was as dry as a bone. One interesting fact on the weatherstripping is found on the round rubber piece that seals the top of the roll-up windows.

When the windows are closed and the door opened, then shut, the seal is made on the side. When the door is closed and the window rolled up the seal is made on the bottom of the roll. It fascinated the test drivers but seemed to make little

difference in sealing out water and wind, both worked equally well.

Outside there are few changes. The new grille is more attractive and appears to be better for protection and wear. One good thing that impressed us was the radio antenna which had a small spring similar to a CB radio antenna. This is an excellent touch and one that should be appreciated by brush drivers. Apparently someone at International skinned his knuckles once too often as the rear latch for the tailgate has been repositioned. Now you can open the gate with one hand and support it with the other. No more skinned fingers and far less comment unfit for children to hear.

All in all the new 800A in the Travel Top style appears to the naked eye to have changed little. But it really has changed considerably. A person has to drive it to appreciate how much different it is from even the previous V-8. And if you are one of those individuals who haven't driven a Scout since its early four banger days — you won't believe it is the same rig. The Scout 800A is that much better.

the *Scout* 800
by INTERNATIONAL®

FAMILY RUNABOUT...WORK-SAVER...SURE-FOOTED TRAIL BLAZER

the *Scout* 800

does anything you want to do, goes anywhere you want to go... with sure all-wheel or lively rear-wheel drive

Like to explore the back woods in comfortable bucket seats . . . pull a boat, push a snow plow, tote a little league team, or run around town without running out of patience? You can do all these things with a new Scout 800.

The Scout has compact size and operating economy, but king-size performance and reliability. It can be a sporty convertible or lead a double life on safari, or as a pickup or utility vehicle—with a choice of all-wheel or rear-wheel drive, a half-dozen cab styles, standard or turbocharged engine, and a three-speed or four-speed transmission.

The new Scout 800 is crisply styled, with a bold look of ability. It's comfortable without being slushy-sprung. It's powerful, but goes easy on the gas.

In short, here's everything a real *action* car should be. No other vehicle can match its proven record of stamina and owner acceptance, nor surpass its usefulness and all-around pleasure. It's carefully built to be what it was meant to be—a thrifty, all-purpose carrier that never says quit.

NEW, EASY-VIEW INSTRUMENT PANEL

No skimping on instruments or squinting to read them. individual gauges and turn signal lights are clearly cluste on a panel that can be lifted out for easy service. Control kr are directly below, where they should be. The instrument tion is balanced by a wide utility compartment, with radio trols and speaker centered between. Defrosting is m efficient—the warm air duct runs the entire length of the w shield for full-vision defrosting.

Other up-front refinements include a new bright, care-anodized aluminum grille; permanently-fixed leakproof w shield; bottom-mounted, variable-speed dual windshield ers that do a he-man job.

FULL COMFORT AND CONVENIENCE FEATURES

New safety-styled steering wheel that provides increased space between wheel and front seat ■ Roll-down windows ■ Tension-adjustable vent wings ■ New extended drip moldings to carry water *below* windows ■ New rotary door locks that can be actuated from inside or outside ■ Pushbutton door handles with separate keyholes ■ Suspended pedals ■ Vibradamp insulated, vinyl-covered acoustical headliner on steel Traveltop models ■ Molded rubber, vinyl-coated floor mats with sound-deadening backing ■ Sound-deadening lining on outer door panels ■ Easy, one-hand tailgate latch-release lever ■ Two-stage support strap on models with tailgate-mounted spare tire to prevent full drop from weight of tire.

CUSTOMIZED
for any kind of action

The Scout's versatility is its virtue, reliability it's stock in trade. It can be adapted for family pleasure, utility or business use with a choice of three seating arrangements and six cab styles . . . all-wheel or rear-wheel drive with standard three-speed or optional four-speed synchromesh transmission . . . standard 93 hp or optional high-performance turbocharged engine . . . plus a power take-off for operating a winch, post-hole digger, or other powered attachments.

REAR-WHEEL OR ALL-WHEEL DRIVE

Scout rear-wheel drive models are ideal for scooting over improved roads or in areas with no roads at all. If you plan to hit really rough country, the all-wheel drive Scout, when in Low Range, doubles torque to all four wheels. You can scramble up and inch down steep grades, plow through mud, sand, snow, and shallow streams.

INTERIORS AND TRIM

Utility Model (Available with hard and soft Cab Top, Panel Top or hard and soft Travel Top.) Full-width, foam-rubber-padded front seat. All-vinyl Champagne upholstery. Ash tray. Silver-gray front bumper.

Custom Model (Available with hard and soft Cab Top and hard and soft Travel Top.) Full-width front seat for Cab Top models only. Deep-contoured bucket seats standard in Travel Top Models,* optional in Cab Top models. All-vinyl Champagne upholstery. Harmonizing vinyl-covered padded door panels. Dual sun visors and arm rests. Front floor mat. Cigar lighter. Chrome outside rear-view mirror. Chrome wheel discs. Chrome front bumper.

*Steel Travel Top has Vibradamp insulated, vinyl-covered acoustical headliner.

Additional Interior and Trim Options — Rear compartment seating for Custom Travel Top models: includes custom-trim full-width back seat with arm rests and rear floor mat. Other options: cushions for built-in benches over wheel housings—available for all models. Driver's or dual arm rests for Utility models. Silver-gray rear bumper for Utility models. Chrome rear bumper for Custom models.

Other popular accessories listed on back cover.

SEAT FOR PASSENGERS OR PAYLOADS

REAR SEATING
Two types: Removable rear seat for two adults; or cushions for the built-in benches over wheel housings. Seats four adults.

BUCKET SEATS
Choice of solid bulkhead or open access to rear. Spare tire can be mounted on inside or outside of tailgate.

UTILITY PICKUP MODEL
One-piece, full-width seat with solid bulkhead. Five-foot pickup box with spare tire mounted on back of steel bulkhead.

COVER UP OR GO "CONVERTIBLE"

You can go part top, full top, hard top, soft top, or no top with the Scout . . . in any of seven colors shown. The standard steel part-top cab enclosure gives you the look of a conventional pickup. The other options shown at right tailor your Scout to the exact style you want for any type of work or weather conditions.

Steel Cab Top
Completely waterproofs driver's compartment. Frames and seals roll-down side windows. Large rear window.

Soft Cab Top
Convertible-quality top instead of steel to enclose driver's compartment. Includes plastic rear window.

Steel Travel Top

Full-length enclosure from windshield to tailgate. Large side windows and large window in lift-up tailgate.

No Top

All tops can be removed (or you can order without top) for a true open-air roadster. Doors and optional sliding windows also removable.

CHOICE OF 7 EXTERIOR COLORS

White

Champagne Metallic

Red

Soft Travel Top

Full-enclosure soft top with fold-down frame. Roll-up curtains contain plastic windows for sides and rear.

Steel Panel Top

Ideal for delivery use with solid sides for business identification sign. Offers full-closure protection for cargo.

Aspen Green

Light Yellow

Apache Gold

Moonstone Blue

Turbocharged Engine

Standard Engine

POWERED fo
stamina and

STANDARD COMANCHE® 93 HP ENGINE

The standard four-cylinder Scout 800 power plant is totally proven. It's patterned after one of the most successful International heavy-duty V-8 commercial engines. Small wonder its 152 cubic inch displacement packs the pep to pull loads under severest conditions —on regular gasoline.

Yet, its abundant lugging ability doesn't sacrifice the performance you want for the open road. The Comanche engine is far from sluggish. You get fast response for passing and smooth running for the straightaway.

OPTIONAL TURBOCHARGED 111 HP ENGINE

This four-cylinder turbocharged Comanche engine gives you the power of many sixes—with a big edge on fuel economy. At engine speeds above 2000 rpm (road speeds above 40 mph in high gear) the turbocharger steps in to sharply boost power and torque. You'll really feel the surge of this high-performance engine when hauling husky loads, towing trailers, and climbing steep grades. Or when you're cruising at high speeds and want extra-quick passing power.

The turbocharged engine is especially valuable for mountain driving. It reduces the power loss most engines start to encounter at altitudes above 5000 feet . . . actually delivers the same net brake horsepower at 9000 feet as the standard Scout engine at sea level.

No groping or grappling when servicing—The Scout's engine compartment is large and low. Components are placed for direct access. In fact, oil, battery and other routine checks can be made from one position in front.

pull,
economy

NO SKIMPING ON QUALITY IN THE PARTS YOU DON'T SEE

CHASSIS
Quality standards on the Scout chassis, as well as body and parts, exceed those for standard automobile components. For example, the sturdy box-section frame, truck-strength axles and suspension system safely shoulder the strain of maximum rated loads on toughest assignments.

BRAKES
Self-energizing hydraulic with commercial-grade, bonded linings. Provide longer wear and safer stops on grades and when carrying full loads.

SYNCHROMESH TRANSMISSIONS
The standard, direct three-speed transmission delivers maximum usable power with either rear-wheel or all-wheel drive, the standard or turbocharged engine.

The optional four-speed transmission is preferred by a large number of owners. Its scientifically-spaced gears permit you to take greater advantage of the Scout's capabilities.

ALL-WHEEL DRIVE
Shifts traction into front wheels and, when in Low Range, doubles torque to all four wheels. Hi-Low Range gives you a choice of six forward speeds. Separate floor-mounted stick shifts for rear-wheel drive, all-wheel drive and hi-low speed. Also has provision for mounting a full-torque power take off.

New quiet transfer case. *Unlike conventional transfer case gearing, the all-wheel drive Scout does not have a pronounced "whine" when in rear-wheel drive. There is no power applied to the idler gears when in rear-wheel drive. You enjoy a quiet, smooth flow of power.*

mph. Then I hit a soft spot. Before you could flick a fly off the end of your nose, the Scout had sunk in.

I quickly tried to reverse to harder ground. No go. I was locked in, axle-deep front and rear, the "four-wheel drive" now became two-wheel, and that was it! The Rover was still on harder sand so we rigged up a chain to try and yank the Scout out backwards. The instant we applied pulling power on the Rover, it too broke through the crust and was up to its axles. We were both stuck, but good. Jim McMichael went on a long hike up the beach and finally reached a telephone, calling a wrecker for help. It was becoming pretty critical, as the tide was moving in and unless we got out within half an hour both cars would have been under a few feet of water. The tow truck almost got stuck trying to reach our vicinity. But with his long wire cable and hook, from a spot a good 200 feet inland, the driver snatched out the Scout first and then the Rover. Fifteen minutes later there was two feet of water over the place where both cars had been.

At this near-sinking, Brewster Shaw, many times Speed Trial Champ on the beach, was with us. When he and Jim and I got back home and began discussing the situation, the first thing we decided was that if the Scout had had 7.50 tires it probably could have kept going without getting into trouble.

For the next day's test we decided to match this new cross-country kid against my Willys Jeep which is now seven years old but as perfect as the day it left the factory. We crashed the Jeep and the Scout over and up dunes. These revealed some pretty interesting findings. Again, the Jeep had better size rubber, 7.00x15. It could out-climb the Scout but not by too much. Actually, though the Scout engine is slightly larger and has much more horsepower (86.9 @ 4400 rpm versus 70 @ 4000 rpm) and a higher torque rating (135 ft. lbs. @ 2400 rpm versus 112 ft. lbs. @ 2000), the Jeep had more torque for real tough climbing. This could be due to transmission gearing but I got the impression that the Jeep engine had a little more whop when under full power and extreme loads. Next we took the Jeep and the Scout close to the water's edge (on Daytona Beach this time, where the sand was as hard as a mother-in-law's stare). We put a chain between the two, back to back, and started a tug-of-war. The result was a dead heat —neither vehicle could pull the other an inch backwards. They just stood there and dug themselves toward China, each time through the hardest sand this side of concrete.

Later, we took both the Scouts to the Daytona International Speedway for some performance runs. I found that the full cab body on the 4x2 could very well do with a mattress-full of sound-deadening material in the roof. The drumming is fairly severe—in fact, much too severe for any real comfort on a long trip. The steering wheels of both cars come out too far on the post and would be much more comfortable to drive if they were recessed toward the instrument panel by two or three inches. The two-wheel drive job is quite agile, batting out 0-60 in 15.6 seconds and 0-30 mph in 5.2. The 4x4 does the 0-60 mph route in 22 seconds and takes seven seconds flat to reach 30 mph. On my high-speed runs made at the Speedway, the top speed of the 4x2 was 80 mph, right on the nose, and I cranked 71 mph out of the 4x4.

I was much more interested in the four-wheel-drive babe. Like the two-wheel drive Scout (which has an identical five-foot-long pickup body) and unlike the Jeep, it has real cargo-carrying capacity. If the steering wheel were better positioned with a shorter post, the 4x4 Scout would be a fairly comfortable car. The ride was good, considering the vehicle, and the fittings and appointments pleasant if not posh. At the comparatively low price this car is selling for I think it's a helluva buy for anyone who does much hunting, farming or just plain woods-whacking. The rear of the standard cab is quite large and should hold at least a half dozen embalmed Chinamen, two kegs of beer and a ukelele.

Both these vehicles are offspring of International Harvester, which means top quality by a major, highly-respected outfit. It wouldn't surprise me to see new versions of the Scout within a year featuring soft, rag or canvas tops that can be quickly lowered, making the car a real popular favorite with sportsmen everywhere. As it is, with the top removed the Scout can be used as a great shooting and safari car although heavier bumper provisions will have to be made to hold a stump-catcher when driving in quail country. I use a piece of quarter-inch armor plate as a stump-catcher on my Jeep; without it, the tie rods would be ripped out several times a day when hunting in Florida. Tree stumps down there have been cut by pixies to grass height (which is tie-rod height) and they can't be seen until you smash into them.

In summing up, I think the Scout is a real fine contribution to our portfolio of American vehicles. The seats are far more comfortable than you get in a Jeep and with slightly larger tires it will go anywhere a Jeep can go. If you're in the market for such a car, don't buy until you've checked over the Scout. •

The do-it-yourself Scout.

See what you can do with all the power, performance and pizzazz options we offer you

People are using the SCOUT® so many different ways we figure they ought to be able to get 'em any way they want 'em.

So we offer you more engines, transmissions, rear axles, seating arrangements, and unusual accessories than anybody else in the class.

You can option yourself into any kind of SCOUT from a sassy little runabout to a gutsy beast that'll take off straight up . . .

from a stick shift that's sync-ed in all three gears to a four-on-the-floor to a smooth automatic . . .

. . . from a stripped-down workhorse to a jazzy creampuff with color-keyed interiors, bucket seats, padding all over and even a stereo tape deck.

Two-wheel drive if you're the conservative type, all-wheel drive if you're not.

We'll start you off with 100 rugged inches of wheelbase . . . and from there on your SCOUT is the most exciting do-it-yourself project you ever tackled.

Your INTERNATIONAL SCOUT Dealer has all the tools and a good price.

 **INTERNATIONAL HARVESTER COMPANY** CHICAGO, ILLINOIS 60611

It's an Aristocrat!

Those who think that International's engineers and sales people are not in tune with modern off-the-road demands for recreational vehicles should take a long, hard look at their new Aristocrat. If these individuals can find one, that is. International is only going to build 2500 of the gems.

The Company chose Playboy's fabulous new resort at Lake Geneva, Wisconsin to debut their new Aristocrat. And this was a good choice for nothing describes the new Scout better than saying: "It is the playboy of the Scout line."

Just a glance at the Aristocrat is enough to set it off from regular Scouts. All 2500 are finished in a distinctive metal blue top and silver body combination. The full-length travel top is complemented with considerable chrome trim accented by a unique "wrap-over" chromed luggage rack. The windows in the back slide open for ventilation and have a positive latch system. The tailgate is lockable and the doors open to the full dimensions of the rear access for added security and convenience.

Convenience and luxury items that will appeal greatly to off

roaders are found among the many deluxe interior appointments. The special blue custom interior has all-vinyl bucket seats with matching full-width rear seat (which can be removed for added cargo capacity. Not only are the door panels padded, an identical treatment has been given the cargo compartment with wheel well pads and side pads. Blue carpeting covers the front and rear with bright finish retaining strips. The dash is also padded and trimmed in silver.

Other features which are standard in Aristocrats are usually found on the extra cost list of Scout dealers. These goodies include chromed dual outside rear-view mirrors, a dashboard courtesy lamp, cigar lighter and a radio equipped with a vibration-absorbing antenna.

While it is obvious to anyone that the Aristocrat is intended as a top of the line luxury rig with special emphasis on this type of improvement, International engineers have had their say too — and the results are good. Some of the innovations are not brand new — they were introduced with the 800A a few months ago. Others, such as the beefed up four-cylinder engine and the first-time-offered Six, are debuting with the Aristocrat.

The new Four is an improved version of the familiar 93 horsepower International in-line four-cylinder which is now

rated at 111 horsepower. Also, this is the first time a six-cylinder engine has been available for any Scout. It is International's 145 horsepower, 232 cubic-inch, in-line Six and gives the Scout line a complete power range to suit everybody's taste. Top of the powerplant line is the 304 cubic-inch, V-8 that has proved to be extremely popular with Scout buyers. Coupled to the engines will be three transmissions. Standard is a three-speed manual with an optional four-speed manual and a three-speed automatic that gives the driver the option of shifting automatically or going through the gears. The new single-lever transfer case introduced in the 800A will be standard.

One detail that many persons might overlook is the simple fact that the Aristocrat will be available only in the four-wheel drive version — no two wheel models will be built. This makes the Aristocrat the first bobtailed recreational unit to admit that there is simply nothing better than four-wheel drive.

Other extra cost, highly desired items that will be standard include a limited-slip differential, dual fuel tanks and undercoating. A 3.31-to-1 axle ratio will be stock for the V-8 with 3.73-to-1 selected for the four- and six-cylinder engines. Spring rate changes have been made in the rear leaf springs to provide a better ride with no loss in longevity. Up front the axle has been re-designed slightly and now is a flanged type.

One of the most significant developments of the Aristocrat are the standard seven-inch wide wheels with glass-belted H 70-15 low profile tires. These are as close to really wide wheels and tires as have ever been offered as original equipment and probably indicate that off road manufacturers are finally realizing that their most important accessory can be wide wheels and tires.

At the introduction, Aristocrats with all three power plants were made available for test drives. Admittedly, no full scale comments could be developed in such a short experience, yet

there are several characteristics that were immediately evident.

The Four is greatly improved and more powerful, but it is still a Four. Most surprising was the Six, which seems to have more power than its 145 horsepower rating would indicate. It is an engine that will bear more investigation and can not be competently commented on until power, cost and economy factors are investigated. The V-8 was the subject of a full length road test in a previous issue and is still rated extremely high by FOUR WHEELER.

But the most significant difference between the Aristocrat and regular Scouts is evident when you sit behind the wheel. There is an aura of luxury and comfort unusual for back country machines. When driving this feeling is deepened by almost complete road silence and comfort. Since there was a good, though short, off road course available, comparisons for general off road travel were also possible. Here, too, the padding, undercoating and carpeting paid off in a quieter, more comfortable ride.

It was hard to understand why International would elect to build only 2500 Aristocrats when it is obviously such a superior Scout. This is only a small percent of their annual production and won't begin to satisfy their 3500 dealers. After a little though, the reasons became more understandable.

First, after the initial Aristocrats are sold, many of the newly developed options will be made available for regular Scout production. Items such as the wide wheels can be evaluated as to customer reaction, feasibility and cost before they are put into regular production thereby eliminating a lot of sometimes costly guessing.

Next, and most important to International undoubtedly, is cost. If present anticipated pricing policy stands, the Aristocrat is at once an "economical costly" car to manufacture. Economical because the usual options are standard equipment – costly simply because it has more to offer.

This was explained by International executives who would not reveal the final retail price of the Aristocrat. They said it would probably cost a few hundred dollars more than a stock Scout but probably would be priced as much as $500 under what the price tag would be if the accessories were selected off the factory option list by the customer for a regular Scout.

Not only is the Aristocrat a luxury four-wheel drive rig, it is one of the better bargains of 1969. Apparently, International is using the rig to test out sales principles in the comfort and luxury department.

Since car manufacturers are not famous for their benevolence, International elected to make only 2500 of the Aristocrats. This may be the only complaint that four wheelers have. There simply isn't going to be enough Aristocrats to go around. Those who want one had better be first in line at their local Scout dealer.

FOUR-WHEELERS

INTERNATIONAL SCOUT

International Harvester has been manufacturing the Scout for close to 20 years now, and it is a highly dependable, fairly good looking little bucket. With most of I-H's sales in the fields of heavy trucks and farm implements, the management's interest in the Scout is purely functional. They have done little in the off-road competition field, either with factory entries or by supporting private or dealer entries. A more-or-less private entry Scout ran in the last Baja 1000 and it did make it to La Paz, which is more than did 60% of the 250-plus other entries.

For many years the greatest failing for high-speed off-road work was the little 4-banger engine that was the Scout's only power. Currently at 196 cubic inches and 111 hp, it's economical to run, but that's about it. In the last couple of years International has also offered a 232-cubic-inch, 145-hp straight-6 and, better yet, a 304-cubic-inch, 193-hp V-8.

This V-8, which is manufactured by International, offers some interesting possibilities for NORRA competition, remembering the ruling that states you can switch engines so long as the block is the same. It would appear that the 345-cubic-inch, 197-hp V-8 offered for the Travelall wagon is a longer-stroke version of the 304, and the Travelall 392-cubic-inch V-8 is a bored version of the 345. The 345 offers only 4 more horsepower than the 304, but gobs more torque. The 392 has both torque and 235 hp with its stock 4-barrel carburetor.

Where most of the other American 4-wheel-drive manufacturers offer various dress-up packages to make their vehicles more presentable for city use, International has a special model called the "Aristocrat." While perhaps not the best selection of a name for a 4-wheel-drive vehicle, the Aristocrat is a rugged little bear. Available with the 196, 232 and 304 engines, it costs about $900 more than the standard

Scout hardtop wagon. While the normal range of body colors is available for the non-aristocratic Scouts, the Aristocrat has its own distinctive dark blue and gray paint job.

Additional standard equipment on the Aristocrat includes a Powr-Lok limited slip, chrome bumpers, carpeting, dual 10-gallon gas tanks, headliners, free-wheel front hubs, a luggage rack, pushbutton radio, bucket front seats and a full-width rear seat, an outside tire carrier, five H70x15 Wide Oval Custom tires, reverse-dish 15x7.00 chromed wheels, undercoating, and sliding windows in the hardtop. While we're talking of $4000 and up for the Aristocrat, dependent on engine, this isn't too bad when you add up the cost of similar options on the other 4-wheel-drive vehicles in the field. Most of these bits and pieces can be purchased separately for the other models of the Scout.

While the open roadster and the travel top models are the most fre-

2

3

quently seen versions of the Scout, there is also a pickup with cab version that sells for a price about midway between the other two. It, like the other Scout models, has 5 feet of length between the seat and the tailgate, which somewhat limits its use for living aboard, but leaves plenty of room for luggage.

The standard transmission for the Scouts is a 3-speed with a 4-speed manual available as a $95 option, and for 1970, a 3-speed automatic. Heavier-duty alternators (52-amp and 61-amp for the V-8 4-wheel-drive models) can be ordered to replace the normal 32-amp job. This option would be a wise one if the owner buys the increased capacity 60 amp-hour battery to run a batch of quartz iodine lights for night use. For a little over $20 you can have an automatic choke on the V-8 Scouts, which will make starting easier and should increase gas mileage slightly.

For heavy off-road use, International sells a skidplate kit for under $50, and heavy-duty front and rear springs will add only about $11 to the tab. As the basic fuel capacity is only 10 gallons, the second tank at $28 is a good buy for any kind of off-road use. All of the standard engines use regular-grade gasoline.

The basic Scout roadster is in the same price bracket as just about all the other basic models of American 4-wheelers, and International has about the same range of optional equipment. The selection of optional tires for the Scout line is fairly expensive, but not really too interesting to the sporting-minded off-roader. The Aristocrat does come with nice, fat wienies, but 8.55's are the biggest normally available through the factory. As with many of the other 4-wheel-drive vehicles, the best plan is to buy the

4

thing with the normal tires, save them for towing or around town, and buy a set of wide wheels and high-flotation off-road tires for the serious work. When doing this, you can ask to have the spare wheel and tire deleted from your original car purchase and save $20 or so.

International is highly oriented toward the rural market, so front and rear power takeoffs are standard. This makes it possible to stick a winch on the front or a post-hole auger on the

SPECIFICATIONS	
Wheelbase	100.0
Overall length	152.5
Width	68.6
Height	66.8
Front tread	56.1
Rear tread	55.7
Ground clearance	7.1
Box length—floor	60.0
Box length—top	56.0
Box width—floor	41.0
Box width—tailgate	38.0
Box depth	20.5
Max. gross vehicle wt.	4200*
* 4700 with H-D rear springs.	

1. *Properly set up, and with the right engine, the Scout will compete with the best of them.*

2. *Scout's styling is comparable with other vehicles' in its class—simple, functional, yet pleasing.*

3. *For the comfort-minded, optional interior package and automatic trans make a neat little parcel.*

4. *Aristocrat, pictured here and above, is the optional ball of wax for those who want something more than good off-road transportation. Beneath the frills and nice 2-tone paint is the same 'ol Scout.*

rear. The Scout can be equipped with a snowplow, a mower or a sweeper, making it one of the most versatile of the 4-wheel-drive vehicles.

The Scout is particularly well designed for rough going, as nothing hangs down below the reinforced welded steel box frame. It is interesting to check how many of the newer 4-wheel-drives have their transfer case, transmission or crankcase mounted where they are extremely vulnerable to rocks and high crowns. You can usually add special skidplates, but this amounts to covering up a failing, rather than eliminating it in designing the vehicle. The Scout's gas tank is fully enclosed and mounted outside and above the frame, giving it better protection. The radiator is protected in front by a steel frame crossmember, and underneath by a steel flange.

As yet unproven in serious competition, there is no reason at all that the 1970 Scout—with one of the bigger V-8 engines, the limited-slip rear, and perhaps the automatic transmission—shouldn't be a real winner for all-around fun driving!

the SR-2

By JON BASTIAN

Road testing a new 4wd vehicle usually doesn't leave the testers perplexed after several hundred miles of on- and off-road operation. In the case of the International SR-2, the latest International refinement of the 800-A, there were many "whys" and not enough good "becauses." The SR-2 is the most effective introduction of luxury to the International line of 800-A's, so it would seem reasonable that it would live up to its claimed ease of operation and comfort. That's a toss-up.

The SR-2 used for the test was powered by a Thrift Six that has a cubic inch displacement of 232. It packs 145 hp. at 4,000 rpm. The power is transferred through the select shift T-39 automatic transmission to the 3.73-to-1 rear axle. The inline six was introduced last year to the Aristocrat line of Scout 800-A's.

Power of the Thrift Six was somewhat hampered by the transmission, which didn't seem to have much going for it. Shifting with the flimsy metal shift lever didn't leave the operator with a feeling of confidence, and the lever pattern wasn't designed to prevent mis-shifts into a wrong gear, mainly reverse or even neutral. In addition, when it was decided to use the transmission like a clutchless three-speed, down shifting from second to first caused a scary lurching forward. The owner's manual explains that downshifting can be accomplished by the simple sliding of the lever forward and backward, 1-2-D. In decelerating, the shift from 2 to 1, if accomplished any faster than 22 mph, would cause a momentary disengagement of gears as the transmission would lapse into neutral. If you're using the transmission for controlled driving on turns or even on a somewhat slippery surface, the lurching forward might cause a panic strike at the brakes. The results are well understood.

The handle itself, topped by a smooth plastic grip, does not lead to a desire to use the automatic transmission in excess. With the rear axle ratio, traveling in the rig down hills off the road was kept under steady control. A few taps at the brake here and there to slow the rig were needed, but the transmission and engine compression kept the rig at a slow speed. Climbing the same hill was much easier as the single-speed transfer case lever was shifted into low. Steady climbing and pulling up hard-packed hills can be easily rated as dependable.

The transfer case caused no headaches when it was time to shift from

Interior features large 17-inch steering wheel and dashboard of gauges. Note position of speedometer on the right side of the steering column. Hard to see?

street operation to off-road readiness. The SR-2 is provided with automatic locking hubs for the front wheel drive, and when locked in, the transfer case can be shifted to the appropriate gearing with minimal shifting of the automatic transmission lever. Automatic locking hubs, however, are automatic as opening the door, walking a few feet, and twisting a dial on each wheel.

The SR-2 suspension is HD, like that of the Aristocrat, which was tested in the July 1969 issue of FOUR WHEELER. Like the Aristocrat, the front suspension is comprised of beefed springs and HD shocks. The front axle is of the flanged type, while the rear axle is also HD and has additional support from HD shocks. On

Engine compartment had plenty of space when a Powerthrift 232 cubic inch engine is included. Dry type of air cleaner is used for the inline six.

street operation, the SR-2 fared well when taken over familiar rough spots where local street repairs were underway. It definitely carries itself well, both on and off the road.

Increasing the riding pleasure of the SR-2 were four Polyglass H70-15 tires mounted on International chrome rims. Polyglass is a remarkable tire for street operation, however, a tire expert advised us that polyglass, a four-ply tire, loses some of its advantages when applied to off-road operation. The sides are only two-ply, so low pressure use would bring the sides into more direct contact with the road. On the road, the polyglass provides astounding gripping ability, while off

the road the tires seemed to adequately carry the rig.

Besides the chrome wheels, the SR-2 has a chromed front bumper, chromed external rear view mirrors, a chromed antenna with whip-coil, chromed gas caps, and the attractive front grille surrounded by chrome.

With the two-tone paint (ours was white and bronze), chromed wheels, tires and striping, the SR-2 is a breathtaking dazzler. The best looking yet from International.

Good appearance also applies to the interior, which featured vinyl upholstered seats, carpeting, sound-absorbing headliner, chromed dash gauges, door panels and arm rests. With the engine

sounding smooth and powerful outside of the rig, it's easy to tell when it's started. However, it took · a concentrated ear to hear when the engine started while behind the wheel. The noise dampeners on the inside are great, especially when driving the freeway for long distances. The seats are also comfortable, from first touch to last, but it's the door ledge that tends to cause a few trips. The seats force a good sitting posture, but with the 17-inch steering wheel located just above the lap and the relatively low foot boards, high-stepping has to be made an effort.

It's also an effort to turn the unpowered wheel. In comparison with a

V-8 (more weight on the front) 800-A, the SR-2 lost the contest. The steering difficulty was present through the entire test, which lasted more than 800 miles. But to criticize the steering without offering a high speed evaluation would be unfair. At high speeds, the steering is good.

Another interesting characteristic of the SR-2 is its waterproofing. While subjecting the SR-2 to the sand and water trial, the water surged below the rig and doused the electrical components and caused the fire to die. The engine sputtered while trying to

Traction on the sand with tires deflated was moderately good. Polyglass tires were excellent on the hard surfaces.

By the sea the SR-2 is au natural. *Vacuum windshield wipers washed away the sea spray. Problems developed when the rig was run along the shore as the engine drowned out.*

start, and finally it did. The drowning wasn't consistent, however, as the surging tide flowed below the rig several times.

For reaching the sand, 4wd was locked in and the tires were deflated. Low gear was used intermittently between high gear as the transfer case lever was tested. No problems there. As the rig was powered through soft sections of sand, the speedometer needle jumped from 0 to 30 in first gear in high. A shift to compound low and the SR-2 whined and dashed.

The seating was fine for two people as we crossed the sand and descended a small embankment that signaled the edge of the ocean line, but the rider in the rear wasn't too happy. The Scout line of 4wd's has a tremendous amount of storage room. The potential is unlimited, almost, with the addition of the chromed rack. This rig had no rack on top. It also had a rear seat. To explain the rear seating arrangement would be to describe sitting in a Japanese restaurant or driving a soapbox derby car. The legs have to be extended straight forward, which means that the rear seat has to be as far back as feasible. What happens to the storage room? There are a few cubic feet of space behind the rear seat for things like a suitcase and sleeping bag, unrolled.

Another nicety of the SR-2 was the rear sliding windows. On hot days it was much nicer to flip the windows back and close the side door windows. The back gate also opened easily and provided pleasure in operation as the tailgate first had to be dropped, the

Front view of the SR-2 shows its bold features. Distinctive grill work adds to its show appearance.

rear window lifted, and the tailgate lifted back into position. Positive locks on the window kept it open while off the road.

The rear view vision through the tail window was hampered by wide corners and a spare tire. A little more glass, possibly? The rear view mirrors were excellent for knowing who was trailing behind during driving on congested freeways after the working day had concluded. The SR-2 seems to become hot, but not overheated, very quickly as it stays at a constant level on the gauge. The heat controlled thermostat lets the engine warm up quickly in the morning. The other gauges—gas, oil, amps—are to the left of the steering column, while the speedometer is uncommonly located to the right of the column. The angle of the column, coming from the steering gear box, necessitates the location of the speedometer to its right. It's a bit unusual, but old habits are soon forgotten.

Below the gauges are the separate instrument controls for the lights and windshield wipers. The latter, vacuum controlled, work independently of each other. It's a strange sight to see two windshield wipers flapping out of time.

In the middle of the dash the radio

rests, slightly above and to the left of the heater control. The glove box offers plenty of room for storing practicals such as flares, maps, or small tools.

Below the passenger seat, which flips forward for easy entrance to the rear, is the jack for tire repair.

On the driver's side and below his seat is the fuel tank selector valve control, which allows gas to flow directly to the engine from either right or left nine gallon tank. With the right combination of driving techniques and road conditions, more than 270 miles can be driven without having to stop to refuel. That's about 15 miles to the gallon.

All during the test, the SR-2 developed no troubles mechanically, except when the radio automatically turned on and off. Hit a bump, and there was music. Hit another bump, and it became silent.

Lifting the front hood to see what could be done reminded us that the engine compartment was very spacious. The Powerthrift Six is a tight fit into the engine compartment when a two-piece mounting bracket is used to secure the forepart of the engine block to the front of the chassis. To the sides of the engine space reigns.

Also neatly tucked into the inner confines of the engine compartment is the brake tandem master cylinder, windshield washer fluid reservoir, vacuum pump for the windshield wipers, the battery and the heating unit.

International reported in early statistics that again they would follow the cautious route and has listed the SR-2 as a limited production model. The SR-2 is the flashiest yet, and appears to be the most dashing of the 4x4 bobtails. It's the little things that have to be worked out.

SCOUT II

International introduced the Scout-type off road vehicle almost a decade ago. Since then nearly a half million of similarly-styled back country ma-more than 300,000 of these are Scouts. chines roam the trails of America and No one needs to go any further in proving that International had a good idea.

Now they have done something almost as revolutionary — introduced a second generation Scout. At first glance it might not seem that the new Scout II is completely new. But those who are familiar with the engineering from frame to spare tire will immediately begin finding the differences.

The total change is not too evident from the outside and the new concept takes a few seconds to soak in. The rear side window treatment strikes the eye first and then the subtle changes in the rounded sections of the body. Soon the old time off road enthusiast finds himself literally checking hundreds of minor changes in styling and trying to

Luxury and ruggedness are the keynotes of the all new Scout II. Ladies will like it for town or off road duty.

64

MAJOR DIMENSIONS

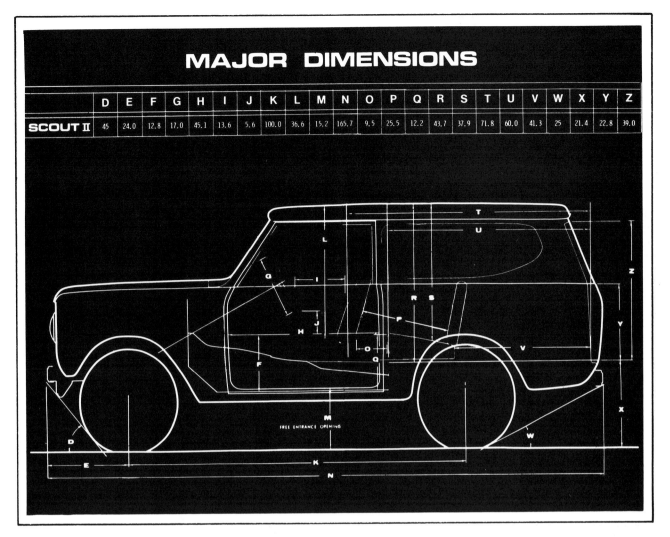

	D	E	F	G	H	I	J	K	L	M	N	O	P	Q	R	S	T	U	V	W	X	Y	Z
SCOUT II	45	24.0	12.8	17.0	45.1	13.6	5.6	100.0	36.6	15.2	165.7	9.5	25.5	12.2	43.7	37.9	71.8	60.0	41.3	25	21.4	22.8	39.0

absorb the Scout's changed look.

Overall the exterior of the Scout is remarkably pleasing. A vehicle that can still be driven off the road and to the market but now has a new function. No one would feel the least uncomfortable in driving up to the finest restaurant in their home town, dressed in their best clothes.

Scout's engineers may have done something that has not even yet occurred to them or International's sales force. The Scout II may be the best bet yet for the single car family that wants to spend their weekends in the back country where four-wheel drive is necessary to get them where they want to go.

A look inside some of the more deluxe versions of the Scout II bear this out. For old timers whose idea of taking off in the toolies was packing a sleeping bag and a six pack, the interior decor of the Scout II will come as sort of a shock, to say the least.

Seats are luxury bucket with a plush vinyl cover. Floor mats . . .? Not really, unless you want the everyday version. Instead the new Two has luxuriant pile carpet in blue, gold, black or red that adds a dash of elegance.

Look around and you'll see that the dash is padded as well as the quilted door panels. Although it is not time to speak of such things, the Scout II can come with automatic transmission, full, across-panel air conditioning and a color matching steering wheel.

It might occur to experienced four wheelers that someone in styling got a grip on International's thinking and what they have offered is simply a jazzed up version of the old Scout with a new skin and a lot of goodies.

Nothing could be further from the truth and a look at the line up of engines will prove that someone in engineering really cares. Of course, there are familiar faces. Standard is the 196 cid Four, a slant four inline that has been around more years than we care to mention. Four wheelers have looked on this engine with scant approval in the past and have almost universally passed it up in favor of the bigger powerplants. This year Californians will have no problems of choosing something else—International apparently agreed with the far westerners and didn't bring the engine up to California's tough air pollution standards.

Instead, the first choice for this state will be the 232 cubic inch, inline Six which develops 135 horsepower. For those who are not economy inclined the V-304, V-8 with its 193 horsepower is back.

But for the first time, a rather remarkable engine is available for the Scout II. Those who like to run down the spec sheets quickly might miss the real meaning of the new powerplant. This is International's V-345 which is rated at 197 horsepower. At first glance it might seem rather foolish to have two V-8 selections, one with only four extra horses. One major clue for the reasoning is in the gross torque output which is rated at 309 foot-pounds at 2200 rpm.

Even this does not tell the whole story and it is necessary to go to the graph to see some of the real potential of this engine. The V-345 is pure truck engine and its torque curve after peaking is as flat as Aunt Tillie's bust. And, like Aunt Tillie, when it puts out—it really puts out.

With full power available over a long range of rpm's this engine will have no trouble with hills, trailers or even off road racing. In this latter respect, it might be one of the most important developments for those who like to bang over hummocks for money. With little modification, it can probably hold its own with any engine running in races today.

Coupled to the engines will be the familiar three-speed manual transmission. A four-speed, choose your gear, is available with the Six and bigger engines, is a three-speed console-stick automatic which also comes in four-wheel drive.

All models have a ten-inch, six-spring clutch as standard. With the Six a 10½-inch version is optional; for the all-out racing or performance enthusiasts, an 11-angle link clutch has been provided as an option with the Four or V-8 engines.

This year both the economy and guts crowd will find an overall axle ratio to suit them with 3:31, 3:73, or 4:27-to-1 available. Also the limited slip differential, trade name Track-Lok, has been completely redesigned for the mid-year model change.

Many changes have been made in the suspension system to improve both the ride and off-road handling characteristics. The front springs are wider and three inches longer, now measuring 40 inches by two inches. The rear springs are 56 inches by two inches, some ten inches longer than those on earlier Scouts. The total design of the suspension includes setting the springs out further which has measureably changed all handling characteristics. For those who demand more, there are heavy duty front and rear springs, heavy duty progressive rear springs and a front spring air attachment listed as extra cost items.

Braking on the Scout II will be excellent with 11-inch by two-inch linings in front and 11 inches by 1¾ inches in the rear. With 175.7 square inches of surface this provides more than the Scout will need when driven solo and ample reserve to handle a medium-sized trailer.

Many off roaders will find the completely re-engineered steering system to their liking. It is now worm-and-roller steering with the front axle using open Cardon joints. International engineers have been able to set their geometry for a 38 degree turning angle. This year, another change in the suspension are the ball-joint kingpins which greatly improve the damping out of shock from irregular terrain while contributing to longer life. From a safety standpoint the steering columns is lockable and energy absorbing. Those who like ease of steering will be able to order power steering on all the optional engines.

One moot point on the steering is the extended left arm which is bored to take what our technical staff throught was a steering damper—something not needed with the newly redesigned steering. After tracking down the head engineer, we discovered that it was simply a forethought. In the event International wins a post office contract, the steering is engineered to swap to right-hand drive with little change.

For off roaders who drive during summer, or in the desert, the Scout II has a greatly increased cooling system which is pressurized with a reservoir which stores water instead of letting it run off. The radiator is a cross-flow and a modulated fan is optional on V-8 engines to increase efficiency.

The fuel tank has been mounted amidships between the rear frame rails. With a capacity of 19 gallons it offers long mileage which ever engine is se-

SCOUT II HAS NEW DIMENSIONS, LUGGAGE AND WIDER DOORS MAKE ENTRY EASY.

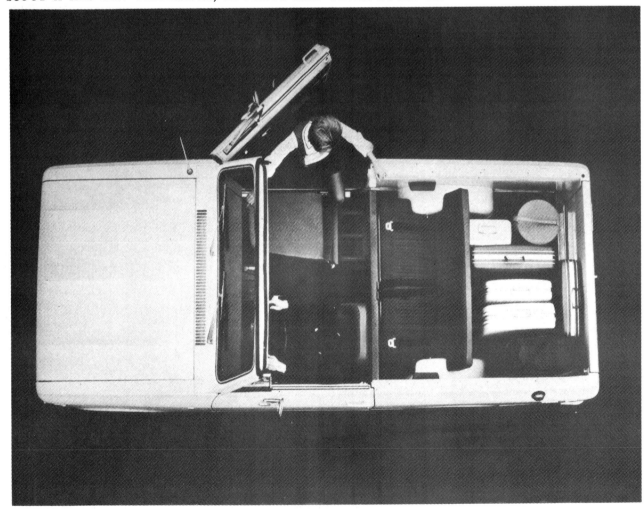

New V-345, V-8 engine is an important accessory for Scout II. Horsepower is slightly more but torque curve nearly flat after peaking at 2200 rpm.

The new Scout II will be far easier to negotiate on tough trails. Steering geometry has been completely redesigned and the turning circle is much smaller.

lected. Accessory manufacturers have been anticipated by International which has already designed a factory installed skid plate for the gas tank as well as one for the entire power train.

A lot of four wheelers will get a big kick out of playing the numbers game with Scout II's new dimensions. Without further ado, let's take a look at what the styling engineers came up with for the specification book. Bumper-to-bumper the Scout is 165.7 inches long, 70 inches wide (at the apex of the fender curve) with an overall height of 66.4 inches (for the station wagon type). Wheelbase is 100 inches.

Those who know will realize what the differences are, but here they are spelled out. The Scout II body is nearly three inches lower and nearly eleven inches longer. And by lower we mean to the ground, yet it has the same generous ground clearance it always had. Longitudinal-wise, if you can say it, the Scout II has six inches more for driver and passengers and a six-foot, six-inch driver will not bang his head on the headliner, if he buckles his seat belt. In the rear there is nearly five cubic feet more cargo space. The rear seat is now full-width and placed on the same level as the driver. This seat is also located ahead of the rear axle which greatly increases riding comfort.

One minor change will be greatly lauded by the stiff side of off roading who have long complained that there is a sexy way, but no dignified way to enter an off road machine while wearing a dress. Scout engineers have flattened the door sill and widened the

door to 45.1 inches. The floor height has also been lowered to 15.2 inches.

International has admitted this year that there are no "idiots" driving off road machines and have eliminated their lights. Instrumentation is full and controlled by printed circuits for reliability. Fuses have been moved to the left side of the steering column for easy accessibility.

With all the previously mentioned changes and the emphasis on luxury, it is only to be expected that the Scout II can be purchased with vinyl twin bucket seats, air conditioning, tinted glass, color keyed interior trim packages, rear dome light, courtesy lights, coat hooks and even a cargo area mat (color keyed) with insulation.

At its introduction on the vast proving grounds of International just south of Phoenix, Arizona, there was not one of the hundreds of automotive experts who did not agree that the Scout II was entirely new. Overall, in appearance, it has not changed greatly, but for the better. The most important changes are under the skin where even the simplest bolt placement has been examined and redesigned if ncessary.

But this engineering triumph may go unnoticed by the general public. International has come up with the first of what is bound to be a trend. An off road vehicle that is also a luxury passenger car. Something that everybody has said was quite impossible. The Scout II proves it wasn't.

Styling changes are more apparent on the station wagon model, but even the pickup style shows the rounded curves of the body. Each of the Scout II versions has a long list of luxury options.

INTERNATIONAL SCOUT

A Drive-Test reveals a performance minded bobtail with plenty of comfort.

With the introduction of International's 1973 line up, we decided to conduct a driving impression of the Scout. To this end we got in touch with Vic Hickey, the inveterate fixer-uper, who had a new Scout. Vic had added some custom touches of his own, which aided driving both on and off-road. Although the new Scout has a standard dash mounted transfer case shifter, Vic had taken delivery of a Scout with the optional floor mounted shifter. We thought this would be a good test, as a future test of a Scout with the dash mounted shifter would make an interesting comparison.

When we picked up our test Scout, we noted with satisfaction that it **looked** like a real off-road machine, due to the Hickey accessories that adorned the vehicle inside and out. The stock, factory gold paint that International uses is a definite winner, and with the

FOUR WHEELER ROAD TEST

Rear view shows fuel tank skid plate and Hickey swing-away tire and can carrier.

addition of a little striping, it looks like a custom paint job.

For a compact bobtail, the Scout is one of the most versatile of all 4x4s. Interior comfort can be extended to that of a passenger car with the addition of a variety of optional packages. Although extensive use of different engines coupled to different transmissions and axle ratios can often cause quality control problems. International has undertaken to endow the Scout with just such numerous powertrain options. You can order several different engines, from a base six to big V8s. These engines can be combined with a number of transmissions, from 3-speed manuals to automatics. And several different axle ratios can be ordered.

POWERTRAIN AND PERFORMANCE

Our test Scout was set up with a 345-cubic inch V8 and a 3-speed automatic transmission. The 345 in the little Scout afforded excellent power and good, fast acceleration. The floor mounted automatic transmission shifter was in an ideal location. The shifter is close at hand for easy, manual shifting if you enjoy down shifting an automatic for compression or upshifting during acceleration. More manufacturers who build 4x4s with automatic transmissions should use this floor position. It might hinder three people riding in the front seat, but it gives much more control to the driver, especially in rough, rugged terrain. The optional, old style, floor mounted transfer case shifter is easy to shift, but it always seemed to grind excessively when shifting into Hi or Lo four wheel drive, even with the transmission in neutral and the vehicle stopped. It will be interesting to test the new dash mounted unit for ease of shifting and to find out if it still grinds gears.

Although the floor mounted automatic tranny costs $235, we think it is an option that is worth the price for enjoyable four wheeling. Our test vehicle also had a # 44 Spicer Power Lok, which at $60 is also a good option for better control in water, mud, sand, or snow.

Fuel economy wasn't as good as expected, or as good as we felt it could be with the big engine and smaller vehicle. Gas consumption ran between 10.2 and 11.6 mpg and averaged about 11.0 mpg even.

HANDLING, STEERING
AND STOPPING AND STOPPING

The Scout was one of the best and easiest handling rigs around. Our test

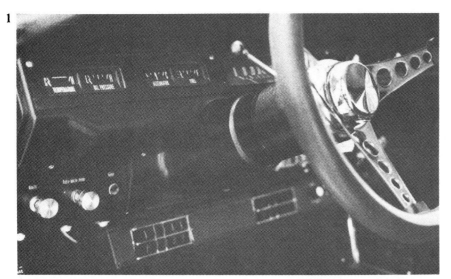

1. Instrument panel has gauges for all engine functions. Small, padded steering wheel is Hickey addition.

2. Floor mounted automatic transmission and transfer case shifter are close at hand.

3. Scout front bucket seats are quite comfortable. Console with folding arm rest adds excellent driver arm support.

4. Factory installed front locking hubs, chrome wheel, and Norseman tire make good combination.

vehicle came equipped with heavy duty front and rear springs, which cost $19 installed at the factory. The HD springs are also a recommended option. In addition, it had 700D Saginaw power steering. That's an option that definitely is worth $128 when you get off road. It is even more true when you add a set of Armstrong Norseman tires, which Hickey obtained from Dick Cepek. To help even more off road, Hickey added his Shimmy Dampner springs ($12.50) and heavy duty front spring shackles ($12.50), plus a steering stabilizer ($25.95). With all that equipment up front, the track of the Scout stayed true and even and never wandered in the slightest. Handling was much improved off road.

International brakes performed well under normal conditions. We didn't have an opportunity to take the Scout to a test track to practice panic brake stops. We put several thousand miles on this test rig and didn't have any brake problems of fading or pulling.

COMFORT AND CONVENIENCE

The Scout becomes quite luxurious when you order some of the convenience trim packages. Our test vehicle had the Custom Interior Trim ($245) and the Deluxe Exterior Trim Package ($116) as factory installed options. When Hickey got the vehicle he added even more: Rollbar ($69.95); foam padded steering wheel ($14.95); spare tire carrier ($56.95); console jump seat ($59.95); dual exhausts ($69.95); front end guard ($59.95); chrome wheels ($35.00 ea.); and chrome tow hooks ($9.95). With all the extra goodies inside and out, the Scout became a dream 4x4.

The Scout dash has a good layout with a padded top. Our test vehicle had an all black interior, upholstery, and carpeting, which kept the dirt from showing too much. The instrument panel had all gauges with no lights for any of the important monitoring functions. Gauges run horizontally across the panel, with the speedometer/odometer on the right. All controls, such as lights and windshield wipers have lighted names just above the control knob so there is no fumbling for the correct knob at night. Unfortunately, the Scout glove box is too small to handle many objects or gear that one has to take off road.

The radio is in the center of the dash and can be reached by either driver or passenger. The same is true of the heater and air conditioning controls. If you are a heavy smoker, you'll find the ash tray

Continued on page 73

SCOUT PRICES AND OPTIONS

Suggested retail price $3388.00

OPTIONAL EQUIPMENT

Heavy duty rear step bumper . . . . $ 23.50	700D Saginaw power steering 128.00	Driver and passenger seats 102.00
Lock-O-Matic front hubs 106.00	AM radio 62.00	Custom interior trim 245.00
Heavy duty front and rear springs . . . 19.00	V345 engine 189.00	Deluxe exterior trim 116.00
Dual hydraulic brake control 43.50	3-speed automatic transmission 235.00	Luggage rack 68.00
	#44 Spicer Power Lok 60.00	Full width rear seat 115.00
	Fuel tank skid plate 16.00	Air conditioning package 402.00

Rear seat in Scout is one of best in production; allows lots of floor space so your feet and legs have someplace to go.

Rear storage space is adequate when seat is up.

Slick New Scout

Sitting in looking out, you'd hardly guess you were driving an off-road vehicle. It's another of those two-car cars

By MICHAEL LAMM, West Coast Editor/Photos by the Author

INTERNATIONAL HARVESTER assumes that the typical off-roader still spends most of his time *on the road*. Thus the new Scout II, while it's perfectly at home in the wilds and woollies, is as much so on the freeway or carting the kids to music lessons.

In 1961, the original Scout became the first recreational workhorse to give the Jeep Universal a run for its money. Soon, with the Scout selling so well,

Ford jumped in with its Bronco, then Chevy with the Blazer, and several imports also entered the field—the British Land Rover, Toyota's Land Cruiser, and the like.

Now I-H feels it's time for a second generation of Scouts. Styling differences aren't drastic, but the changes inside and underneath are quite thorough. The key word is *refinement*. The Scout II has been greatly refined, and by doing so, I-H is trying to make this vehicle the Cadillac of its class.

You can order it any of 1000 ways—from spartan to ultraluxurious. Airconditioning, power steering, power drum brakes, automatic transmission, two big V8s, All-Wheel drive with power take-off, Trac-Lok limited-slip differentials, locking hubs and fancy interiors are only the beginning. And if you think it's sissy to drive through the

ALL-WHEEL-DRIVE Scout II uses open Cardon joints to give a 38° turn angle. Brakes have 11-in. drums

WITH 4WD, power takeoff is standard. Gearbox options include four-speed manual, three-speed auto

WIDE CHOICE of colors and trim brighten Scout II, and luxuries include airconditioning, power options

boonies with power steering and airconditioning, you ought to try it sometime. The thing is, these luxuries don't impede the Scout II's ability to go odd places—they just make it more flexible and comfortable, and they also make this the car you and your wife can use *willingly* for daily transport. So again, this is one of those two-car cars.

The Scout II in its underwear comes as a roadster, but with doors this time (it used to be available without doors). Since almost no one ever bought a roadster, you can now get one only via special dealer order, and since there's not yet a folding cloth top available, these little impediments add up to I-H's way of discouraging the roadster's sale.

Next rung up the ladder is a Scout II pickup, which is merely the roadster with a cab top. But for more general use, a full-length Traveltop transforms the Scout II into a small wagon, with plenty of room for a family of five plus all their camping gear.

Available engines, transmissions, and general specifications are given on page 102, so we won't repeat those here except to say that one of the V8s—either the 193 or the 197-bhp—is recommended if you're planning to load yours down with options and trailers. The bigger V8 is new to the Scout this year, although it's been available in Travelalls for some time.

The Scout II gives you a choice of

TAILGATE opens with one hand, thanks to spare tire being moved inside. Cargo deck is 5 inches longer

BUCKETS or 30/70 split bench may be trimmed in a variety of styles. Instruments include full gauges

SCOUT
Continued from page 70

is too small.

If you live in a climate that stays warm all year 'round, the Scout air conditioning unit will be a welcome guest. It is by far the best 4x4 air conditioner we've seen. It cools the Scout interior almost instantly, even in 104° summer heat. And there are no leaks, no drips, and no failures. The Scout heater is equally as efficient.

One of the most salient features of the Scout, from the driver's view, are the bucket seats. Our test vehicle had them and they were ultimately comfortable.

With the addition of the Hickey built center console that has a fold-down arm rest, Scout driving was a dream. The center console acts as a third seat when the folding arm rest is up. You can rest your right elbow on the cushioned top when it is down, and the automatic tranny shifter is just an inch away for easy shifting.

As an all-around family car that can be used daily on the road and on weekends for off-road excursions, the Scout combines the best of both worlds. With a few dress-up items, such as those offered by Vic Hickey, a four wheeler can have himself quite a rig.

□

---

toeboard leaks, and the trans hump is now smaller even though the floor stands lower.

The Scout II's ventilation system has been redesigned, with a remote-controlled vent on the driver's side and an easy-to-reach lever for the front passenger. The tailgate may be opened with one hand, because the spare tire now rests inside the car, not continental-style as before, and doesn't hamper tailgate operation. The hood now has an inside lock. It hinges from the front and opens almost vertical to give better engine access.

The Scout II's All-Wheel drive system, made by Dana, can be ordered in the same package with automatic transmission. A separate lever controls the transfer case, and on Scouts equipped with locking front hubs, four-wheel drive can't be engaged except after turning the hubs.

We drove several Scout IIs briefly at I-H's Chandler, Ariz., proving grounds and found them amazingly comfortable and easy to drive. It's impossible to give detailed impressions in so short a space, but we will say we were extremely impressed with the performances the new Scouts turned in.

The base Traveltop wagon with the standard 111-bhp Four sells for $2622. All-Wheel drive adds $822, and from there the sky's the limit. With most of the luxury options, the tab can easily top $5000.

★ ★ ★

SCOUT II stands lower, longer; gets re-engineered suspension for a greater on or off-highway comfort

front bucket seats or a bench with a 30/70 split. Gauges are just that—no idiot lights. The 19-gallon gas tank nestles between the rear (and fully boxed) frame rails. Optional skidplates are a must for rough country, because the Scout II has longer leaf springs than before, thus more suspension travel. This means the body dips lower on hard bumps, but it also means a more comfortable, softer ride both on and off the road. We recommend skidplates both front and rear.

Other differences between the old and the new Scout are briefly these: The new body stands 3 inches lower and nearly 11 inches longer, giving half a foot more passenger space and a 5-inch longer cargo bed. Doors are wider and now use flat sills so you don't have to step over them. The doors have check straps and better insulation to cut wind noise at higher speeds. Pedals are suspended for the first time to eliminate the chance of

---

1972 SCOUT II SPECIFICATIONS

Available engines: ohv 4, 196 c.i.d. (std.); ohv 6, 232 c.i.d.; ohv V8, 304 c.i.d.; ohv V8, 345 c.i.d.

Available transmissions: three-speed manual, floor shift (std.); four-speed manual, floor shift; three-speed automatic, floor shift.

Differential types and ratios: All-Wheel drive with power takeoff (opt.); Trac-Lok no-spin differential; manual locking hubs; ratios 3.31, 3.73, 4.27:1.

Brakes: hydraulic drums, 11-in. dia.; 175.7-sq.-in. total lining area; opt. vacuum assist.

Steering: worm and roller; power steering opt.; All-Wheel drive has open front Cardon joints, ball-joint kingpins.

Suspension: Solid front axle, longitudinal semielliptic leaf springs, double-acting, tubular hydraulic shock aborbers, torsional front stabilizer bar; rear is same but without stabilizer bar.

Frame: ladder type, fully boxed side rails, three cross members.

Dimensions: Wheelbase, 100 in.; overall length, 165.7 in.; width, 70.0 in.; overall height, 66.4 in.; front and rear tread, 57.1 in.; curb weight, 3569 lbs.

INTERNATIONAL SCOUT II

A 6-CYL VERSION WITH GOOD PERFORMANCE

THE INTERNATIONAL SCOUT II for 1974 is basically a carryover from the outstanding '73 model, however, there are enough changes to make this vehicle an even better on/off-road performer than it was last year. Power front disc brakes, front anti-sway bar, heavier front and rear suspension and increased trailer towing capabilities are some of the major refinements and these are especially important to people who like to camp and venture into the outback.

The Scout II is available in two models—a Traveltop and a steel Cab Top, both on a 100-in. wheelbase. The Traveltop is a compact wagon style vehicle whereas the Cab Top is a short pickup with a 5-ft cargo box.

The power lineup remains the same as last year with the 258-cu-in. inline 6 as the standard engine. Options include a 304 and 345-cu-in. V-8. Horsepower figures are 113 for the 6, 137 for the 304 and 144 for the 345. A dual exhaust option ups the 345 to 156 net horsepower.

PV4 TEST

The 304 V-8 is not available in California, nor is the 2-bbl carburetor version of the 345. For California only, there is a 4-bbl 345 equipped with electronic ignition. A 3-spd fully synchronized manual transmission is basic with a 4-spd manual and 3-spd floor-mounted automatic available.

The Scout is offered as a 2-wheel drive as well as a 4wd (International calls the 4wd an all-wheel drive). The two wheeler goes for about $700 less than the 4wd. This difference in price might appeal to the people on a budget but who still would like to have a good off-pavement vehicle. A chain-driven, single-speed transfer case is standard in the 4wd. This is a dash mounted, push-pull control and can be engaged or disengaged without stopping the vehicle or going to neutral. A 2-spd floor-mounted transfer case is optional. Manual locking or automatic locking hubs can also be specified.

With an optional heavy-duty rear step bumper and hitch

REPRINT INTERNATIONAL TRUCK SERVICE PUBLICATIONS FROM BINDER BOOKS

Binder Books™

Post Office Box 230269
Tigard, Oregon 97281-0269
Phone (503)-684-2024
Fax (503) 684-3990
E-mail: sac@binderbooks.com
www.binderbooks.com
Retail Store: 8110 SW Durham Rd, Tigard
© Copyright 2000 Binder Books, Updated 04/00
Prices & Availability Subject to Change without Notice.

About the truck manuals we sell:

Our truck publications are licensed and approved by International Truck & Engine Corporation (Formerly International Harvester). Currently, we stock or have available over 190 separate publications for your needs. In addition, we stock thousands of original manuals. Please contact us if you do not see the manual you are looking for.

Truck and Scout Owners Manuals

#	Title	Price Each
1.	Auto Wagon Model MW, AW, MA, & AA	$19.95
2.	1917-1923 Model F	$19.95
3.	1917-1923 Model G	$19.95
4.	1917-1923 Model H	$19.95
5.	1917-1923 Model K	$19.95
6.	International Speed Truck	$19.95
7.	Model 43	$19.95
8.	Model HS-74	$19.95
9.	Special Delivery Truck (1500 lb.)	$19.95
10.	Speed Truck Model SF-34 & 36	$19.95
11.	Six-Speed Special	$19.95
12.	Special Delivery Model AW-1	$19.95
13.	Six Speed Special Model AW-2	$19.95
14.	Model B-4	$19.95
15.	1934-1936 Model C-1	$19.95
16.	1934-1936 Model C-30	$19.95
17.	1934-1936 Model C-35	$19.95
18.	1934-1936 Model CS-40	$19.95
19.	1937-1940 Model D-2 & D-15	$19.95
20.	1937-1940 Model D-30 & DS-30	$19.95
21.	1937-1940 Models D-35, DS-35, D-40 & DS-40	$19.95
22.	1941-1946 Model K-2	$17.95
23.	1947-1949 Model KB-1	$17.95
24.	1947-1949 Model KB-5, KBS-5	$17.95
25.	1947-1949 Model KB-7 & KBS-7	$17.95
26.	1947-1949 Model KB-8 & KBS-8	$17.95
27.	Military M-3L-4-269, M-3H-4-269	$17.95
28.	1950-1952 Model L-110 to L-112	$17.95
29.	1950-1952 Model L-120 to L-122	$17.95
30.	1950-1952 Model L-130 to L-132	$17.95
31.	1950-1952 Model L-160 to L-165	$17.95
32.	1950-1952 Model L-170 to L-175	$17.95
33.	1950-1952 Model L-180 to L-185	$17.95
34.	1953-1955 Model R-100	$17.95
35.	1953-1955 Model R-110 to R-112	$17.95

The Scout II is a comfortable and easy-to-drive vehicle. We like it.

The interior of our test model was not fancy nor was it plain. It had a good balance of both. The front seat was a 1/3-2/3 split bench.

The instrument panel layout is quite good in the Scout II and all of the gauges are there. The controls are easy to reach and they all work simply.

The 6-cyl engine in our test model was lively though not as economical as expected.

ball, the '74 Scout can tow camping trailers up to 2000 pounds. For larger trailers up to 5000 pounds, an equalizer hitch receiver can be dealer installed. The front and rear suspension is conventional with semi-elliptic leaf springs on live axles. Last year's optional 3200-pound capacity front axle is now standard with the V-8 engine and optional with the six. Gross vehicle weight ratings are 5200 (standard) or 5500 (optional).

The dash is fully instrumented and there are dual padded sun visors, arm rest and adjustable window vents. The standard interior is sage-colored vinyl. Two levels of interiors can be specified. The deluxe cames with a vinyl nylon 1/3-2/3 split-back front seat. The top of the line is the Custom. Front bucket seats can be ordered with any interior as can a folding rear bench seat. Two-tone appliques made of vinyl are production line installed and are offered in four decor treatments ranging from white stripes and white side panels to wood grain side panels.

The radial tire package consists of 15 x 7-in. slotted wheels, HR78 x 15B steel belted radial tires, chrome lug nuts and chrome rear axle end plates. This package carries a price tag of just over $300. Other options for the '74 Scout include chrome bumpers, power steering, air conditioning, panel sides in lieu of glass in the Traveltop, AM/FM radio and a skid plate kit that comes detached.

TEST & IMPRESSIONS

Our test Scout was the Traveltop model with the 258-cu-in. 6-cyl engine with 4-spd manual transmission. Unlike the '73 Scout we tested in the October issue, which was loaded to the gunwales, the '74 was rather spartan with a minimum of accessories. The option list for our test vehicle included manual locking front hubs, 11-inch clutch, increased cooling, hand throttle, 2-spd transfer case, deluxe interior trim, folding rear bench seat and H78 x 15 tires. The West Coast list price was just under $5000.

The first thing we noticed in sliding behind the wheel was that the hood seemed much higher than previous models. Visibility to the roadway directly in front of the vehicle was restricted. We knew the actual body dimensions had not been changed so we passed it off as perhaps it was just our imagination. In pulling away from the parking lot one thing was definitely obvious. This Scout did not have power steering. The effort required to steer the vehicle was not necessarily greater than other non-power trucks but the steering ratio was extremely slow. Much winding of the steering wheel was needed to negotiate a street corner and the wheel did not want to return to straight forward without some help on the driver's part. When driving down the freeway the steering wheel could be turned slightly and it would stay there until brought back to center. In all fairness, this was a zero miles vehicle when we picked it up and perhaps with use the steering would loosen up some. At any rate, we don't believe anyone should consider the Scout without power steering. It would be extremely tiring off road without it.

The ride in town and in the boonies was very good. The suspension had a happy medium; it was neither too soft nor too stiff. It soaked up the uneven terrain but retained good stability at all times. Other than the slow steering, the maneuverability and handling were also very good. The bench seat was comfortable and set well to the steering wheel although perhaps a little closer than we would have liked. The instruments were easily readable but somewhat on the small side. The horizontal speedometer was located to the right of the steering column rather than in the middle but this posed no problem.

While thrashing around the perimeter of Saddleback Park test facility, we found that it was not our imagination that the hood obstructed the forward view. When topping a rise we found ourselves leaning forward and stretching our neck to get a glimpse of the ground ahead. Traveling off pavement at speed could create some anxious moments. The seat height

may be lower in the '74 than last year. This was not as much of a problem with the taller members of the staff.

The 6-cyl engine ran beautifully from the first moment we fired it up. It was a good combination coupled to the 4-spd manual transmission. The Scout became only the third vehicle to climb Test Hill No. 2 (63 percent grade) in 2-wheel drive, however, we had to go to 4wd low range to get it over Hill No. 3. The 6 just didn't have enough power to make it in high range. But that's nothing to be ashamed of as most PV4s won't make it up No. 3 in high range either.

The 4-spd is a stout transmission and requires a healthy tug to change gears. Low gear is sometimes hard to engage when stopped but should loosen up with more miles. Synchronization is in the top three gears. The 2-spd transfer case is very smooth and positive. The lever is easily reached from the driver's seat.

At Orange County International Raceway a pleasant surprise was in store for us. Last year's Scout, which had drum brakes on all four corners, was miserable in the braking department. Not so with the '74. We knew the brakes were better from just driving the vehicle around town but adding the power disc brakes up front really made a difference. The '73 Scout required over 200 feet to make a panic stop from 60 mph—the '74 needed only 154. The stop was straight and there was a minimum of nosediving. From an initial pedal pressure of 32 pounds for a ½-g stop, the brakes faded only 56 percent for a 50 pound reading on the 6th stop. The Scout rated excellent in this department.

We didn't expect miracles in the acceleration tests and we didn't get any. However, the 6 did well enough for a 3900-pound vehicle with a 3.73:1 rear axle ratio. The standing start quarter mile was turned in 21.4 seconds at 63 mph. This compares to what the mini-pickups are doing. Gas economy was about what we expected from the 6-cyl engine. At 13.9 mpg, it's better than the V-8 we tested last year. With the gas shortages seeming to get worse, the 6 will be in more demand than ever. We believe the Scout with this engine is strong enough for most everyone's needs.

We thought the '74 Scout was well built, comfortable to drive, with a certain beauty about it. You can get one as plain or as fancy as you like. For the money, it has to be considered a good buy. ●

Seeing over the hood seemed a bit of a problem for some of our staff members. Scout II is outstanding off the road.

There is adequate space behind the rear seat for some cargo. We like the spare tire placement.

The 6-cyl Scout II is one of the best riding and handling vehicles we have tested, especially off the pavement.

INTERNATIONAL SCOUT II

PRICES

Basic list, FOB Ft. Wayne, Ind.
Scout II Cab Top $3790
Scout II Traveltop $3943

Standard equipment: 258-cu-in. inline 6-cyl engine, 3-speed manual transmission, full instrumentation, front bench seat, backup lights, heater/defroster, 2-speed electric wiper/washers, painted front bumper, power front disc brakes, F78 x 15LRB tires.

ENGINES

Standard . . . . 258-cu-in. inline 6
Bore x stroke, in . . . . 3.75 x 3.89
Compression ratio 8.0:1
Net horsepower @ rpm . . . . . 113 @ 4000
Net torque @ rpm, lb-ft . . . . . 191 @ 2000
Type fuel required . . . . 91 octane

Optional 304-cu-in. V-8 . . . . $118
Bore x stroke, in . . . . 3.875 x 3.218
Compression ratio 8.19
Net horsepower @ rpm . . . . . 137 @ 4000
Net torque @ rpm, lb-ft . . . . . 233 @ 2400
Type fuel required . . . . 91 octane

Optional 345-cu-in. V-8 . . . . $153*
Bore x stroke, in . . . . 3.875 x 3.656
Compression ratio 8.05:1
Net horsepower @ rpm: 144 @ 3600; 156 w/dual exh.
Net torque @ rpm, lb-ft: 263 @ 2000; 269 w/dual exh.
Type fuel required . . . . 91 octane
*For Calif., engine has 4-bbl carb and electronic ignition. Cost is $258.

DRIVE TRAIN

Standard transmission . . . . . 3-spd manual
Clutch dia., in. . . . . 10.5 & 11
Transmission ratios: 3rd 1.00:1
2nd 1.85:1
1st 2.80:1
Synchromesh . . . . 2nd & 3rd gear

Optional 4-spd manual $107
Transmission ratios: 4th 1.00:1
3rd 1.41:1
2nd 2.41:1
1st 4.02:1
Synchromesh . . . . . . 2nd, 3rd & 4th gear

Optional 3-spd automatic $249
Transmission ratios: 3rd 1.00:1
2nd 1.45:1
1st 2.45:1
Rear axle type . . . . . semi-floating hypoid
Final drive ratios: 3.31:1, 3.73:1, 4.27:1
Overdrive . . . . none
Free-running front hubs:
Manual $77
Automatic $113
Limited slip differential $64
Transfer case . . . . single spd & 2-spd
Transfer case ratios . . . . 1.00:1 & 2.03:1

CHASSIS & BODY

Body/frame: ladder-type frame with separate steel body
Brakes (std): front, 11.75-in. dia. disc; rear, 11 x 2.5-in. drums
Brake swept area, sq in. 417
Swept area/ton (max load) 151
Power brakes . . . . std

Steering type (std) . . . . . . worm & roller
Steering ratio 24:1
Power steering $136
Power steering ratio 17.5:1
Turning circle, ft 34

Wheel size (std) . . . . 15 x 6.0JK
Optional wheel sizes . . . . 15 x 7.0JJ
Tire size (std) . . . . F78 x 15LRB
Optional tire sizes: G78 x 15LRB, H78 x 15LRB, HR78 x 15B

SUSPENSION

Front suspension: semi-elliptic leaf springs on live axle with tube shocks
Front axle capacity, lb 2500
Optional 3200

Rear suspension: semi-elliptic leaf springs on live axle with tube shocks
Rear axle capacity, lb 3500
Optional . . . . none

Additional suspension options: HD spring and shock pkg, $22; front air type level ride springs, $45

ACCOMMODATION

Standard seats: full width front bench
Optional seats: 1/3-2/3 split back front bench, $33; folding full width rear bench seat, $108; front buckets, $92

Headroom, in. 36
Pedal to seatback, max 44
Steering wheel to seatback, max 15
Seat to ground 32
Floor to ground 18

Heater & defroster . . . . std
Tinted glass: $18 (Cab Top), $30 (Traveltop)
Air conditioning $427

Unobstructed load space (length x width x height) in.
With seats in place . . . . . 41 x 42 x 41.5
Rear folded . . . . 59 x 42 x 41.5
Tailgate (width x height) . . . . 53 x 23

INSTRUMENTATION

Instruments: 0-100-mph speedometer, 99,999.9-mi. odometer, fuel gauge, oil pressure, water temp, ammeter
Warning lights: hazard warning, brake system warning, front axle engaged signal light
Optional . . . . none

GENERAL

Curb weight, lb (test model) 3875
GVW (max. laden weight) 5200
Optional GVWs: 4600 (std Cab Top), 5200 (optl Cab Top), 5500 (both models)

Wheelbase, in. 100.0
Track, front/rear 51.7/51.7
Overall length 165.8
Overall height: 65.8 (Cab Top) 66.2 (Traveltop)
Overall width 70.0
Overhang, front/rear 27/39.5

Approach angle, degrees 38
Departure angle 23

Ground clearances (test model):
Front axle 9.1
Rear axle 8.2
Oil pan 15.5
Transfer case 12.8
Fuel tank 14.0
Exhaust system (lowest point) . . . 11.7

Fuel tank capacity (U.S. gal) 19
Auxiliary tank . . . . none

PERFORMANCE DATA

TEST MODEL

Traveltop, 258-cu-in. 6-cyl. engine, 4-spd transmission, painted rear bumper, locking hubs, AM radio, chrome wheel covers, increased cooling, hand throttle, deluxe interior trim, full width folding rear seat, 2-tone paint, H78 x 15B tires, 11-in. clutch, 2-spd transfer case, 3.73 rear axle.
West Coast list price $4990

ACCELERATION

Time to speed, sec:
0-30 mph 5.2
0-45 mph 10.4
0-60 mph 18.4
0-70 mph 22.5
Standing start, ¼-mile, sec 21.4
Speed at end, mph 63

SPEED IN GEARS

High range, 4th (3500 rpm) 77
3rd (4000 rpm) 63
2nd (4000 rpm) 36
1st (4000 rpm) 22
Low range, 4th (4000 rpm) 44
3rd (4000 rpm) 31
2nd (4000 rpm) 18
1st (4000 rpm) 11

BRAKE TESTS

Pedal pressure required for ½-g deceleration rate from 60 mph, lb 32
Stopping distance from 60 mph, ft . . .154
Fade: Percent increase in pedal pressure for 6 stops from 60 mph 56
Overall brake rating . . . . excellent

INTERIOR NOISE

Idle in neutral, dBA 61.5
Maximum during acceleration 83
At steady 60-mph cruising speed 79

OFF PAVEMENT

Hillclimbing ability . . . . excellent
Maneuverability . . . . very good
Turnaround capability . . . . . . very good
Handling . . . . very good
Ride . . . . very good

GENERAL

Heater rating . . . . very good
Defroster effectiveness . . . . very good
Wiper coverage . . . . good

FUEL CONSUMPTION

Normal driving, mpg 13.9
Off pavement 10.4
Range, normal driving, miles 264
Range, off pavement 197

INT'L SCOUT VS. FORD BRONCO

ONE IS EXCELLENT ON THE PAVEMENT,
THE OTHER IS EXCELLENT OFF THE PAVEMENT

SCOUT VS. BRONCO. That sort of has a nice ring about it and when we decided to do this comparison of the two popular mid-size 4-wheel-drive utility vehicles we felt that it would be worthwhile to make a long-distance trip in them to really learn what they are like. In addition, we wanted to get in some snow time and the nearest white stuff we could find was in the mountains of Utah near Salt Lake City. Well, we reasoned, that's only 750 miles away and the round trip would enable us to become thoroughly familiar and conversant with the two vehicles.

The Scout from International and the Bronco from Ford are two of the older 4wd utility vehicles around. The Scout seems to have been with us since year one and the Bronco made its appearance in 1966, both predating the Blazer, Ramcharger, Cherokee and others. Over the years both vehicles have built up a substantial following among off-pavement enthusiasts and a good argument can be

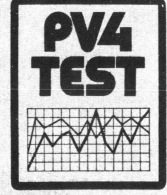

heard on either side any time 4wd folks get together.

These two vehicles are essentially similar in size although the redesign of the Scout in 1973 with the concomitan change in designation to Scout II has put thi vehicle in a sort of in-between state. . .large than the Bronco but smaller than the Cherokee Blazer and Ramcharger.

The Bronco has a wheelbase of 92 inche and an overall length of 152.1 inches while th Scout II stands on a 100-in. wheelbase with total length of 165.8 inches. Conversely, th Scout II is less tall than the Bronco—66.2 versu 70.6 inches. It could be argued that the siz difference between the two puts the Scou more in the class with the bigger 4wds, but w are resisting that train of thought due to tradition and the fact that we still feel they ar close enough to be valid competitors. Also, anyone who ha done much off-pavement driving in all of these vehicles as w have will realize that the difference in size between the Scou

Ford's Bronco, shorter and taller than the competition from International, appeared on the U.S. 4wd market in 1966.

International's Scout II, product of 1973 re-design, has a longer wheelbase and lower profile than the Ford product.

INT'L SCOUT

PRICES
Basic list, FOB Ft. Wayne, Ind.
Scout II Traveltop 4wd $4712

Standard Equipment: 196-cu-in. inline 4-cyl engine, 3-spd manual transmission, single-speed transfer case, full instrumentation, front bench seat, heater/defroster, 2-spd electric wiper/washers, backup lights, painted front bumper, power front disc brakes, H78 x 15B tires, electronic ignition

ENGINES
Standard . . . . . . 196-cu-in. inline 4-cyl
Bore x stroke, in. . . . . 4.125 x 3.656
Compression ratio 8.02:1
Net horsepower @ rpm . . . . . 92 @ 3600
Net torque @ rpm, lb-ft . . . . 164 @ 2000
Type fuel required . . leaded or unleaded

Optional 304-cu-in. V-8 . . . . $99
Bore x stroke, in. . . . . . . 3.875 x 3.218
Compression ratio 8.19:1
Net horsepower @ rpm . . . . 141 @ 4000
Net torque @ rpm, lb-ft . . . . 243 @ 2400
Type fuel required . . leaded or unleaded

Optional 345-cu-in. V-8 . . . . $135
Bore x stroke, in. . . . . . . 3.875 x 3.656
Compression ratio 8.05:1
Net horsepower @ rpm . . . . 158 @ 3600
Net torque @ rpm, lb-ft . . . . 288 @ 2000
Type fuel required . . leaded or unleaded

DRIVE TRAIN
Standard transmission: . . . . 3-spd manual
Clutch dia., in. . . . . 10.5 & 11.0
Transmission ratios: 3rd 1.00:1
2nd 1.85:1
1st 2.80:1
Synchromesh . . . . all forward gears

Optional 4-spd manual $125
Transmission ratios: 4th 1.00:1
3rd 1.41:1
2nd 2.41:1
1st 4.02:1
Synchromesh . . . . . . 2nd, 3rd & 4th gear

Optional 3-spd automatic $269
Transmission ratios: 3rd 1.00:1
2nd 1.45:1
1st 2.45:1
Rear axle type . . . . semi-floating hypoid
Final drive ratios: 3.07:1, 3.54:1, 4.09:1
Overdrive . . . . none

Free-running front hubs:
manual $82
automatic $120
Limited slip differential $68
Transfer case . . . . single & 2-spd
Transfer case ratios . . . 1.00:1 & 2.03:1

CHASSIS & BODY
Body/frame: ladder-type frame with separate steel body

Brakes (std): front, 11.75-in. dia. disc; rear, 11 x 2.5-in. drums
Brake swept area, sq in. 417
Swept area/ton (max load) 134
Power brakes . . . . std

Steering type (std) . . . . . . worm & roller
Steering ratio 24.1
Power steering $159
Power steering ratio 17.5:1
Turning circle, ft 34

Wheel size (std) . . . . 15 x 6.0JK
Optional wheel sizes: . . . . . . 15 x 7.0JJ
Tire size (std) . . . . H78 x 15LRB
Optional tire sizes: HR78 x 15 steel belted radials

SUSPENSION
Front suspension: semi-elliptic leaf springs on live axle with tube shocks
Front axle capacity, lb 3200
Optional . . . . none
Rear suspension: semi-elliptic leaf springs on live axle with tube shocks
Rear axle capacity, lb 3500
Optional . . . . none

Additional suspension options: HD front springs and shocks, $10; HD rear springs, $18

ACCOMMODATION
Standard seats . . . full width front bench
Optional seats: 1/3-2/3 split back front bench, $40; folding full width rear bench, $136; front buckets, $121
Headroom in. 36.0
Accelerator pedal to seatback, max . 46.0
Steering wheel to seatback, max . . . 18.7
Seat to ground 31.5
Floor to ground 17.5

Unobstructed load space (length x width x height) in.
With seats in place . . . . . 40 x 41 x 41.2
Rear folded or removed 66.5 x 41 x 41.2
Tailgate (width x height) . . . . . . 53 x 22

INSTRUMENTATION
Instruments: speedometer, odometer, fuel gauge, oil pressure, water temp, ammeter
Warning lights: hazard warning, brake system warning, front axle engaged signal light
Optional: . . . . none

GENERAL
Curb weight, lb (test model) 4400
GVWR (test model) 6200
Optional GVWRs . . . . none

Wheelbase, in. 100.0
Track, front/rear 57.1/57.1
Overall length 165.8
Overall height 66.2

Overall width 70.0
Overhang, front/rear 23.0/43.0

Approach angle, degrees 42
Departure angle 21

Ground clearances (test model):
Front axle 8.2
Rear axle 8.2
Oil pan 13.7
Transfer case 11.9
Fuel tank 13.3
Exhaust system (lowest point) . . . 11.3
Fuel tank capacity (U.S. gal) 19
Auxiliary tank . . . . none

PERFORMANCE DATA

TEST MODEL
Scout II Traveltop, 304-cu-in. V-8, automatic transmission, 2-spd transfer case, rear stepbumper, free-running front hubs, HD front springs & shocks, HD rear springs, power steering, dual exhausts, trailer wiring, AM radio, 2-tone paint, modulated fan, fuel tank skid plate, evaporative emission control, bucket seats, custom interior, deluxe exterior trim, luggage rack, folding rear seat, air conditioning, storage box console, 3.54:1 limited slip rear axle, H78 x 15B tires
West Coast list price $7570

ACCELERATION
Time to speed, sec:
0-30 mph 5.0
0-45 mph 9.2
0-60 mph 15.3
Standing start, ¼-mile, sec 19.6
Speed at end, mph 68

SPEED IN GEARS
High range,
3rd (4000 rpm) 90
2nd (4000 rpm) 63
1st (4000 rpm) 38

Low range,
3rd (4000 rpm) 44
2nd (4000 rpm) 31
1st (4000 rpm) 19
Engine rpm @ 55 mph 2500

BRAKE TESTS
Pedal pressure required for ½-g deceleration rate from 60 mph, lb 38
Stopping distance from 60 mph, ft . 158
Fade: Percent increase in pedal pressure for 6 stops from 60 mph 52
Overall brake rating . . . . excellent

INTERIOR NOISE
Idle in neutral, dBA 63
Maximum during acceleration 79
At steady 60 mph cruising speed . . . 78

OFF PAVEMENT
Hillclimbing ability . . . . excellent
Maneuverability . . . . very good
Turnaround capability . . . . . . very good
Handling . . . . very good
Ride . . . . excellent

ON PAVEMENT
Handling . . . . very good
Ride . . . . very good
Driver visibility . . . . good
Driver comfort . . . . very good
Engine response . . . . good

FUEL CONSUMPTION
Normal driving, mpg 14.4
Off pavement 10.8
Range, normal driving, miles 273
Range, off pavement 205

FORD BRONCO

PRICES
Basic list, FOB Detroit
Bronco U-100 . . . .$4973

Standard Equipment: 302-cu-in. V-8, 3-spd manual transmission, 2-spd transfer case, bucket seats, free-running front hubs, heater/defroster, 2-spd electric wiper/washers, painted bumpers, backup lights, E78 x 15B tires, full instrumentation, electronic ignition

ENGINES
Standard 302-cu-in. V-8
Bore x stroke, in. . . . . .4.00 x 3.00
Compression ratio 8.0:1
Net horsepower @ rpm . . . . 125 @ 3600*
Net torque @ rpm, lb-ft. . . . 218 @ 2200*
Type fuel required . . . . . . .unleaded only
*For Calif. hp rating is 121 @ 3400 and torque is 216 @ 1600
Optional . . . . none

DRIVE TRAIN
Standard transmission: . . . . 3-spd manual
Clutch dia., in. 11.0
Transmission ratios: 3rd 1.00:1
2nd 1.75:1
1st 2.99:1
Synchromesh . . . . .all forward gears
Optional . . . . .3-spd automatic $246

Transmission ratios: 3rd 1.00:1
2nd 1.46:1
1st 2.46:1

Rear axle type . . . . . .semi-floating hypoid
Final drive ratios: 3.54:1 front/3.50:1 rear; 4.09:1 front/4.11:1 rear
Overdrive .none
Free-running front hubs . . . . std

CHASSIS & BODY
Body/frame: ladder-type frame with separate steel body
Brakes (std): front, 11 x 2-in. drum; rear, 10 x 2.5-in. drum (11 x 1.75-in. w/3300-lb. axle)
Brake swept area, sq in. 295 (258)
Swept area/ton (max load) . . .120 (105)
Power brakes . . . . .none
Steering type (std) . . . . . .worm & roller
Steering ratio 24:1
Power steering $173
Power steering ratio 17:1
Turning circle, ft. 31

Wheel size (std) . . . . .15 x 5.5K
Optional wheel sizes: . . . . .none
Tire size (std) . . . . E78 x 15B
Optional tire sizes: G78 x 15B, G78 x 15D, L78 x 15B, 7.00 x 15C

SUSPENSION
Front suspension: trailing arms and coil springs on live axle with tube shocks
Front axle capacity, lb. 3000
Optional . . . . .none
Rear suspension: leaf springs on live axle with tube shocks
Rear axle capacity, lb. 2900
Optional 3300
Additional suspension options: HD front and rear springs, $14

Limited slip differential . . . . $106 (front), $56 (2900 lb. axle); $63 (3300 lb. axle)

Transfer case . . . . .Dana 2-spd
Transfer case ratios: . . . . 2.46 & 1.00:1

ACCOMMODATION
Standard seats . . . . front buckets
Optional seats . . . . .rear bench $107
Headroom in. 38.6
Accelerator pedal to seatback, max. . . 43.7
Steering wheel to seatback, max. . . .14.8
Seat to ground 33.5
Floor to ground 22.0

Unobstructed load space (length x width x height) in.
With seats in place . . . . . . .13 x 39 x 38
Rear folded or removed . . .49 x 39 x 38
Tailgate (width x height) . . . . . .58 x 21.5

INSTRUMENTATION
Instruments: speedometer, odometer, fuel gauge, ammeter, oil pressure, water temp
Warning lights: hazard warning, brake system warning
Optional: . . . . .none

GENERAL
Curb weight, lb. (test model) 3660
GVWR (test model) 4500
Optional GVWRs 4300, 4450, 4900
Wheelbase, in. 92.0
Track, front/rear 57.4/57.4
Overall length 152.1
Overall height 70.6
Overall width 69.1
Overhang, front/rear 26.0/33
Approach angle, degrees 38
Departure angle 29
Ground clearances (test model):
Front axle 8.2
Rear axle 8.3
Oil pan 17.0
Transfer case 14.3
Fuel tank 15.5
Exhaust system (lowest point) 12.9
Fuel tank capacity (U.S. gal) 12.1
Auxiliary 7.5-gal. tank $40

PERFORMANCE DATA

TEST MODEL
Bronco U-100, 302-cu-in. V-8, automatic transmission, rear bench seat, remote control side mirror, reduced sound level exhaust, 55-amp alternator, extra cooling radiator, hardboard headliner, 70-amp battery, auxiliary fuel tank, chrome bumpers, 3.50:1 limited slip rear axle, L78 x 15B tires, Calif. emissions certificate.
West Coast list price $6122

ACCELERATION
Time to speed, sec:
0-30 mph 4.5
0-45 mph 8.1
0-60 mph 13.6
Standing start, 1/4-mile, sec 19.2
Speed at end, mph 69

SPEED IN GEARS
High range
3rd (4000 rpm) 90
2nd (4000 rpm) 64
1st (4000 rpm) 39
Low range
3rd (4000 rpm) 36
2nd (4000 rpm) 26
1st (4000 rpm) 16
Engine rpm @ 55 mph 2500

BRAKE TESTS
Pedal pressure required for ½-g deceleration rate from 60 mph, lb 83
Stopping distance from 60 mph, ft . 206
Fade: Percent increase in pedal pressure for 6 stops from 60 mph 102
Overall brake rating . . . . fair

INTERIOR NOISE
Idle in neutral, dBA 54
Maximum during acceleration 82
At steady 60 mph cruising speed 80

OFF PAVEMENT
Hillclimbing ability . . . . .excellent
Maneuverability . . . . .excellent
Turnaround capability . . . . . . .excellent
Handling . . . . .very good
Ride . . . . .good

ON PAVEMENT
Handling .good
Ride . . . . .good
Driver visibility . . . . .very good
Driver comfort . . . . .good
Engine response . . . . .good

FUEL CONSUMPTION
Normal driving, mpg 14.0
Off pavement 10.5
Range, normal driving, miles 170
Range, off pavement 128

Both Bronco and Scout are fitted with 3-speed manuals as standard equipment, but Scout offers 4-speed optional gearbox while the Bronco has only a 3-speed automatic optionally available.

Bronco has drum brakes all around, trailing arm and coil spring suspension in the front and longitudinal leaf springs in the rear. Ford offers limited-slip differentials for both front and rear drive units. Free-running front hubs are standard.

and the Bronco does not *feel* as great as the difference between the Scout and the Blazer, for example. Size differentials seem to take on a geometric rate of growth at a certain point and become accentuated.

A quick rundown of the vehicles shows that the Scout II comes with a 4-cylinder engine as standard equipment and this is new for 1975. Actually, it's a return to the past when the old Scouts always came with a 4-cylinder powerplant and was done in recognition of the interest in fuel saving. The base engine for the Ford Bronco is the 302-cu-in. V-8 and, in fact, this is now the only engine for the Bronco. The emission situation has caused the loss of the 6-cylinder Ford engines for Bronco application due to its low volume output in comparison with the remainder of the Ford truck line. Both the Scout and the Bronco have a 3-speed manual transmission as standard equipment but the Scout offers a choice of a 4-speed manual or 3-speed automatic for extra money while the Ford only has a 3-speed automatic on the option list.

Other dissimilarities worth mentioning are the Scout's choice of manual or automatic front hubs, both costing extra while the Bronco has free-running front hubs as standard equipment, but not automatic. Ford is the only manufacturer of 4wds which offers limited-slip differentials for the front as well as the rear. The Scout has front disc brakes as standard equipment and the Bronco has drums all the way around with no provision for the discs. In terms of suspension, the Scout utilizes the more common leaf springs on a live axle both front and rear while the Ford has trailing arms and coil springs on the front with the leaf spring arrangement at the back.

In terms of money, the basic list price for the Scout is $4712, FOB Fort Wayne, Ind. while the Bronco has a base price of $4973 at Detroit. However, it should be pointed out that the Bronco price does include the V-8 engine and the front hubs along with the 2-speed Dana 20 transfer case instead of the single-speed as in the Scout's base price.

We were quite lucky to get our hands on two of the first

Side-by-side placement of Bronco and Scout II emphasizes longer wheelbase of the International vehicle. And this photo emphasizes Scout II's longitudinal front springs in contrast to the Bronco's coil spring setup.

Scout II interior has the look of a family station wagon rather than the look of a rough country utility vehicle.

Column shift, stark panel, floor-mounted transfer case shift lever, lend a spartan look to the Ford Bronco.

'75 models of each vehicle with the Bronco coming to us through the courtesy of Dick Landfield at Fairway Ford in Placentia, Calif. Early on a Wednesday morning we began the long drive to the Utah snow, planning on being back in southern California by Friday night. We got our first glimpse of snow on the peaks of Utah late that afternoon and after spending the night in Salt Lake, we bundled our California bodies up and proceeded to take the Scout and the Bronco into that magical white ground.

We were delighted to find that both of the vehicles performed in an admirable style throughout the day but, of course, we were never in any powder deeper than about seven inches. On the other hand, it was such a sunny day the snow was melting and that gave it a nice slippery quality which allowed us to obtain a good feel for the tractive power of both vehicles.

The trip totalled just about 1600 miles and was primarily highway driving. We did some 75 or 80 miles off the pavement in Utah at the upper elevations and threw in a short off-pavement drive in the desert area near Zion National Park to get a few more photos.

Let's take a look now at the measurable differences we found in our normal tests of the two 4wds and then get into the impressions we received druing our driving of them.

Acceleration measurements at Orange County International Raceway showed that the Bronco was somewhat better than the Scout, getting to 60 mph in almost two seconds less time. The difference in the quarter-mile run, however, was much less with the Bronco beating the Scout by only .4 seconds. Both

Scout II's spare tire stowage permits easy cargo loading, and ready access when tire change becomes necessary.

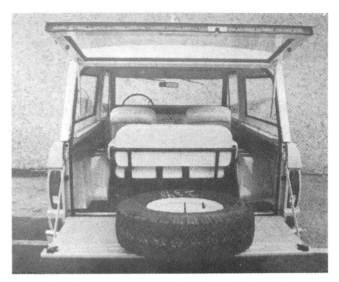

Bronco's tailgate mounting interferes with loading and takes up space that could be used for carrying cargo.

vehicles were equipped with limited-slip differentials and the axle ratios were as close as possible: 3.50 in the Ford and 3.54 in the International. Also, we had asked for and received the Scout with the 304-cu-in. V-8 so that it would be as close as possible to the Bronco's 302. We should point out that the Scout had almost all the extra equipment available from the factory while the Bronco was pretty much a plain-jane which could easily account for the Bronco's slightly quicker performance. The weight of the Scout's air conditioning and power steering, plus all the interior refinements, could easily make the difference. On the other hand, the Bronco was outfitted with all of the necessary emission control equipment including a catalytic converter while the Scout had a Gross Vehicle Weight Rating (GVWR) of 6200 lbs so it did not have as much smog-prohibiting machinery.

The largest difference between the Scout and the Bronco in our tests was in the braking ability where the Scout performed excellently while the Bronco achieved a rating of fair. This should be no great surprise to anyone as we have long contended that Broncos may have the worst brakes on an average of anything we have driven since our last outing in the Editor's late '41 Ford pickup. To give you some numbers for comparison, the Scout braked from 60 mph to zero in a very short 158 feet while the Bronco rolled up more than 200 feet in accomplishing the same test.

Getting down to the crunch, we like the Scout better than the Bronco in most cases. Obviously, our experience with the two vehicles was primarily on the road for all-day cruising. We also did a lot of around-town driving in both and found the Scout was a more pleasant vehicle to drive. Off the pavement, we have a draw with the Editor preferring the Bronco and the Technical Editor preferring the Scout.

Looking down a list of features, the Scout was bound to be the winner of the highway portion of the trip by reason of its high-backed bucket seats; its ample carpeting and paneling, which offer good noise insulation; plus its air conditioning and other comfort features. When you spend 16-18 hours driving, it's impossible not to prefer the more comfortable of the two. Also, of course, the longer wheelbase of the Scout gave it a better ride and the lower noise level helps in keeping fatigue down.

In terms of fuel economy, both the Scout and the Bronco gave a fairly decent account of themselves. The figures on the data panels accompanying this report show very little differ-

ence: 14.4 mpg for the Scout and 14.0 for the Bronco. Those figures are taken with our special fuel metering equipment and include driving out to the freeway through town and then cruising at a steady 55 mph. On the trip to Utah we found there were more variances between the two vehicles. Generally, the Scout was getting about 1.5 mpg better than the Bronco on the highway but we were driving at fairly rapid speeds and this undoubtedly accounts for the disparity.

Off the pavement, the ride is somewhat smoother in the Scout but the handling of the Bronco is superior. It gives you the feeling that you can go just about anywhere, any time and not be too concerned about whether you will fit between the trees, canyon walls or along side another vehicle on a narrow trail. The visibility from within the Bronco is second only to a CJ-5 without a top, although we do object to the windshield wiper position (at the top of the windshield) which forces the tallest drivers to slump a bit in the seat in order to see out. The ride of the Bronco is not as good as that of the Scout in the rougher areas but it is not punishing at all and is worth putting up with for the maneuverability and agility.

So, we come down to the same old dilemma. Which vehicle is best for you depends on your personal driving. From our offices here in southern California and keeping in mind that we are on the fringe of the Los Angeles megalopolis, we would probably choose the Scout. We do a lot of freeway driving into the city for entertainment so that our ratio of on-pavement versus off-pavement driving is probably about 80/20, which is still more than the average for off-pavement trips. Under those conditions we would want the highway capability of the Scout and be willing to sacrifice a little in terms of off-pavement characteristics. Also, this is qualified by the fact that we are making this choice in terms of this being our only vehicle. Obviously, if you own more than one vehicle, your choice may be altered.

The Bronco is an outstanding off-pavement vehicle. It does everything asked of it, within reason, and seems pleased to deliver miles of going even in the roughest of conditions. On the pavement, as a town car, it suffers only by comparison with the Scout. It is not bad. . . .in fact, it is good. . .but it is not *as good* as the Scout.

We like both of these 4-wheel drives. We would not hesitate to own either one of them. But, we like the Scout just a little bit better considering we have to exist in a world of paved roads and highways. ●

1976 PREVIEW: WHAT'S NEW AT

INTERNATIONAL

Two brand new vehicles
and the first diesel engine
in the 4 x 4 market
should make 1976 a very
promising year for
International Harvester.

Story and photos by Bill Sanders

Rear tailgate treatment of Traveler is smooth and clean.

The truck division at International Harvester can really surprise you sometimes. Considered by many to be a rather stodgy, conservative truck builder, they seldom have extravagant press previews or introductions. That's probably because they haven't changed their product substantially for some time. But, for 1976, that has all changed. As someone else's advertisement has said: "You've come a long way, baby!"

While many manufacturers are waiting around to see where emission controls, safety restrictions and everything else is leading, International has gone ahead and completely redesigned and restructured their entire light-duty truck lineup, including four wheel drive vehicles.

In fact, there is so much big news from International for 1976, one has difficulty in determining just where to start. For four wheelers, all the new changes are quite exciting.

To start, the square, old Travelall has mercifully been laid to rest. In it's place is an entirely new 4x4 called the "Traveler." The Traveler is based on a Scout chassis, but is longer and has a roof line that looks strangely like a Blazer!

Secondly, the old pickup is gone also. In its place is an all new unit, also based on the Scout chassis, but with a longer wheelbase. The new pickup is called the Scout "Terra," and is one sharp looking rig. The new Terra is available in one body size and thus isn't designated as either a ½-ton or ¾-ton, but rather as an intermediate. All three vehicles; the Scout, which remains in the lineup virtually unchanged, except for a few modifications, the Traveler, and the Terra, have GVW ratings of 6200 lbs., which gets them above the 6000 lb. limit for catalytic converters. Thus all three vehicles can use any type gasoline available, unleaded, regular or premium. And they don't have the added inconvenience of worrying about a converter.

The last big news, but not the least, is the introduction in 1976, in all three vehicles, of an optional diesel engine. You heard it right! International will be the first major manufacturer to offer a diesel in a 4x4 vehicle.

NEW DIESEL ENGINE

The first American manufacturer to make diesel power available for light trucks and recreational vehicles, IH is introducing the new engine as the result of a continuing program where a variety of existing diesel engines were extensively tested and compared. Following the tests the Nissan CH6-33 was selected as being the most compatible with the International Scout chassis.

"Fuel economy, naturally, is the most established reason for choosing a diesel power plant over a gasoline engine," stated W.W. Johnson, IH light truck marketing manager to questions posed by FOUR WHEELER. "But long life and low maintenance costs are important advantages as well," he continued. "Any diesel truck has a substantially higher initial cost that normally is paid back to the owner during the life of the vehicle in terms of less operating expenses for fuel and maintenance. We expect that owners of diesel Scouts will have the same experience."

The new six cylinder diesel totals 198 cubic inches, with a 3.27 inch bore and a 3.94 inch stroke and a compression ratio of 22:1. It develops a maximum of 92 brake horsepower at 4000 RPM and 137.5 ft. lbs. of torque at 2000 RPM, which is pretty good torque for a six banger off-road engine. Weight is 662 lbs.

Mileage testing on the diesel with all three models — Traveler, Terra, and the Scout II — is continuing, but estimates at this writing showed improvements from 50 to 60 percent over current gasoline engines. A firm price for Scouts equipped with the new engine had not been determined when this was being written.

HATCHBACK SCOUT "TRAVELER"

This all new 'intermediate' 4x4 looks as though it may certainly give its competitors some competition in the years ahead. The Traveler is built on a Scout II chassis, but has a 118 inch wheelbase (18 inches longer than the Scout II) and an overall length of 183.8 inches. Width is 70.0 inches. The Traveler is more compact in outside dimensions than some competitors — as much as 40 inches shorter and 10 inches narrower. Size alone should allow it to get into more out-of-the-way places than some larger rigs. Yet a Traveler can hold more than a standard American station wagon. Its cargo capacity is 2400 lbs., and it has 103 cubic feet of storage space with the second seat folded. The tailgate is a nifty hatchback design that lifts all as one unit.

This is the all new 6-cylinder diesel engine from IH. It will be available in the Scout II, Traveler and Terra pickup. It has 198 cu. in. displacement and develops 92 brake horsepower with 137.5 ft. lbs. of torque.

Traveler rear roofline is strangely reminiscent of Blazer.

New Traveler should be great for camping, with full lift-up tailgate. This arrangement for tailgate should keep dust from getting into interior as it does with other models when tail gate window is lowered.

Bill Mason, IH public relations, shows how easy it is to lift tailgate on Traveler with air assist cylinders.

Traveler has 1/3-2/3 type bench seats for easy entry to rear seat on passenger side.

Dick Bakkom, the IH Light Truck Sales Manager, told us: "The hatchback tailgate affords a great deal of convenience since it lifts out of the way and leaves an opening 38 inches high and 50 inches wide. That's larger than almost any station wagon — standard, compact, or utility. And the tailgate's air assist cylinders make opening and closing easy for anyone." Bakkom added, "With its 118 inch wheelbase, the Scout Traveler can turn a circle in 38 feet — maneuverability comparable to a "mini" import, but for a vehicle that provides far greater towing capacity and a half-ton more load capacity."

A steel-reinforced fiberglass station wagon top with integral headliner is standard on the new Traveler. The second seat folds forward and out of the way easily — as opposed to the bolted-type available with some competitive makes of 4x4 vehicles. Only the Jeep Cherokee and Wagoneer have fold down rear seats besides the Scout and Scout Traveler.

Dick Bakkom also said, "With the rear seat folded forward, this wagon can carry two full-sized trail bikes in the cargo area. But with four wheel drive, automatic transmission, automatic hubs, and a two speed transfer case, I'd bet a Traveler can reach spots where even the bikes wouldn't make it!"

The new Traveler, like its cousin the Scout II, has a 196 cu. in. 4-banger gasoline engine as standard. A 304 V8 and a step-up 345 V8 are also available as well as the new diesel 6-banger. Axle ratios range from 4.09:1 with the 4-banger and a 3-speed manual tranny, to 3.07:1 with the 345 V8 and an automatic tranny.

NEW "TERRA" PICKUP

It's sort of in a class all by itself; there really isn't any other pickup like it. Some are smaller, some larger, but the Terra fits an all new category. It has a compact, 118 inch wheelbase, with a six-foot bed and a new, roomy fiberglass cab.

With an overall length of less than 184 inches and width of only 70 inches, the new Scout pickup is considerably smaller than standard-size pickups, but has a surprisingly roomy cab and a substantial load capacity.

About the Scout Terra, Dick Bakkom said, "While the Terra may be inter-

The all new "Terra" pickup is also a nifty looking rig.

New cab for Terra pickup is made of strong, inner and outer molded fiberglass for added durability.

This photo gives you an idea of how much gear can be stowed behind the seats of a Terra

The Scout II has a variety of exterior trim packages. This is the Rallye stripe package.

The '76 Scout II is built on a 100 inch wheelbase and has received only minor exterior changes.

88

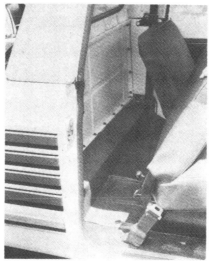

Interior mounted roll bar is option for Terra pickup.

Terra has 11 cubic feet of storage space behind seats as a *standard* feature.

Tailgate of Terra pickup is easily opened, has strong hinges.

It was a hot, humid summer day at the IH national press preview, but journalists were quite impressed by 1976 IH lineup.

mediate in size, it cannot be termed a compromise in any way. Rather, it is a response to a need; a vehicle that will match the changing requirements of a growing number of pickup users — both for commercial and personal transportation."

The Terra cab has been designed with lots of storage space in mind. Behind the 1/3-2/3 split seat or optional bucket seats there is 11 cubic feet of storage space — more than the entire trunk capacity of some passenger cars. This area will hold sleeping bags, suitcases, tents, camping gear or a multitude of other items. This inside storage area is a *standard* feature. The cab is made of strong inner and outer molded fiberglass shells for added durability.

The six-foot pickup bed has double wall construction and a load capacity of 2400 lbs. Front and rear axle capacity is 3200 and 3500 lbs. respectively.

Four wheel drive models of the Terra are available with Scout's 2-speed transfer case with floor mounted shifter, or the single-speed transfer case with a dash operated shifter.

The Terra's 118 inch wheelbase affords a smoother ride than shorter wheelbase mini pickups, yet the high clearance (eight inches, front and rear axles) and narrow width combined with 4x4 ability will allow it to maneuver in many places larger 4x4 pickups can't go.

As with the Traveler, the standard engine is the IH 196 cu. in. 4-banger with step up V8's, the 304 and 345. The all new diesel is also available. Three transmissions are also available, a 3-speed manual, 4-speed manual and a 3-speed automatic.

SCOUT II

The familiar Scout II will be continued in the 100-inch wheelbase model for 1976. The Scout II also has a GVW of 6200 lbs. and therefore doesn't require a catalytic converter or unleaded fuel. Scout II drivetrain components are the same as those for the Traveler and Terra.

Primarily, the Scout has undergone only appearance changes for '76. There is a restyled, vertical grille design and special side panel appliques. These include: white, woodgrain with a cork finish, and a red "feature" design. A fourth applique is part of a special "Rallye" package and consists of racing stripes extending along the sides and onto the hood.

From the appearance of the entire IH line, with two new vehicles and an all new diesel engine available, IH should give competing 4x4 manufacturers some reason to sit up and take notice in 1976. □

In past years, whenever an International 4x4 truck drove past, we could all hear the affectionate jokes about "Corn Binders."

But since the introduction of the 1976 model line, that has all changed, or is changing. IH completely changed their light truck model lineup in '76, and with the introduction of the "Traveler," came into direct competition with the big guys from Detroit with an outstanding, longer wheelbase 4x4.

International also dropped their unprofitable, big pickup models from the team. In their place is a neat unit that IH calls a "mini" pickup, based on the same wheelbase (and other dimensions) as the Scout II.

Called the "Terra," this 4x4 pickup is a unique truck package, with short, bobtail-type wheelbase, but with all the capacity of a true pickup. You can order out your Terra pickup as plush as you like, and with almost any engine/transmission combination you might want. As a four wheeler, it can make the trek into any location a bobtail can go, yet has the bed capacity to carry plenty of camping, hunting, fishing, or other gear you may have.

SCOUT"TERRA"PICKUP

FROM INTERNATIONAL HARVESTER

This nimble little rig is truly a four wheel drive "mini"

By Bill Sanders

POWERTRAIN AND PERFORMANCE

Performance can be dealers' choice. You can build as much performance into your Terra as you want, starting with the Comanche 196-cu. in. four-banger, the 304 V-8, or the big bomb 345 V-8. We purposely ordered the 345 for our truck because we wanted as much useable horsepower as possible.

The 345 V-8 is rated at 163 hp, and 292 ft.-lbs. of torque at 2000 RPM, which is plenty of torque to pull this little rig through the roughest terrain. Curb weight for the Terra is listed at something over 3800-lbs., so the big V-8 can really move this truck. We were, quite frankly, amazed at acceleration response when we first got behind the wheel. Foot to the wood brought on some great getaway power, which left many so-called performance passenger cars sitting at the stop light. This isn't to say the Terra is a drag racing machine, but it does show the power potential to get through rough spots off road.

The V-8 was hooked into a 3-spd. automatic tranny and a 3.07:1 axle ratio. The 3.07 is an optional ratio. Standard ratio is a 4.09, which should make for some really exciting acceleration, although it would probably also make for some disappointing gas mileage figures. There is also a 3.54:1 ratio that probably would be a better all-around compromise ratio for best performance and best fuel economy. Our test truck came equipped with street radial tires, so if you planned to put some big off road rubber on your Terra, it would be better to order the 4.09 or the 3.54 so the ratio wouldn't get too tall.

In the Terra, both the automatic transmission shifter and transfer case shifter are mounted on the floor. We like this arrangement quite well, especially for the 3-spd. automatic tranny. It is much easier to work with the transmission, both on and off road, manually when the shifter is mounted on the floor, rather than on the steering column. It may sound like an old magazine cliche, but the transmission shifter is always at your fingertips for a quick down-shift. With the shifter in that location you tend to use engine braking much more than you normally would with a column-mounted shifter.

Shifting the transfer case is also a piece of cake in the Terra. The shifter is conveniently located and shifts easily.

Performance overall was fantastic. Acceleration was great, and yet we managed to get between 10.9 and 12.1 mpg in our driving. Probably a little less

throttle foot would bring fuel economy down even more.

HANDLING, STEERING, STOPPING

Because it is, relatively speaking, a bobtail rig, the Terra is an exquisitely nimble vehicle. On road handling is a dream; it corners beautifully and gets around through traffic like a compact. Off road the same characteristics are evident; handling is great.

Our test vehicle came equipped with optional power steering. This is a $178 option, but, as we've said many times before, one we think is worth it for an off road machine. Power steering is an integral unit and really saves a lot of backbreaking work, especially if you add big rubber. With the street radials, steering the Terra was also easy and great to operate.

Standard brakes on the Terra consist of discs up front, drums in the rear and a power assist. That is definitely a package you can't beat for a standard item. Braking was quiet, swift and sure. Crossing deep streams, there was never any brake fade as the discs just threw the water off. After heavy use off road coming down numerous steep trails, we never experienced any fade or pulling.

COMFORT, CONVENIENCE, OPTIONS

Our test rig was just about fully loaded with options. It had air conditioning, the custom interior, an electric clock, and other niceties. One of the first items we noticed when we got behind the wheel was the tilt steering wheel. This item goes for $67, but if you've got long

Terra dash has all instruments implanted for easy readability. Air conditioner vents are add-on units and hang down too low.

Full compliment of gauges comes in handy for four wheeler.

Bucket seats may not look it, but are quite comfortable.

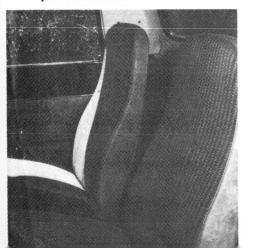

Even though Terra is smaller than average pickup, bed still holds plenty of cargo.

IH SCOUT `TERRa`

PRICES AND OPTIONS

Base price as tested $5,394.00
Locking hubs 42.50
Tilt steering wheel 67.00
AM/FM radio 173.00
Electric clock 22.00
Two tone applique 108.00
Radial tire package 345.00
345 V-8 . . . . 198.00
Modulated fan 38.00
Two-speed transfer case 63.00
Three-speed
  automatic transmission 279.00
Trac-Lok axle 77.00
Bucket seats 95.00
Custom interior 206.00
Deluxe exterior trim 50.00
Air conditioner 462.00
Bucket seat console 45.00

SPECIFICATIONS

Engine . . . . 90°OHV V-8
Bore & Stroke (ins.) . . . . . 3-7/8 x 3-21/32
Displacement (cu. in.) 345
HP @ RPM . . . . .163 @ 3600
Torque: lbs.-ft. @ RPM . . . . .292 @ 2000
Compression Ratio/Fuel . . 8.05:1/Regular
Carburetion . . . . 1 4-bbl.
Transmission . . . . Automatic
Transfer Case . . . . .2-spd.
Final Drive Ratio (axle ratio) 3.07:1

Steering type . . . . Power
Steering Ratio . . . . N.A.
Turning diameter (ft.) 38.10
Tire Size . . . . HR78x15PC Radial
Brakes . . . . Disc Front/Drum Rear
Front Suspension . . . . Leaf; Driving Hypoid
Rear Suspension . . . . . Leaf; Semi-Floating
Wheelbase (ins.) 118.0
Overall length (ins.) 184.2
Width (ins.) 70.0
Height (ins.) 66.0

Front tread width (ins.) 57.1
Rear tread width (ins.) 57.1
Fuel tank capacity (gals.) 19.0
Auxiliary fuel tank capacity (gals.) . . . N.A.
Engine oil capacity (qts.) 5.0
Ground clearance,
  front & rear differential (ins.) 7.6
Approach angle . . . . 49.0 degrees
Departure angle . . . . 22.0 degrees
Curb weight (lbs.) 3890

PERFORMANCE RATING

On Road

Acceleration . . . . Excellent
Passing speed . . . . Excellent
Steering Response . . . . Excellent
Maneuverability . . . . Excellent
Cornering . . . . Excellent
Braking . . . . Excellent
Interior noise . . . . .Low
Ride . . . . Smooth
Seating comfort . . . . Good
Accessibility of dash controls . . . . . . Good
Accessibility of transmission shifter Excellent
Entry/Exit height to ground . . . . . . .Low
Glove box size . . . . Fair
Instrument readability . . . . Excellent
Head room . . . . Fair
Seat belt location . . . . Good

Off Road

Traction in soft,
  sandy or muddy soil . . . . Good
Hillclimbing characteristics . . . . . Excellent
Rollover angle stability
  (center of gravity) . . . . Good
Suspension load
  without bottoming . . . . .Fair
Turning circle . . . . Excellent
Ride . . . . Smooth
Tire flotation (stock tires) . . . . .Fair
Vehicle control . . . . Excellent
Hi-Range 4WD performance . . . . . . Excellent
Lo-Range 4WD performance . . . . . . Excellent
Accessibility of
  transfer case shifter . . . . Excellent
Ease of shifting transfer case . . . Excellent
Steering Response . . . . Excellent
Brake, (clutch), accelerator
  pedal location . . . . Excellent
Roll bar installation . . . . N.A.
Occupant seating stability . . . . Good
Close proximity visibility
  over hood . . . . Good
Sun visor capability . . . . .Fair
Headlight illumination for
  off road driving . . . . Good
Storage capacity (camping gear etc.) Excellent
Fuel tank filler accessibility
  (for funnels etc.) . . . . Excellent
Low gear lugging capability . . . . . . Good
Brakes/Compression
  downhill capability . . . . Good
Ease of access to spare tire . . . . . . Excellent

Fuel Consumption

On road . . . . .10.9 to 12.1 mpg.
(Normal driving—highway and surface streets)
Off Road . . . . .10.6 to 11.5 mpg.

Accessories and Options

Air conditioning effectiveness . . . . . . .Good
Heater/Defroster effectiveness . . . Excellent
Windshield Wiper/
  Washer effectiveness . . . . Excellent
Wiper area covered . . . . Good
Horn (Loudness) . . . . .Good
Dash lighting . . . . Excellent
Interior lighting . . . . Excellent
Door handles
  (operation and location) . . . . .Fair
Door locks . . . . Fair
Hood latch . . . . Excellent
Jack/Lug wrench location . . . . .Fair

Big 345 V-8 and jumble of hoses fills engine compartment.

Automatic locking hubs are good option to get.

legs and are tall, we think it is well worth the price.

Locking front hubs are $42.50 (automatic) and a good option to install at the factory. Another good option, even though it doesn't add too much to creature comfort, is a modulated engine fan that is priced at $38.

As mentioned previously, our rig came equipped with the radial tire package. The cost of radials from the factory is listed at $345. If you plan to do all your driving on the pavement, which we doubt, the radials might be a good buy, as they are super-comfortable riding. But, for an off road machine, we wouldn't recommend them, and the money could be better spent on equipment that would be more conducive to four wheeling.

SUMMING UP

The new Terra, like the Scout II, is a really neat four wheel drive rig. It is in a size category that isn't too small, yet is small enough to get into some of those tight back country spots.

The number of powertrain options gives each buyer a specific choice as to the type vehicle he wants, whether it be four-banger with low axle ratio or V-8 with plenty of horsepower. And, it's definitely a fun truck to drive! ◻

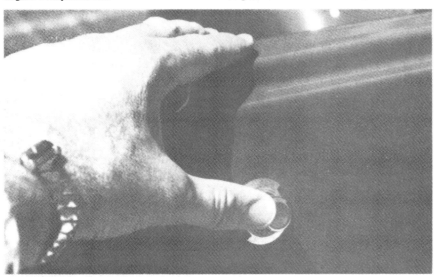

Versatility personified; just push a button . . .

Cargo light lights up bed at night and . . .

. . . has conveniently located switch on dash.

. . . and the tailgate drops down.

DIESEL
INTERNATIONAL SCOUT TERRA

PV4 TEST

Powered by the Nissan CN6-33 compression ignition powerplant, this midi shows plenty of potential...

WHEN INTERNATIONAL said diesel-powered Scout pickup trucks were going into series production, *Pickup, Van & 4WD* snapped to attention immediately, with deep interest. Here was a possibility for durability, longevity, load capacity and fuel economy all rolled into one vehicle. Review of these possibilities only served to bring up additional questions about the effectiveness of small displacement diesel engine power in the current context of gasoline-burning, large-displacement, 6-cylinder engines and the even bigger bore V-8 powerplants that are the motive force for the majority of U.S.-made, light-utility vehicles that are used daily in myriad on- and off-pavement activities, both commercial and recreational. Basically, the question was: "Where does the diesel Scout fit into America's light truck picture?" This road test report will attempt to review exactly what comprises this diesel-engined, midi-sized Scout pickup truck, explore its possibilities, and answer questions about its performance on the freeways, wintered country roads,

desert drywashes and mountain fire lanes.

First, though, it must be reported that diesel power for IH's Scout Terra pickup series was not a spur of the moment decision, or a whim of International management. Rather, the decision to install the Nissan CN6-33 powerplant in 400 Scouts during the 1976 model year was made on the basis of information gathered in both marketing and engineering surveys.

The marketing people determined that among Americans there is a definite interest in diesel power as the alternative to gasoline for light trucks. The marketing people were off the mark only in their assessment of the demand potential for diesel Scouts. The first production run of 400 was changed to 1200—on the basis of firm orders taken for the diesel vehicle by IH dealers. And, at this writing, the production figure has been raised to more than 2000 on the basis of what IH dealers consider firm demand.

Diesel power is nothing new at International. From 1963 through 1968, IH

offered an in-line 6-cylinder diesel powerplant, the company's 130-hp D-301 engine, in either the now discontinued full-sized pickups or Travelalls. But there was that nagging marketing department note that said some people wanted diesel power in their Internationals.

In 1971, the IH engineering department undertook evaluation of the Peugeot XDP-6.90, the Perkins 6-247, the IH D-301 and the Nissan CN6-33. In the U. S., the CN6-33 is identified as a Chrysler-Nissan engine because, at present, Chrysler Corp. is the licensed U. S. distributor for "Made in Japan" Nissan diesel powerplants.

For comparative evaluation of the engines, a Scout was sent to Peugeot in France for custom installation of the diesel engine in a Scout. Ultimately, the Peugeot was rejected because its use for production vehicles would have required extensive purchases of new tooling and redesign of the Scout firewall. A Perkins also was installed in a Scout, and was also rejected because, though it offered up to 105 hp, it proved to be not as

DIESEL SCOUT

economical as other engines under consideration, and IH people viewed the Perkins replacement parts situation as less than optimum.

International's own compression ignition engine, because of its size and weight, also was turned down for the midi truck application.

During test runs, IH engineers also looked at fuel consumption figures and compared them with the performance level desired for future diesel Scouts. The Peugeot delivered 26.6 mpg; the Perkins 16.6 mpg; the IH 14.7; and the Nissan 23.1 mpg. The Nissan, though not the top fuel economizer, was the compromise choice, mainly for other considerations.

The original Nissan diesel Scout was hand built in 1973 as a test bed for development of cooling, noise suppression and drivetrain systems. This was well prior to advent of the so-called "Energy Crisis," and the IH plan then was to market diesel Scouts elsewhere than in the U. S., in countries where diesel power is an accepted way of light truck transportation life.

METRIC NECESSITIES

Factors that accelerated the IH decision to series produce Nissan diesel powered Scout trucks were: The Energy Crisis and Associated demands for petroleum fuel conservation, and the hard facts that the CN6-33 could be slipped easily into the IH Scout chassis with only minor assembly line modifications, that the Japanese-built engine offers replaceable cylinder sleeves, that it bolts readily to the Chrysler T-407 TorqueFlite automatic transmission and that the heart of its injection system is a Kiki pump, built on Bosch license, and hence has proven ultimately reliable in numerous diesels worldwide.

One of the chief problems encountered in putting Nissan diesel Scouts into production was tuning the linear demand throttle linkage system to the automatic transmission for shift points that would insure acceptable driveability. A couple of other problems that plagued IH assembly people were the necessity to tool up with metric wrenches on the production line, and to provide a source of diesel fuel on the line in order to get the trucks running when built. These, in writing, appear to be minor difficulties, but solutions required time, hence the Nissan diesel Scout Terra did not become available for retail sale until the 1976 model year.

Moreover, an additional problem was that the goal of 400 units for the year was soon exceeded by at least 800 additional firm orders, which required revisions in both production schedules and assembly line utilization. These

unexpected changes, to a degree, slowed initial deliveries of diesel Scouts to IH dealers.

The Nissan engine, in use in many parts of the world in marine, industrial and vehicular applications, is a 4-cycle in-line Six with a piston displacement of 198 cu in. Peak power development is 92 bhp at a fuel system governed 4000 rpm. Maximum torque delivery of 137.5 lb-ft occurs at 2000 rpm. The engine's compression ratio is 22:1. Its weight, with standard accessories, but not including transmission, is 662 lb, which puts it in about the same weight range as a small V-8 gasoline powerplant.

The CN6-33's fuel injection is comprised of a fuel feed pump that draws No. 2 diesel from the Scout's 19-gal. tank and delivers it to a large sized fuel filter; a return line that directs filter overflow through a return line to a tank; a filtered fuel line to the injection pump; and the pump itself which both meters fuel on throttle demand and pressurizes the fuel for pump-timed injection atomization into swirl precombustion chambers inside the cylinders. Ignition, of course, occurs in each cylinder when the atomized fuel charge is injected into the superheated intake air compressed on the upstroke of the piston.

In the Scout tested by *Pickup, Van & 4WD*, the Nissan CN6-33 diesel was coupled to the Chrysler TorqueFlite 3-speed automatic, and a Dana 2-speed 4wd transfer system which incorporated Warn free-wheeling hubs at the front axles, with exception of diesel power, a very conventional drive layout. The diesel Scout's drive axles carried 3.54:1 final drive gearing, which is IH standard

for the vehicle. IH offers 4.09 gearing as an option with the diesel Scout.

The Torqueflite transmission carried a small diameter (9-in.) torque converter so that the engine would spin the converter quickly to stall at 2000 rpm, the CN6-33's torque peak, for as brisk as possible acceleration from a standing start.

Special systems associated with the diesel engine that were fitted to the test Scout included an 85-ampere/hour battery and 45-ampere alternator to supply the electrical demand of starting the engine against that stiff 22:1 compression; a nichrome wire glow plug dash indicator to show when combustion preheat is in operation; and an induction butterfly to shut off intake air to stop the engine.

Otherwise, the diesel midi was equipped much as would be a deluxe Scout ordered to an owner's taste. The package included folding front bench seat, front floor mat, energy absorbing steering column, undercoating, dual exterior mirrors, HR78 x 15 Goodyear F-32 All Winter Radial tires (a test report on which appears elsewhere in this magazine), AM radio, electric clock, deluxe interior with color keyed trim and upholstery, deluxe exterior trim with bright finish grille and moldings, air conditioning, door edge guards, heavy-duty rear step bumper with trailer hitch ball, power assisted steering, trailer wiring, and special painted side panels.

The 4wd Scout, with a standard 6200-lb GVWR (Gross Vehicle Weight Rating), was fitted with heavy-duty front springs of 3200-lb capacity (at the ground), rather than the 3100-lb capac-

PRICES

Basic list, FOB Ft. Wayne, Ind.
Terra Diesel 4wd pickup $8042

Standard Equipment: 198-cu-in. diesel in-line Six engine, 4-spd manual transmission, power disc brakes, tilt steering wheel, 85 amp/hr battery, 45 amp alternator, glow plug indicator, gauges, 2-spd transfer case, folding front bench seat, front floor mat, undercoating, tinted glass, 2-spd electric wiper/washers, heater/defroster, chrome front and rear bumpers, H78 x 15B tires

GENERAL

Curb weight, lb (test model)	4180
GVWR (test model)	6200
Optional GVWRs	none
Wheelbase, in.	118.0
Track, front/rear	57.1/57.1
Overall length	183.8
Overall height	66.0
Overall width	70.0
Overhang, front/rear	24.0/41.8
Approach angle, degrees	39
Departure angle, degrees	19

Ground clearances (test model):

Front axle	7.6
Rear axle	7.7
Oil pan	13.5
Transfer case	11.0
Fuel tank	14.6
Exhaust system (lowest point)	11.7
Fuel tank capacity (U.S. gal.)	19
Auxiliary	30-gal. dealer installed tank

ACCOMMODATION

Standard seats full-width folding bench, 1/3-2/3 split

Optional seats	bucket seats
Headroom, in.	34.8
Accelerator pedal to seatback, max	42.5
Steering wheel to seatback, max	14.9
Seat to ground	32.5
Floor to ground	16.8
Unobstructed load space (length x width x height)	72.4 x 42.0 x 21.3
Tailgate (width x height)	54.8 x 21.3

INSTRUMENTATION

Instruments: speedometer, odometer, ammeter, oil pressure, water temp, fuel gauge
Warning lights: hazard warning, front axle engaged indicator, glow plug indicator, parking brake
Optional: none

ity standard front springs. All Scouts carry 3100-lb capacity (at the ground) rear springs, with no optional rear springs available. The test Scout received heavy-duty shock absorbers during assembly in Ft. Wayne, Ind.

Pickup, Van & 4WD's test crewman was flown to Ft. Wayne to pick up the test Terra, and was scheduled to drive the diesel midi truck in as many adverse conditions as he could discover during his solo Atlantic-to-Pacific evaluation run.

In starting out on a diesel junket, it's well to learn how to start and stop a diesel engine. The first step in the procedure is to determine that the stop valve knob is pushed in, else the engine can be cranked until the battery is completely drained and still not start

for lack of intake air. The next step is to thumb a red button on a special control panel until the glow plug indicator glows red. This requires from 20 sec in

Glow plug button, nichrome element and shutoff pull effect go, stop.

mild temperatures to as much as a minute and a half or more in sub-zero temperatures; and in cold weather the glow plugs in the precombustion chambers can be used to augment compression heat until the engine is sufficiently warm to fire regularly unaided. While the glow plug button is depressed, and the indicator is glowing, the starter (not ignition) key switch on the steering column is rotated clockwise to engage the starter, and cranking must be continued until engine heat builds sufficiently to support compression ignition. Once the Nissan "smoker" is chuckling with its typical cold diesel knock idle characteristic, both glow plug button and starter key switch are released. From that point onward, the IH Scout Terra with diesel power is operated in very much the same manner at a gasoline powered truck of the same ilk.

With the Dana drive system in 2wd, high range, and with the Chrysler TorqueFlite automatic in "Drive," full pressure on the accelerator pedal brings the engine up to speed and the torque converter to stall rather rapidly. What occurs is that things grab hold at the diesel engine's torque peak and the Scout leaps off the line rather abruptly. However, acceleration from this juncture is rather slow, as compared with gasoline powered vehicles of any kind, yet not as sluggish as had been anticipated by the test driver who is conditioned by some 100,000 miles of driving in his personal Mercedes-Benz 190D sedan, powered by a 4-cylinder, 121-cu.-in. diesel engine.

A BIT STARTLING

The Torqueflite automatic, under full acceleration, achieves the 1-2 gear change at 38 mph, and rather abruptly at that. Likewise, the 2-3 upshift, which occurs at just under 60 mph, is abrupt, too, but not a true neck-snapper. The shifts are firm and positive, but they're not of smooth passenger sedan quality. In pulling grades, under full throttle, downshifts definitely occur with more of a snap, and the first few times a diesel Scout driver encounters these down changes, he's inclined to be a bit startled. However, the automatic shifts downward help to keep the small displacement diesel engine's rpm upward, which is important. Maintenance of rpm is very important because, on an upgrade, lost rpm can't be regained until the next downslope.

In level cruising at the legal 55 mph in third gear, the engine seems relaxed and breathing easily. Moreover, in "convoy" with the giant tandem freight trucks that ply the interstates, the little diesel has no trouble in keeping up at the legally abusive speed of 70 to 75 mph. At 79 mph, the governored diesel simply quits adding rpm, but on level paved surfaces it will maintain that 79

International assembly workers use an electric hoist to swing a Nissan CN6-33 diesel engine into a Scout Terra 4wd chassis.

ENGINES

Standard ... 198-cu.-in. diesel in-line Six
Bore x stroke, in. .... 3.27 x 3.94
Compression ratio 22:1
Net horsepower @ rpm ...... 92 @ 4000
Net torque @ rpm, lb-ft .. 137.5 @ 2000
Type fuel required .... No. 2 diesel

DRIVE TRAIN

Standard transmission: .... 4-spd manual
Clutch dia., in. 11.0
Transmission ratios: 4th 1.00:1
3rd 1.68:1
2nd 3.09:1
1st 6.32:1
Synchromesh .... all forward gears

Optional 3-spd automatic $124*
Transmission ratios: 3rd 1.00:1
2nd 1.45:1
1st 2.45:1
*The automatic transmission is a mandatory option at the present time.

Rear axle type .... semi-floating hypoid
Final drive ratios: 3.54:1, 4.09:1
Overdrive .... none
Free-running front hubs automatic . $43
Limited slip differential $77
Transfer case .... Dana 20 2-spd
Transfer case ratios: 2.03:1, 1.00:1

CHASSIS & BODY

Body/frame: ladder-type frame with separate steel body
Brakes (std): front, 11.75-in. dia disc; rear, 11.03 x 2.25-in. drum
Brake swept area, sq in. 381
Swept area/ton (max load) 123
Power brakes .... std
Steering type (std) .... recirculating ball
Steering ratio 24:1
Power steering $162
Power steering ratio 17.5:1
Turning circle, ft 38.8
Wheel size (std) .... 15 x 6.0JK
Optional wheel sizes: .... 15 x 7.0JJ
Tire size (std) .... H78 x 15B
Optional tire sizes: ...... HR78 x 15C

SUSPENSION

Front suspension: semi-elliptic leaf springs on live axle and tube shocks
Front axle capacity, lb 3200
Optional .... none
Rear suspension: semi-elliptic leaf springs on live axle and tube shocks
Rear axle capacity, lb 3500
Optional .... none
Additional suspension options: HD front springs and shock absorbers, $17

DIESEL SCOUT

mph until the red or blue lights flash in the rear view mirror.

Where the small diesel engine, coupled to automatic transmission and 4wd system, really shined was in the uphill/downhill, off-pavement terrain of thoroughly wintered-in New England. In 4wd mode, with Warn front hubs locked, and employing the healthy bite of the Goodyear F-32 All Winter Radials, the diesel Scout traversed packed snow, new snow, slush, ice ridges, sharp bends and whatever with seeming enthusiasm. When lesser vehicles were being dug or towed out of untoward situations, the diesel Terra just kept chuckling right along.

In the transcontinental trip, the diesel engine suffered visibly only in the Rocky Mountains, traversing Loveland Pass at 11,999 ft above sea level. The rarified air at that altitude resulted in a rich fuel-to-air mixture ratio, and consequently the Scout's engine produced significantly less power and blew black, sooty smoke on trailing vehicles. Though down on power, the diesel, in conjunction with the 4wd system, provided the combination of strong torque and surefootedness that resulted in safe, secure handling in high altitude, winter icing conditions.

Back in the desert country of the Southwest (home to the now thoroughly chilled test crewman), the Scout was put through its off-pavement paces. In off-road running, the trick with the diesel is to keep rpm up through judicious manual gear selection with the automatic transmission. A drop in rpm must be anticipated and the down gear change made well in advance of where a gasoline engined vehicle would be downshifted in the same terrain. The diesel's throttle response is such that there is no quick spurt of power to straighten out a slide in loose surfaces, hence driving technique must be modified accordingly.

TORQUE TO TERRAIN

In 4wd, low range, locked up, with the Goodyear F-32s biting effectively, the diesel Scout is a rock crawler second to none. The trick is to keep the torque converter at stall, at just 2000 rpm, and change gears manually to meet obstacles as they come into the vehicle's path. It is simply a match of the engine's torque through the gears to the terrain.

In terms of ride and handling, the diesel Scout is identical to any other Scout with heavy-duty front springs. On seamed freeway concrete, the ride tends to be choppy, but is solid and firm on regular pavement. The wheel suspension system—stiff leaf springs all around—does not obviate handling characteristics that are more than acceptable in con-

text of a midi truck. The Terra goes where it's pointed without protest. The single failing in handling is that the Dana 44 front drive axle, in 2wd mode, tends to "hunt" a good deal, particularly at low speeds. However, when the 4wd system is engaged, the "hunting" tendency disappears for the most part, probably because the axle steering joints are loaded, rather than free, as in 2wd mode.

With respect to noise, that the truck was diesel powered was only apparent when the engine was cold, particularly at cold idle, when diesel knock was most audible. Once the engine was thoroughly warmed and brought up to cruising rpm, the sound settled into a pleasant, low-pitched hum. Both the 4-cylinder gasoline and diesel Terras registered 76 dbA in standard 55-mph sound level testing. The only objectionable sound in the truck came from the Dana transfer case shift lever which transmitted a persistent shifter-finger jingle into the cab. One test driver fixed this by fitting his ski glove over the transfer shift lever knob to serve as a vibration damper and sound limiter.

NONLINEAR SWOOP

As with the 4-cylinder gasoline engined Scout Terra pickup truck tested earlier (PV4, Feb., '76), driver and passenger comfort left something to be desired. Though fitted with a tilt wheel for driver ease, rearward seat travel was insufficient to permit elbow room in the cab for quick steering maneuvers. IH makes much of the 11 cu ft of cargo

space behind the bench seat; this could well be employed for additional seat travel and significant improvement in driver comfort.

Seemingly insignificant at first was the Terra's nonlinear fuel gauge. When topped off, the tank reading would remain at the full mark for a long driving period, then after the half-full mark was passed would swoop quickly to "E." On one occasion, before the test driver became fully aware of this characteristic, addition of a couple of gallons of kerosene, with some motor oil mixed in, was necessary to take the Terra to the next fuel stop. Later on, the driver determined that at the half-full mark, the CN6-33 had burned 14.6 gal. of its 19-gal. supply.

Another fuel problem occurred in New Hampshire, where nighttime static air temperature was 16 degrees below zero, and the wind chill factor was registered at more than 50 below zero. Either water in the diesel fuel froze at the fuel tank pickup screen, or fuel jellied in the tank at low temperatures. Whatever the direct cause was, it was winter temperature related. With the fuel delivery line blocked by ice or overly viscous fuel, the injection pump purged the fuel lines and itself, and the engine ran dry. A restart required a tow to a warm service station lube bay, direction of forced air heat onto fuel tank and engine block, priming the fuel system with the Nissan diesel's integral hand pump, a battery recharge, addition of methanol and kerosene to the fuel, and a shot of ether in the induction

---

TEST MODEL.
Terra 4wd pickup, 198-cu-in. diesel Six engine, automatic transmission, automatic locking hubs, HD front and rear springs and shock absorbers, AM radio, electric clock, custom interior pkg, deluxe exterior pkg, air conditioning, door edge guards, rear step bumper with hitch ball, power steering, 6-way trailer wiring, exterior decor side panels, 3.54 axle ratio, HR78 x 15C tires

West Coast list price . . $9596 plus freight

ACCELERATION
Time to speed, sec:	
0-30 mph	8.4
0-45 mph	16.0
0-60 mph	26.6
Standard start, ¼-mile, sec.	24.0
Speed at end, mph	58

SPEED IN GEARS
High range,	
3rd (3700 rpm)	78
2nd (4000 rpm)	58
1st (4000 rpm)	34
Low range,	
3rd (4000 rpm)	42
2nd (4000 rpm)	28
1st (4000 rpm)	16
Engine rpm @ 55 mph	2600

BRAKE TESTS
Pedal pressure required for ½-g deceleration rate from 60 mph, lb	35
Stopping distance from 60 mph, ft	121
Fade: Percent increase in pedal pressure for 6 stops from 60 mph	42
Overall brake rating	excellent

INTERIOR NOISE
Idle in neutral, dbA	60
Maximum during acceleration	83
At steady 60 mph cruising speed	76

OFF PAVEMENT
Hillclimbing ability	excellent
Maneuverability	very good
Turnaround capability	very good
Driver visibility	very good
Handling	very good
Ride	good

ON PAVEMENT
Handling	very good
Ride	good
Driver comfort	fair/good
Engine response	good

FUEL CONSUMPTION
City/freeway driving, mpg	12.7 to 21.4*
Off pavement	12.0
Range, city/freeway driving, miles	240 to 400
Range, off pavement	228

*During cross country trip, the Terra diesel's fuel consumption ranged between 12.7 and 21.4 mpg.

system to get things running again. Methanol or isopropyl alcohol, plus some kerosene, in the fuel beforehand in all likelihood would have prevented the engine stoppage, even in super cold conditions.

Most of the questions asked by diesel neophytes are about fuel availability and fuel economy.

Diesel fuel, succinctly, is readily available everywhere in the U. S. that the Terra was driven—some 4500 miles through a total of 17 states. "Truck Stop" or "Truck Service" are what the diesel driver must look for. In 17 states, only Colorado required a special diesel fuel permit, at $2. Let it be said, though, that the majority of diesel fuel pumps are on Interstate throughways, so an off-pavement enthusiast diesel Terra owner would do well to consider the optional dealer-installed 30-gal. fuel tank (which really should be a factory option for diesels, but isn't at present). In terms of economy, fuel prices varied a great deal from state to state, ranging in per-gallon price from 41 cents to 65 cents. And, in miles-per-gallon economy, the Nissan engine delivered anywhere from a low of 12.17 mpg, in fast uphill running in deep, wet slush in upstate New York to 21.4 mpg chugging about on packed snow in New Hampshire. Average fuel consumption for the 4500-mile trip was 16.86 mpg.

When the diesel idles, the transfer shift lever, lower right, vibrates with a bad case of the jingles.

This is reasonable fuel economy in view of the keep-up-with-the-big-rigs speeds at which the diesel Terra was driven. The mpg figure also includes extended periods of idling while fueling or dining, when it seemed more prudent to keep the compression ignition engine nice and warm, rather than to let it cool out and drain the battery unnecessarily on a balky restart of the cold smoker.

The 16.8 mpg figure offers a no-reserve fuel range of 336 miles—which surely could be extended through the medium of lighter foot pressure on the throttle pedal. The 30-gal. tank conceivably could take the Terra non-stop more than 500 miles, but that distance extends farther than human endurance.

In the 4500-mile trip, only two minor troubles were encountered: One was a fuel filter fitting unscrewing itself slightly, which required 10 seconds with a crescent wrench. The other was self-destruction of the Saginaw power steering pump, which gave up while pushing heavily against snow and ice accumulated in the front drive axle knuckles and steering linkage. The pump did not fail entirely, but squealed its protest mightily all the way from Vermont to California.

ASTONISHING BRAKES

In terms of quarter-mile performance, the Terra's speed and elapsed time reflect directly the torque and rpm development characteristics of the small displacement Nissan diesel engine. That is to say, the diesel powered Scout is neither quick nor fast. From a standing start, best 0-60 mph time was 26.6 sec. Best quarter-mile e.t. and terminal speed were 24.0 sec at 58 mph. For reference, this e.t. and speed can be compared to those for a Scout Terra with a gasoline-burning 196-cu-in. Four. The conventionally powered Scout turned the quarter in 21.5 sec at an e.t. of 61 mph. The gasoline Terra was obviously quicker, but not all that much faster than its compression ignition counterpart.

Shod with Goodyear F-32s, the diesel Scout at 4180 lb put on a much improved braking performance, as compared with the gasoline Scout that weighed 3690 lb and was fitted with General Jumbo tires. In an all-out panic stop from 60 mph, the gasoline Terra came to a halt in a very acceptable 145 ft. However, with the multiple siping of the sticky F-32s gripping dry dragstrip asphalt, the diesel Terra was stopped from the carefully calibrated 60 mph in an astonishing 121 ft. The stop was made with no break-away whatsoever, and with no rear lockup. But, as forward weight transfer occurred during rapid deceleration, the front set of radials tended to squirm slightly, which resulted in minor directional changes—wiggles—that were easily correctable. During almost 5000 miles of driving,

test crewmen sensed that the excellent stopping potential of the Terra's front disc/rear drum braking system was significantly improved with the F-32 radials. The controlled braking tests show that drivers were correct in their early assessment of the braking effectiveness of the F-32-shod Terra.

To sum up, the IH Scout Terra, powered by the Nissan CN6-33 diesel Six, may not be quick, but it can be fast and steady. It may not be an off-road thunder machine, but it is a sturdy, almost indestructible, creeper/crawler of any kind of terrain. The diesel Terra is economical in terms of fuel price and miles per gallon fuel use. However, the unit tested by *Pickup, Van & 4WD* carried a list price of $9596. The premium paid for the diesel powerplant, over and above the base gasoline powered Scout price, roughly would require more than four years of driving more than 20,000 miles per year to achieve the "payoff" at which time the diesel Terra would become truly, and increasingly economical.

The diesel Scout Terra certainly would fit right into a ranch situation in which the rancher fueled other equipment with No. 2 diesel oil, purchased in bulk at a cost saving. And the diesel Scout would be well suited to the recreational plans of touring buffs headed for Mexico where diesel fuel still goes for 15 cents per gallon (at this writing). In between, the prospects are so-so for the diesel Scout. In considering a diesel powerplant as part of an order for a Terra, a prospective Scout buyer must consider very long-term uses of his proposed purchase, and whether the economies beyond a four- or five-year "payoff" period are truly worthwhile.

'ABOUT THAT RAISE?'

In these considerations there remains the knowledge that out there in fun-truck land there are numerous, though uncounted, diesel nuts who'll pay the premium and live with less than brilliant performance simply for the sake of ownership of a diesel powerplant and sheer enjoyment of the operational parameters of diesel power that are far different, though no less rewarding, than gasoline power.

The test of this is that *Pickup, Van & 4WD*'s diesel nut who accomplished the majority of the test driving came around asking about a raise, hopeful that he might someday get it financially together sufficiently to make the down payment on an IH Scout, with Nissan diesel engine, but with a Traveltop and bucket seats and the big fuel tank, "and the heck with air conditioning." This, in itself, after 4500 miles and more, solo, across the worst terrain and through the worst weather that the U. S. has to offer, is a worthy recommendation for the diesel Terra Scout. ●

Terrarizing the U.S. of A.

A wintertime transcontinental solo run puts the diesel powered Scout on ice... BY DAVE EPPERSON

PHOTOS BY THE AUTHOR

TO MAKE A transcontinental run, Atlantic to Pacific, in any kind of a vehicle, it's first necessary to achieve proximity with the eastern shore, right? Right! That may not always be as easy as it seems.

The plan was to secure a Nissan diesel powered International Scout Terra 4wd pickup at IH's plant in Ft. Wayne, Ind., then drive it to the East Coast, sniff some Atlantic Ocean salt air, pull a quick U-turn, and head for California. This sounded fairly non-complex on paper, and the red felt pen route tracings on various pages of a *Rand McNally Road Atlas* foreshortened distances involved to mere desktop dimensions.

Golfers were going 'round the course in 86-degree California sunshine as departure flight time neared—but the temperature was 13 degrees F when the Boeing 727 landed at Ft. Wayne, then it dropped to 2 above early on the day of arrival at International's manufacturing facility.

Lanky IH sales engineer Larry Ehlers

provided a thorough briefing on the Nissan CN6-33 diesel engined Scout, then dropped its starter switch (not ignition, of course) keys into the outstretched palm. The diesel engine starting drill (detailed in the accompanying road test report) brought the little Japanese-built compression ignition Six to a happy power chuckle. Then, in 2wd, high range, on a set of new Goodyear F-32 winter tires, the pale yellow and white Terra was set eastward through the sleeted, salted, slushed afternoon traffic of Ft. Wayne.

The city left behind, the diesel Terra devoured the two-lane secondaries, Highways 24 and 6, northeastward through Ohio's midwest midwinter, temperature in the teens. Barns, silos, homes, slush, ice, and Currier & Ives kinds of wintry scenes reeled inward at 55 mph, perhaps more now and again, until Highway 6 intersected U.S. 90 at Fremont, Ohio. There the little diesel joined battle with the big diesels in the darkening grayness of cold dusk.

Ohio became Pennsylvania, one

indistinguishable from the other in the black ribbon environment of crimson taillights, moving, shifting, always rolling forward on flat land or through low hills. The Terra's AM radio reported snow flurries and descending temperatures were due throughout the area, with more severe weather forecast for the New England area and the Atlantic seaboard.

And then Pennsylvania became New York, and U.S. 90 became the New York Throughway and 70 mph in gently rolling blackness. Glimpses of high voltage transmission line towers elicited a weird bit of unrelated history, Orson Welles' Mercury Theatre broadcast of the "War of the Worlds," in the days of radio drama. Welles and his cast convinced the northeastern U.S. that Martians had landed. For a moment, the towers became Wellesian visitors from another planet—and then they flicked back into reality as simple benevolent carriers of power from generating plants at Niagara Falls to energy-hungry Manhattan some 400 miles away.

OHIO PENNSYLVANIA NEW YORK VERMONT ATLANTIC NEW HAMP

Midnight: Day one became day two. And Upstate New York had long since pulled quilts and comforters up to its collective chin. But the giant Macks, Peterbilts, Whites, Internationals and Kenworths, and the tiny Terra, just kept on keepin' on, until overweight eyelids, Rochester, N.Y., and a red and green Holiday Inn sign merged. It was 1:30 a.m., and the Atlantic remained some nebulous distance eastward in below freezing blackness.

The 6:30 a.m. wakeup call, unwelcome in the blanket warmth, came on the minute, and a not quite hot shower and breakfast, with a very large jolt of coffee, set blood flowing again. Restarting the diesel in the 12-degree cold was merely a 90-second glow plug exercise to compression ignition on the first flick of the starter keyswitch. And everything was as before on U.S. 90, eastward bound, except that now go-to-work, commercial traffic and snowplow/salter equipment were mixing it up with the diesel rigs, large and small.

DAY THREE, 1 ABOVE 0

A turn northward on U.S. 91 let the little pickup skirt Troy, N.Y., for a bit, then a turn eastward put the Terra on New York Highway 7, and the Terra was soon across the ice-jammed Hudson River, climbing through the low hills of western Vermont.

New Hampshire Highway 9 took the Terra to Keene, which appeared to be at once busy smalltown U.S.A. and Hollywood's idea of what a gracefully aged New England town should be. Supermarket and car wash were side by side with buildings that were beginning to weather and age some 150 years ago. Through Keene on Highway 9, then a turn south on New Hampshire 31 brought the Terra to Day Two's goal. Textile designer person and friend, Annie Dillon, had promised to serve as a guide for off-pavement exercises in the New England woods—along with a snow scene photo session.

Day Three broke at 1 above zero, and an overcast dissolved to sunshine, but a wind of almost 30 knots resulted in a chill factor significantly lower in terms of tingles in toes, fingertips and ends of noses.

The Terra's drive system, small torque converter, 3-speed automatic and 2-H/4-H/4-L transfer case, with Warn locking front hubs, was now in 4-H with the hubs thrown to "Lock."

Trekking over New Hampshire ice and snow at 35 mph, off-pavement, is much like a loose gravel road at 90 mph. Concentration and awareness are necessary, as is a sense of "feel," to keep the truck on the slippery surface. But the advantages of 4wd traction and the toothy bite of the Goodyears in combination offered not one single instant of pit-stomach insecurity.

Annie, usually a 2wd Opel station wagon pilot, drove a bit for photographic purposes. In exchange, she was invited to dinner at David's, a country inn located in a brick house built just at the turn of the 19th Century. It was a very nice dinner, but the time arrived to take Annie home.

The Nissan Six fired immediately, and the little diesel clucked merrily—until it was turned up a shallow grade toward the center of Antrim. Here the diesel engine lost rpm progressively, then apparently died of fuel starvation in mid-road. Nervous laughter masked the fact that this could develop into an untoward situation as the outside air temperature was 15 degrees below zero—and dropping.

All attempts at restarts were all failures. A crew of passersby helped to push the diesel Terra rearward some 70 feet into the driveway of a house which, at 10:30 p.m., still had a light burning (and some hope, too) inside.

A knock at the door brought on-the-spot friendship and, eventually, the kindest kind of help. Jim and Ruth Herne were just brewing a last cup of coffee before bedtime in their house—built in 1828—and offered some for drinking while Jim phoned the local wrecker operator, Wayne's Texaco. Upshot of the conversation was that there had been an accident and the tow truck would be delayed for a time.

Some time! At 1:30 a.m., the tow truck dispatcher phoned to report that the wrecker itself was now stalled, victim of the cold, and couldn't make the run to retrieve the Terra. Jim Herne was able to start his Chevy and delivered Annie and *Pickup, Van & 4WD*'s truckless driver to their respective abodes.

Morning of Day Four arrived at 20 below. And the walk to Wayne's Texaco station was brisk indeed. The wrecker was not yet operating, so it couldn't haul the Terra in.

A phone call to Ehlers in Ft. Wayne brought the initial diagnosis that, in all probability, water in the No. 2 diesel fuel had frozen in the lines. A few minutes later, however, Ehlers called back that the IH consensus opinion was that the fuel pickup filter inside the Terra's 19-gal. tank had collected some water and had frozen solid, and that the condition could be remedied by warming up the truck indoors, and adding a couple of cans of methanol "Heet" or "Dri-Gas" to the fuel to disperse the water into diesel oil. This advice was well and good, but the Antrim, N.H.,

Texaco tow man had yet to retrieve his own truck, and the little International Terra remained, literally, on ice, in Jim and Ruth Herne's driveway.

Finally, at 3:30 in the afternoon, the Terra was towed in and lodged in a lubrication bay at Wayne's Texaco. A quick-charger was hooked up to the Terra's battery, then a kerosene/electric space heater's warm blast was directed at the fuel tank, and later the forced air heat was blown onto the now frosted engine block.

As the freeze-up of the fuel system had caused the entire diesel fuel injection system to starve, purge itself of fuel, it was necessary to bleed the air out of the purged injection system with use of the hand priming pump on the injection pump. Only a few strokes of the pump were required to bring fuel to the Nissan's injection pump. Bleeder screws were snugged tight, and, with a couple of shots of ether in the induction horn on the air cleaner, the CN6-33 fired reluctantly, then warmed to a clacking idle. Pwhew! That diesel knock had the quality of music just then.

So, it was away into the night, heading for the Atlantic, in the finally un-iced Terra. The thermometer was indicating a chill of just above zero as the IH pickup finally reached the Atlantic shore at Hampton Beach, N.H.. The sea was black and still in the past-midnight cold.

HEADING HOME! WOW!

Forty winks in a motel, an early call, breakfast and a balky restart of the cold engine were the sequence that, finally, led to the actual start of the Atlantic-to-Pacific diesel run.

Going *WEST*! Heading *HOME*! Wow! The Terra's odometer read 1302.9 miles. And it was just after 8 a.m. (EST) when the IH pickup was started rolling. Signs said "Clams" and "Lobster" and "Go-Go Golf" as the Terra wended its way toward the Massachusetts Turnpike. Snowy towns and villages flashed past. Hartford, Conn., was traversed well before noon.

At 2 p.m., the Terra was herded into a truck stop for a tank of No. 2. And it was only because the windshield washer reservoir needed filling that the hood was raised with the engine still running. This revealed that a fuel leak had developed at the banjo fitting atop the Nissan engine's primary fuel filter. A little wrenching plugged the leak.

The George Washington Bridge led the pickup again to New York State for the brief run through New Jersey, southwestward to intercept the Pennsylvania Turnpike, U.S. 76, and later U.S. 70.

CONNECTICUT NEW YORK NEW JERSEY PENNSYLVANIA WEST VIRGINIA

DIESEL SCOUT

Just a few minutes before 10:30 p.m., the Terra was turned off the Turnpike and onto U.S. 70, the Interstate Highway that would lead eventually to I-15 and California.

In East Wheeling, W. Va., it was just short of midnight, and it had been a long day. The motel room bed could have been cobblestones and it would have made little difference.

A soul-rock version of "The Battle Hymn of the Republic" was playing as the Terra crossed into Ohio again. Then the radio said it was 29 degrees outside. A light rain was falling.

As tiny spits of ice began to form on the windshield, the faint thought began to form that now would be a great time to slow down, stop, engage 4wd/high and lock the Warn hubs for added driving security on possible patches of ice.

But, before the thought could be completely formed, the Terra had started to skate lightly on a patch of fresh, smooth ice, gently left, then right, then left and—HOLY MACKEREL!—all the way around. It's not a nice feeling to be backing down the freeway at 50 mph or so, trying to keep the truck on the road while peering through the cab's rear window. The pickup ultimately slid off the pavement and onto a stubbled median strip, also very icy, bumped over a shallow ditch and came to rest with no damage whatsoever to the truck.

Pride and nerve, of course, were completely shattered. And, with the truck's drivetrain in 4H/4wd/lock, 25 mph on the ice seemed altogether too great a rate of speed.

DOING THE DIRTY DUFFLE

And now there was another problem developing for the Terra—scarcity of fuel. At Zanesville, Ohio, home of the western novelist Zane Grey, what appeared at a distance to be a diesel fuel pump turned out to be a kerosene pump—so a couple of gallons of coal oil were taken aboard anyway to extend the No. 2 diesel remaining in the tank in order to go truck stop hunting.

There was a diesel dispensary just around the next bend. The fuel halt was a mixture of Lawrence Welk on the radio and clear ice on the fuel pumps. Next came Columbus, almost hidden in gray mist, light snow and intermittent sleeting rain. Still more ice and, as yet, nonappearance of salt-spreaders prompted the decision to (1) eat lunch and (2) wash the clothing that had accumulated in the dirty duffle during a week on the road. The sleet turned to rain, the ice was salted and the Terra was set rolling once again.

The popular "Convoy" was playing as the pickup, in its own convoy of freight trucks, crossed into Indiana once again. In Indianapolis, the temperature was 46 degrees, but going down. Hard rain was the situation, and icing was the forecast.

At 7:20 p.m., the Terra crossed into Illinois. The necessity to refuel was met in Effingham at 8:50 p.m. By 9:25 p.m., the truck was running on dry pavement, so a halt was made to set the hubs for free-wheeling, and to change transfer gearing to 2H. By 10:30 p.m., the arch in St. Louis was in sight, and a little later a sign directed visitors to the memorial for Lindbergh's solo flight across the Atlantic. In his Ryan M-2, Spirit of St. Louis, he had it much tougher than driving solo from Atlantic to Pacific in "Spirit of Ft. Wayne."

The motel keeper in Columbia, Mo., bore a close resemblance to Harry S Truman. It had been a 700-mile day—with spinout. The prospect of rest was golden. Just after 8 a.m., the journey was resumed. Independence, then Kansas City, then the Kansas state line flashed past.

Supper—a burger and a bowl of Kansas bean soup—in a truck stop provided an opportunity to reflect upon Kansas: This state is an all-day drive, but dry pavement is a treat. This state is endless, but Colorado was now closer. It was 5:50 p.m. when the Terra departed Oakley, Kan. The news was Patty Hearst, the music was Elton John. Just after 7 p.m., the Terra zipped through Kanorado, then, a minute later, crossed the border into Colorado. It was 10:12 p.m. and 29 degrees when the pickup rolled through Denver and turned northward on U.S. 25 for Longmont, Colo., for a visit with a friend.

High altitude and temperatures in the low teens made for a hard start of the Nissan diesel engine the next morning—and the cold weather and accumulated slush and collected ice were resulting in grievous noises issuing from the Terra's hydraulic steering pump. The visit and a late lunch preceded a restart of the trip at 2:28 p.m.

Refueled, the Terra started the long climb up the eastern slope of the Rocky Mountains to Loveland Pass at 11,992 ft above sea level. As the Terra gained in altitude, the air/fuel mixture became considerably more rich and the Nissan's exhaust smoke blew very black indeed.

Down is the most satisfactory way to go from 11,992 ft. Gravity came to the aid of Nissan and things improved to a great degree. On the upslope, heavy packed snow, some of it iced, had precipitated a gearing change to 4H/lock, and now the 4wd system and

F-32s once again provided that sure-footed feel in the slick going.

At 9:47 p.m., the IH Terra crossed the Utah border. And the little International and a giant Peterbilt tandem hauler loaded with sheets of drywall board played uphill/downhill, fast/slow games, racing downhill, slowing at the next upgrade, the Terra passing the big rig, then in turn being passed by the Pete on the next descending slope.

Salina, Utah, sidewalks tightly rolled, appeared on the horizon at 1 a.m., The motel "Vacancy" sign, in rose neon, said "Welcome."

It was an effort to turn the Terra's tailgate to the sunrise in Utah morning chill, but the Pacific seemed to be beckoning just over the next rise. As the day warmed, the IH pickup scampered happily homeward through a brief corner of Arizona, across the brown sand and red rock of southern Nevada, pausing only for a fillup of No. 2 diesel in Las Vegas.

THE COMFORTABLE MOJAVE

The desert hills, black rock, Joshua trees, mesquite, dunes, dry lakes and thorny cactus spelled home. The temperature was between 70 and 80 degrees F, sufficiently warm to reactiviate a cardiovascular system that had a surfeit of New England temperatures, zero and below, an overdose of Midwest ice, snow and freezing rain, and more than a sufficiency of Rocky Mountain slush and wind. Never did the wide, harsh Mojave seem so comfortable.

Barstow, then Victorville, then down the coastal mountain slope to San Bernardino, and the Terra was fitted into the going-home traffic of urban Southern California freeways. Radio traffic reports said things were normal: The Hollywood Freeway had come to a stop in both directions, and there had been a major wreck on the Harbor Freeway, south of Los Angeles.

Friday night, Saturday, Sunday, Monday, Tuesday and Wednesday, just into evening, the 4435-mile trip had been completed, Atlantic to Pacific, in some tough driving conditions.

And the Terra had traveled from where the Pilgrims landed to where Junipero Serra built missions at about the time the folk in the eastern part of the continent were thinking about self-government. The Terra had traveled across the great Ohio, the wide Missouri, the plains where buffalo roamed, the Rockies where silver and gold had brought civilization, across Brigham Young's Utah, across Death Valley desert to Los Angeles, Hollywood, and to the Pacific Ocean where surfers hotdog and hang ten. Some trip! ●

MISSOURI KANSAS COLORADO UTAH ARIZONA NEVADA CALIFORNIA

Lo /H t R tion hip:
UNTANN R
In the desert, this International convertible's top has its ups and downs...

PV4 TEST

Right from the start it was a Love/Hate relationship between the International Suntanner and **PICKUP, VAN & 4WD** test crewmen. It was love at first concept, the concept of a rugged, capable IH 4wd vehicle with a convertible vinyl top and taut white bed cover. And a little hate welled up in the struggle to refit the folding top during a stiff wind, and in trying to snap the bed cover into place with icy fingertips on a very cold morning. As one staff driver, former owner of a couple of ragtop sports cars, said, "Loved the idea, the concept; hated the bad weather inconvenience."

International supplied the test Suntanner, the convertible version of the Scout midi pickup on the 118-in. Terra wheelbase. The Suntanner was powered by a 304-cu-in. V-8 IH's mid-sized engine. The engine was fitted with a California emission control package. The powertrain was comprised of a Chrysler 3-speed automatic transmission, a 2-speed Dana transfer case and Dana/Spicer drive axles front and rear, carrying 3.54:1 final drive gearing, and Spicer locking hubs.

Suspension was straight Fort Wayne: Semi-elliptical leaf springs and tubular shock absorbers at all four corners of the rigid Terra ladder frame. Power disc brakes of 11.75-in. diameter at the front, drum brakes of 11 x 2 in. at the rear and General Belted Gripper 780 H78 x 15 tires all-around completed the Suntanner's running gear. The General Grippers, in Load Range B, offer a per-tire load capacity of 1770 lb at 32 psi inflation pressure.

The Suntanner's Gross Vehicle Weight Rating (GVWR) was 6200 lb, the only GVWR available in the 1977 IH Scout Terra line. Both front and rear axles carried a capacity figure of 3500 lb, but the unit's official Gross Axle Weight Rating (GAWR) was 3100 lb per axle, front and rear.

The Suntanner's empty weight was 4125 lb, with a 57/43 percent front/rear weight bias. With a 6200-lb GVWR and 4125-lb empty weight, the Suntanner offered a full ton, plus 75 lb, in cargo carrying capability.

On top of the very basic IH Terra

truck, however, was what could be called full-house trim. The Suntanner's options list included Saginaw power steering, a modulated cooling fan, automatic cruise control, fuel tank skidplate, driver and passenger individual bucket seats, air conditioning, and an AM pushbutton radio. In addition, the Suntanner Terra carried deluxe interior and exterior bright trim packages, door edge guards and body protector moldings. Exterior paint was in "Terra Cotta," a metallic red/brown; and interior vinyl upholstery was in "Saddle" and "Tanbark," tan and olive green tones, respectively.

As tricked-out, the test Suntanner carried a list price of $7552, plus $461 in freight charges, and not including taxes or license fees. The optional Suntanner top/tonneau kit also was not included in the list price. The fiberglass cab top is standard equipment.

International supplied the Terra for test fitted with the dealer-installed pristine white vinyl Suntanner option kit, comprised of a fitted pickup bed cover, a "tonneau" cover for the otherwise exposed forward section of the bed, just behind driver and passenger seats, and the convertible top, with fold-up window frame and top bow components. The Suntanner top option kit retails for $246.15, not including installation costs.

Another dealer-installed option fitted to the Suntanner was a tailgate/quarter-panel mounted swing-away jerry can and spare wheel/tire carrier. This assembly, not installed, lists for $60.

Now back to love/hate, concept/practice: The Suntanner and two-member evaluation team was scheduled for five days with the vehicle in California's "low desert" badlands, a region of soft blow-sand, hardrock, drywash boulders, narrow sandstone canyons, dunes and, of course, sun for suntanning and wind for windburning.

The Terra cargo bed easily accommodated sleeping bags, ground pads, propane stove, food, cooking utensils, charcoal and firewood, clothing and miscellaneous gear. The behind-the-seats Terra cab bay, 11 cu ft of it, more than accommodated Hi-Lift jack, short-handled shovel, axe, snatch straps, tools and parts box, coats, sweaters and Texas hats (the latter to provide shade while driving the Suntanner top-down in the desert).

Loading was made difficult by rain that had puddled in both the vinyl bed cover and in the Suntanner's top. Unsnapping the bed cover and rolling it forward for access to the bed without drizzling some water into the cargo area was impossible; and water that had collected in the top sloshed down the vehicle's sides when doors were slammed. It was a wet evening for crewmen as they departed for some dry desert.

On paved highways, with cruise control set for the legal 55 mph, the Suntanner's top thumped and buffeted noisily, out of syncopation with the steady whining buzz of the General Belted Grippers' cleated teeth on asphalt. It must be said, no two ways about it, that the Terra Suntanner, like most convertible passenger cars of times past, is significantly more noisy inside than are conventional all-metal utility trucks or passenger cars. The initial impression of high noise level was later borne out in sound level testing with a precision meter. At idle, the meter showed 61.5 dbA. This sound level rose to 85.5 dbA at a constant 60 mph. As compared with other IH vehicles tested recently, that's a lot of sound on the exponential decibel scale. For example, a fiberglass cabbed Scout Terra with 196-cu.-in. in-line Four engine generated 55.5 dbA at idle and 76.0 dbA at 60 mph; a likewise enclosed Scout Terra with 198-cu.-in. Nissan diesel Six produced 60 dbA at idle and 76.0 dbA at 60 mph; and a station wagon styled Scout Traveler with 354-cu.-in. V-8 sounded off at 58.5 dbA at idle and 75.0 dbA at 60 mph.

The Suntanner, with top up, and at highway speeds is not for conversationalists or radio music lovers.

The first night's camp, made easily out of the Suntanner's now dry cargo bed, was effortless and convenient. At daylight the next morning, water canisters were filled, tire pressures checked, and then it was time to head for the hard stuff—the *really* hard stuff. But icy fingers pressing painfully on misaligned cargo-bed cover snaps somehow reduced the keen anticipation of the off-roading, four-wheeling day ahead.

The vehicle was loped into a 25-mph drywash, with a whoopee here, a washboard there, and potholes and boulders just about everywhere, but with sufficient traction available to avoid a shift into 4wd and low transfer range. Then, "Cla-bang!" And, "Whattwassat??!!"

The swing-away jerry can/tire carrier had come adrift and swung away, its latching mechanism shaken loose by the brief period of moderately rough running. A 1/4-in. flathead bolt, a couple of flat washers, a lock washer, a nut and some wrenching in the right place corrected the situation, but made the tailgate inaccessible for the remainder of the desert trip, inconvenient, but not really annoying.

Now the trail zig-zagged through a gigantic geologic fault, a boulder-strewn watercourse for flash floods (for which this desert area is deadly famous). But still the Suntanner plugged along easily in 2wd/high range, the gutsy General tires finding bite in rock, loose gravel and rough sandstone exposures. The crew began to believe the entire trip could be accomplished in 2wd, which is something of a waste of time for people who specialize in off-pavement driving of 4wd machinery.

Then the gorge opened into a wide, sandy wash, the grains coarse at first, then taking on the character of talcum-powder-fine blow-sand. The Generals' tread edge cleats began to chew ever more deeply into the runny sand, and the Suntanner groaned to a protesting halt. It was 4wd time.

One crewman hopped out to the left, the other to the right, and the vehicle's locking front hubs were quickly engaged. The driver encountered the usual gritch-and-glatch trouble in stirring the transfer gears into 4wd/low range. From then on, even with the rather narrow Generals inflated to a fairly firm 22 psi, sand simply was not any sort of problem.

The drywash closed in again and branched off into steep canyons, one of which was chosen at random for a hard-rock run. Round boulders, sharp boulders (to the detriment of the right front General's sidewall) were on the creep-and-crawl agenda. Working over the rocks, footing slipping away under the tires, showed that a vehicle with a 118-in. wheelbase is not as effective in slow, arduous, lumpy going as is one of shorter wheel-to-wheel center dimension—the 100-in. wheelbase Scout II, for example. The Suntanner displayed its long wheelbase hang-ups here, one the tendency to high-center over some of the larger lumps, the other to come perilously close to canyon walls and boulders in tight turns on trails that are normally negotiable in 4wd by Jeep CJ-5 and Toyota Land Cruiser. The terrain became much too tight for comfort. Discretion became the better part of valor (in thinking the potential cost of body panel repair). And, in a convenient spot, the Suntanner was turned around and ambled to wider, less threatening surfaces. Neither traction nor power available were problems. The tires grabbed and held; the 304 V-8 offered husky, reliable torque at low rpm. Only the vehicle's dimensional length prevented it from climbing over or angling around obstacles in the trail.

"No more narrow canyons, huh?" said one crewman.

"Okay with me," agreed the other.

Neither of these two enjoys getting stuck, especially high-centered. They enjoy even less the sweaty, lower back pain process of getting unstuck.

Evening found the test crew at the foot of a narrow, sandy draw, an ideal place to make camp—had not the cool

PHOTOS BY DAVE EPPERSON

SUNTANNER

desert wind been whistling at an estimated 40–50 mph.

The next day, corned beef hash and coffee water soft-boiled eggs stowed away, the crew readied the Suntanner for a top-down day of running in the hardrock wilderness.

Removal of the convertible Suntanner top requires several steps: (1) unsnapping the rear of the top at the bow over the cargo bed; (2) release of Velcro window frame closures, and sliding the metal ribbed forward edge of the top from underneath a flange on the windshield header; (3) unrigging both left- and right-hand folding window frames; (4) removal of the single top bow by releasing two keyed mounting pins and a tightening strap, also secured with Velcro, between the center of the bow and an eye on the inside of the windshield header; and (5) folding, gathering and stowing away all the top paraphernalia.

The top-drop drill was worth the trouble. The morning sun was poking its bright golden nose over canyon wall tops as the top-down Suntanner trickled off into the still, now windless, terrifying and rugged beauty of a desert badlands morning. This is what generated test crew enthusiasm (much of the love) for this vehicle.

PRICES

Basic list, FOB Ft. Wayne, Ind
Scout Terra 4wd pickup	$5637
Scout II 4wd	$5751
Scout Traveler 4wd	$6122
Scout SS-II 4wd	$5168
Scout Diesel add approx.	$2648

to above prices

Standard Equipment ....196-cu.-in. in-line Four engine, 3-spd manual transmission, single-speed transfer case, heater/defroster, 2-spd electric wiper/washers, power front disc brakes, full instrumentation, folding front bench seat, tinted glass, chrome front and rear bumpers, fiberglass cab top, H78 x 15B tires

GENERAL

Curb weight, lb (test model)	4125
Weight distribution, %, front/rear	57/43
GVWR (test model)	6200
Optional GVWRs	none
Wheelbase, in.	100/118
Track, front/rear	57.1/57.1
Overall length	166.2/184.2
Overall height	66.0
Overall width	70.0
Overhang, front/rear	24.0/42.2
Approach angle, degrees	30
Departure angle, degrees	19

Ground clearances (test model):
Front axle	7.5
Rear axle	8.0
Oil pan	13.3
Transfer case	12.0
Fuel line	15.6
Exhaust system (lowest point)	12.6
Fuel tank capacity (U.S. gal.)	19
Auxiliary	none

ACCOMMODATION

Standard seats	full-width folding bench seat
Optional seats	bucket seats, $79; center console, $48
Headroom, in.	34.0
Accelerator pedal to seatback, max	44.3
Steering wheel to seatback, max	16.7
Seat to ground	33.6
Floor to ground	17.6
Unobstructed load space (length x width x height)	72.0 x 42.0 x 21.3
Tailgate (width x height)	54.8 x 21.3

Instruments ....speedometer, odometer, fuel gauge, ammeter, oil pressure, water temp
Warning lights ....front axle engaged indicator, parking brake warning, hazard warning
Optional ....none

ENGINES

Standard	196-cu.-in. in-line Four
Bore x stroke	4.125 x 3.656
Compression ratio	8.02:1
Net horsepower @ rpm	86 @ 3800
Net torque @ rpm, lb-ft	157 @ 2200
Type fuel required	leaded or unleaded
Optional	304-cu.-in. V-8, $166
Bore x stroke, in.	3.875 x 3.218
Compression ratio	8.19:1
Net horsepower @ rpm	144 @ 3600*
Net torque @ rpm, lb-ft	247 @ 2400*
Type fuel required	leaded or unleaded

*For Calif., hp rating is 133 @ 3800, torque is 228 @ 2400

Optional	345-cu.-in. V-8, $220
Bore x stroke, in.	3.875 x 3.656
Compression ratio	8.05:1
Net horsepower @ rpm	163 @ 3600*
Net torque @ rpm, lb-ft	292 @ 2000*
Type fuel required	leaded or unleaded

*For Calif., hp rating is 146 @ 3600, torque is 275 @ 2000

Optional	198-cu.-in. in-line diesel Six*
Bore x stroke, in.	3.27 x 3.94
Compression ratio	22:1
Net horsepower @ rpm	92 @ 4000
Net torque @ rpm, lb-ft	137.5 @ 2000
Type fuel required	No. 2 diesel

*Diesel engine is available only as a package at a cost of approx. $2648

DRIVETRAIN

Standard transmission	3-speed manual T-332
Clutch dia., in.	11.0

Transmission ratios:
3rd	1.00:1
2nd	1.55:1
1st	2.99:1
Synchromesh	all forward gears

Optional	4-spd wide ratio manual T-427, $165

Transmission ratios:
4th	1.00:1
3rd	1.68:1
2nd	3.09:1
1st	6.32:1
Synchromesh	all forward gears

Optional	4-spd close ratio manual T-428, $165

Transmission ratios:
4th	1.00:1
3rd	1.41:1
2nd	2.41:1
1st	4.02:1
Synchromesh	all forward gears

Optional	3-spd automatic, $306

Transmission ratios:
3rd	1.00:1
2nd	1.45:1
1st	2.45:1

Rear axle type	semi-floating hypoid
Final drive ratios	3.07:1, 3.54:1, 4.09:1
Overdrive	none
Free-running front hubs	std
Limited slip differential	$82
Transfer case	TC-143 single-speed (std), TC-145 2-spd (opt)
Transfer case ratios	1.00:1 (TC-143), 2.03:1 and 1.00:1 (TC-145)

CHASSIS & BODY

Body/frame	ladder-type frame with separate steel body
Brakes (std)	front, 11.75-in. dia. disc; rear, 11.03 x 2.25-in. drum
Brake swept area, sq in.	381
Swept area/ton (max load)	123
Power brakes	std
Steering type (std)	worm and roller
Steering ratio	24:1
Power steering	$189
Power steering ratio	recirculating ball 17.5:1
Turning circle, ft	34.3 (Scout II), 38.8 (Terra)

Wheel size (std)	15 x 6.0JK
Optional wheel sizes	15 x 7.0JJ
styled chrome	
Tire size (std)	H78 x 15B
Optional tire sizes	HR78 x 15B, 7.00 x 15C, 10 x 15B

SUSPENSION

Front suspension	semi-elliptic leaf springs on live axle with tube shocks
Front axle capacity, lb	3200
Optional	none
Rear suspension	semi-elliptic leaf springs on live axle with tube shocks
Rear axle capacity, lb	3500
Optional	none

Additional suspension options ....HD front and rear shocks, $13; HD front springs includes HD shocks, $19; HD rear springs includes HD shocks, $29

TEST MODEL

Scout Terra pickup, 304-cu.-in. V-8, automatic transmission, 2-spd transfer case, air conditioning, cruise control, dealer installed convertible top, dealer installed spare tire carrier, Calif. emission certification, AM radio, modulated fan, fuel tank skidplate, bucket seats, deluxe interior trim, deluxe exterior trim, door edge guards, 3.54 axle ratio, H78 x 15B tires West Coast list price (includes $461 freight but does not include dealer installed options) $8013

ACCELERATION

Time to speed, sec:
0–30 mph	4.7
0–45 mph	8.2
0–60 mph	13.7
0–70 mph	19.6
Standing start, ¼-mile, sec.	19.6
Speed at end, mph	70

SPEED IN GEARS

High range, 3rd (3500 rpm)	82
2nd (4000 rpm)	65
1st (4000 rpm)	39
Low range, 3rd (4000 rpm)	46
2nd (4000 rpm)	32
1st (4000 rpm)	19
Engine rpm @ 55 mph	2300

BRAKE TESTS

Pedal pressure required for ½-g deceleration rate from 60 mph, lb	35
Stopping distance from 60 mph, ft	164
Fade: Percent increase in pedal pressure for 6 stops from 60 mph	77
Overall brake rating	excellent

INTERIOR NOISE

Idle in neutral, dbA	61.5
Maximum during acceleration	75.5
At steady 60 mph cruising speed	85.5

OFF PAVEMENT

Hillclimbing ability	excellent
Maneuverability	very good
Turnaround capability	very good
Driver visibility	very good
Handling	very good
Ride	very good

ON PAVEMENT

Handling	very good
Ride	very good
Driver comfort	good
Engine response	very good

FUEL CONSUMPTION

City/freeway driving, mpg	12.7
Off pavement	8.2
Range, city/freeway driving, miles	238
Range, off pavement	155

For the dwellers in the out-of-doors, there's simply nothing like being out-of-doors while driving out-of-doors. The sky is in the driver's seat, the visibility is fantastic, the enjoyment is terrific. And this is what the Suntanner is all about.

The one day of top-down running was extended to two (as the wind had hustled away elsewhere), and then it was time to return to alleged civilization. So long, creosote bush and kangaroo rat; hello, megalopolis and smog.

Back on the pavement again, the crew kept the top in the down position, cruising back two-laners at 40 mph or so in absolute sunshine comfort. However, the return road to the home office climbs to more than 5000 ft above sea level, and the chill began to nip at about 4000 ft elevation.

So, it was top-up time. The process, of course, is the reverse of top-down. However, by now, the wind had sprung up again, and the mountain chill had caused the once desert-warmed vinyl top to contract. Both crewmen were required to bulldog the vinyl material into position over the bow and window frames, wrestling the flapping fabric against the blustering wind. On reinstallation, the bow, with the windshield header strap, was drawn up and set more tightly than it had been secured on delivery from International. Snapping the cold vinyl to the lower rear bow required one crewman to pull on the fabric, with other to press with all his might on the chilly snap studs. Some of the love of the open vehicle dissipated into mild hate here. However, and at length, the top was in place, and the Suntanner resumed its homeward course at a controlled 55 mph. The test crew agreed that the top, now secured

Right, Grippers dug in a bit in sand, showed firm traction on rock. Below right, carrier latch came adrift in lumpy running and needed a bolt. Below, Suntanner's interior was color coordinated in "Saddle" and "Tanbark."

in place more tightly, produced somewhat less noise than it had earlier—but it was still a bumper/buffeter that offended the ears recently attuned to wilderness quiet.

As for the "suntanner" aspect of the Suntanner, one crewman who spends a great deal of time in the desert anyway simply added to the leathery, wrinkled brown texture of his facial skin. The other, who spends more time indoors, picked up a decidedly red beak and some windburned cheeks. Probably the Suntanner should be treated like a swimming pool deck or an ocean beach—20 minutes a day until a tan builds up sufficiently to avoid a burn.

So, the top-down period of enjoyment ended and it was back to work at the local dragstrip where, top up, the Terra Suntanner's 304 V-8 propelled the vehicle from zero to 60 mph in 13.7 sec, and zapped the standing-start quarter-mile in 19.6 sec at 70 mph. These figures indicate the Suntanner has no difficulty in urban traffic merging and passing.

The Suntanner's disc/drum braking system turned in a highly acceptable panic stop effort, halting in only 167 ft from 60 mph. In a six-stop series of 1/2-g stops, the Suntanner showed 77 percent brake fade. All stops were smooth and straight, accomplished with no untoward decelerative acrobatics and no

rear wheel lockup. Test crew people regarded the vehicle's brakes in the same light as memories of some of that fine top-down desert running.

At a cruise speed of 55 mph, the truck's engine turned at 2300 rpm. At this city/freeway speed and rpm combination, the Suntanner delivered 12.7 mpg, which fell off to 8.2 mpg in off-road driving situations.

As test crewmen are wont to do with vehicles they drive, the subject of "What I Would Do If I Owned a Suntanner" came up one morning over coffee.

"The Suntanner is really a neat idea," said the leathery-faced one. "But if I owned it, I sure wouldn't want that bed cover and top the way they were fitted to the test unit. I like riding outdoors—but with a roll bar, baby, a roll bar. I'd put a roll bar in, then get some boat top fitter to make me a lid that would fit better, keep out the water and not make so much noise."

"I'd go for a roll bar, too," said burned beak. "But I'd stow the tire inside the bed, along with the jerry cans. That swing-away rack is great as long as you don't have to turn that 118-in. wheelbase truck around in a narrow canyon."

Dealer installed accessories are what make the Suntanner concept attractive, along with International's tried-and-trew 4wd drivetrains, but ill-fitting and cumbersome accessories detract from the pure pleasure that's derived from off-roading in an open vehicle.

For the test crew's part, they loved the desert from their seats in the open Suntanner, but hated the snaps, the pins, the bows and the downright poor fit of the components.

From the start, it was a love/hate relationship between machine and men—about 95 percent love and 5 percent hate.

Love and hate are changeable emotions, like the Suntanner's up-down top and open-closed bed, like—well—the weather. ●

SCOUT TRAVELER

PV4 TEST

First, the bad news, and now the good news can't get much better...

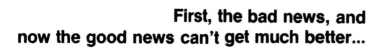

RARELY DOES A test of a vehicle get off to a bad start. Usually, in this business, a vehicle that seems highly acceptable at first will display its faults progressively. It's something like: "First, the good news . . . Now, the bad news."

In the case of a test International Scout Traveler, it was: "First, the bad news."

The vehicle, a '76 model with 118-in. wheelbase, 345-cu-in. V-8 engine, automatic transmission, 2-speed transfer case, reinforced fiberglass top, deluxe trim and upholstery, and plenty of additional extras, was collected at an IH dealership some 30 miles from PICKUP, VAN & 4WD's editorial office. The freshly waxed Traveler's odometer showed but 53 miles. The trip from dealership to office involves about 25 miles of freeway travel at 55 mph during non-rush hours, and 5 miles on city streets at 15 to 40 mph. There are no crossgrain, drywash whoopies, boulders, stream beds, sand, mud or snow on this Southern California route. The freeway was negotiated without undue hardship, with FM radio blasting a bit of mid-morning rock music. There were no jumps, no wheelstands, no rollovers on the paved urban grid. But, when the Traveler was turned hard right onto the home office street, a loud "GRUNCH" was heard and–panic of panics, the steering locked-up tight at almost full right, while the Traveler was aimed directly at a curb, a tree, a lawn and a house. The staffer/driver stomped the brakes and wrenched the steering wheel hard to the left. "KLUNK" ensued and the steering was once again free–to the driver's immediate relief. What had happened?

The Traveler seemed a bit wobbly during the remaining half-mile run to the office. A parking lot inspection revealed the cause of the trouble. The main leaf of the left front longitudinal semi-elliptical spring had fractured about 10 in. rearward of the front eye. The second leaf of the spring and the loose end of the broken main leaf had pinched the steering Pitman arm and main steering link ball joint in a very effective vise. Only IH's husky power steering–and quick reaction by the driver –had avoided an unscheduled over-the-curb junket onto somebody's private greensward. The Traveler returned to the dealership behind a wrecker, front end forlornly slung aloft.

IH folk quickly fitted a new spring, and the vehicle pickup trek was made once again. Now, the good news!

From the initial untoward "bad news" experience, day-to-day evaluation work and play with the 1976 IH Scout Traveler was all easy "good news." The tough little midi station wagon/utility truck trundled willingly everywhere in the urban environment and up and over rugged mountain terrain. After that first flash of bad news, the good news simply got better and better.

First look showed the Traveler painted in "Grenoble Green" with broad "Winter White" side panel striping, and white "glass" top, a combination both comfortable to the eye, and comfortable to the being, as the white top tends to reflect the sun's heat rays, keeping the vehicle's interior cool.

Far from utilitarian in interior appearance, the test vehicle carried optional "Ivy Green" fabric upholstered bucket seats forward and folding 3-passenger bench in the rear. Deep green cut pile carpeting covered the deck forward, and tough green vinyl matting was laid over the cargo deck. The inside mounted spare tire and wheel were protected by a fitted green vinyl cover, a match for the vinyl of seat backs. It's difficult these days to find a truly hard core off-roader that's as tastefully done, with full utility in mind.

Options? The Traveler was a veritable showcase of what IH offers the off-pavement enthusiast who likes–and has the bucks–to go first class. The add-on equipment list included the V-8 engine, automatic transmission and 4wd system, plus made-by-Warn automatic locking front hubs. And, also installed on the test vehicle were power steering, tilting steering wheel, AM/FM radio, electric clock, 3-speed vent fan, transfer engagement warning light, air conditioning, wood grain instrument panel and locking storage console between the front buckets. More? Yes, outside glitter included bright finish grille, window trim, parking and taillight bezels, dual outside mirrors and side moldings, all at extra cost.

As part of the air conditioner installation, the Traveler was assembled with a

PHOTOS BY DAVE EPPERSON

61-ampere alternator and a 72-ampere/ hour battery to meet the cooling load.

Base price of the Traveler was listed at $5844. With charges for California emission control certification, and including options, but not adding freight costs, the Traveler's total price, as tested, was $8312.

Underneath all the soft stuff and brightwork, however, was fitted the hardworking 4wd hardware that extends the vehicle's capability for both utilitarian and recreational activities.

The Traveler's engine, designated 345A, was fitted with California emission control plumbing and a dual exhaust system, and thus was rated as delivering a net 146 bhp at 3600 rpm and peak torque of 275 lb-ft at 2000 rpm. However, the elsewhere 345A V-8 with dual pipes delivers 163 bhp at 3500 rpm and peak torque of 292 lb-ft at 2000.

The 345-cu-in. ohv V-8's motive force was coupled through a 3-speed T-407 (Chrysler TorqueFlite) automatic transmission with first-to-third ratios of 2.45:1, 1.45:1 and 1.00:1, and 2.20:1 in reverse.

Next down the line was a Dana Model 20 2-speed transfer case with 1.00:1 high range and 2.03:1 low range gearing.

(Standard transfer case in Scout models is a single-speed 1.00:1 unit manufactured by IH.)

Front and rear drive axles, Dana Model 44 (FA-44), carried 3.07:1 final drive gearsets.

Hence, in high range, the Traveler's overall gearing, first to third, by the numbers, was 7.52:1, 4.45:1 and, of course, 3.07:1. In low range, employing 2.03 4wd transfer case reduction, overall gearing, first to third, was 15.27:1, 9.04:1 and 6.23:1. Thus the Traveler's gearing range, even with the tall-geared automatic, approaches the "stump-puller" category when everything is locked up in "Low-Low."

The front hubs, manufactured by Warn Industries, but stamped IH, were for automatic selective front drive capability. This means the front hubs engage (lock up) automatically under torque loading when the transfer case is engaged for 4wd. These hubs also may be positively locked manually, if the driver so desires. The hubs were tried both ways, and proved effective in either mode, automatic engagement under 4wd load, or manually engaged.

IH offers a broad variety of 4wd power-

train combinations that can increase the pulling power of the Traveler. Available components include a 3-speed manual with 2.99:1 first gear, a 4-speed manual with 4.02 low, and another 4-speed with a "granny" low gear ratio of 6.32:1. The latter, with the optionally available lower (higher numerically) 3.54:1 drive axle ratio, and the 2.03:1 gearing of the optional 2-speed transfer case, can provide 45.42:1 "Low-Low" gearing that, with properly aggressive tires, could pull the stump of a giant redwood.

Structurally, the 118-in. wheelbase Traveler starts with a 3-crossmember ladder type frame of mild carbon steel rails 4 x 3 x 0.12 in. dimensions. The Traveler's suspension system is completely straightforward with longitudinal semi-elliptical leaf springs, a 43-in. pair at the front, a 56-in. pair at the rear, and telescopic shock absorbers all around (with plenty of space to double-up for hard running). The Traveler's Gross Vehicle Weight Rating (GVWR) was 6200 lb, precluding the installation of a catalytic converter and use of unleaded gasoline. Gross Axle Weight Rating (GAWR), front and rear, was 3100 lb, respectively.

The smart looking exterior, the tasteful

TRAVELER

interior and the nuts-and-bolts details of powertrain and suspension are one thing, but how they work together in the 1976 IH Scout Traveler is decidedly another.

The Traveler's convenient air cylinder assisted hatchback tailgate was lifted and camping gear for three (food for six, though only three were going on the weekend outing) were pitched into the rearmost cargo area behind the optional rear bench. Simply put, everything fitted in with little attention to careful packing.

A couple of hours of 2wd, high transfer range running on freeways and some rural two-laners brought the Traveler to the base camp site, a secluded sandy flat. The three intrepid vehicle testers ate enough for six, then sleeping-bagged it until daylight, time for a mountain run with the now empty Traveler.

The terrain at first included a Forest Service fire road that, disappointingly, had been freshly graded. But, once past the parked grader, things deteriorated into some prime off-pavement activities. The Traveler was trucked over rain-cut crossgrain, water washed ruts, kingsized potholes, rocks of the smooth, stream-worn variety, the broken granite kind, in sizes from gritty sand to body-sized boulders, and soft, sandy forest floor, loose with pine needles and dry leaves.

Though the vehicle's factory fitted HR78 x 15 General Dual Steel Radial tires were designed for street/utility use, traction was broken only rarely, and full use of the vehicle's 4wd system (front manually locked) was available at all times.

The only difficulty encountered with the Traveler presented itself at the dead end of a fire road that obviously hadn't been used in a very long time. Slides partially blocked the way. Boulders littered the path. And, at the very bitter end was an almost vertical shale cutbank on one side, a drop–about 2000 ft almost straight down–on the other, and 3 ft of space on either end of the vehicle for backing and filling.

Maneuvering with a low-geared manual 4-speed and clutch would have made the 180-degree turn a piece of cake. However, with the automatic and relatively tall gearing of the 3.07:1 drive axles, things became difficult. To move ahead or backward, it was necessary to hold the power assisted brakes with the left foot and feed in throttle with the right, building up engine rpm until torque converter stall speed was attained, then ease off the brakes to permit the vehicle to move forward or back. This method isn't nearly so precise

PRICES
Basic list, FOB Ft. Wayne, Ind.
Scout Traveler Four 4wd $5844

Standard Equipment: 196-cu-in. in-line Four engine, 3-spd manual transmission, single-spd transfer case, heater/defroster, 2-spd electric wiper/washers, power front disc brakes, full instrumentation, folding front bench seat, tinted glass, chrome front and rear bumpers, H78 x 15B tires

GENERAL
Curb weight, lb (test model)	4450
GVWR (test model)	6200
Optional GVWRs	none
Wheelbase, in.	118.0
Track, front/rear	57.1/57.1
Overall length	184.2
Overall height	65.7
Overall width	70.0
Overhang, front/rear	24.0/42.2
Approach angle, degrees	30
Departure angle, degrees	19

Ground clearances (test model):
Front axle	6.5
Rear axle	7.1
Oil pan	11.2
Transfer case	10.4
Fuel tank	14.3
Exhaust system (lowest point)	11.7
Fuel tank capacity (U.S. gal.)	19.0
Auxiliary	none

ACCOMMODATION
Standard seats	full-width front bench
Optional seats	front bucket seats, $74; rear folding bench, $135
Headroom, in.	35.9
Accelerator pedal to seatback, max	45.1
Steering wheel to seatback, max	16.4
Seat to ground	31.6
Floor to ground	15.7

Unobstructed load space (length x width x height)
With seats in place	53.6 x 41.5 x 42.3
Rear folded or removed	87.5 x 41.5 x 42.3
Tailgate (width x height)	49.6 x 42.5

INSTRUMENTATION
Instruments . . . . . speedometer, odometer, fuel gauge, ammeter, oil pressure, water temp
Warning lights . . . . hazard warning, parking brake warning, front axle engaged indicator
Optional . . . . none

as use of manual gears and clutch slipping.

The results of the entire process were some indrawn breaths on the part of passengers (driver, too) as the Traveler lurched toward the rocky precipice and relief when the operation was completed.

The assessment here is that the automatic transmissioned Traveler may be well and good for most kinds of off-pavement work but, in a pinch, the manual gearbox and foot operated clutch remain the off-roader's standby. So, an individual who is intent on selecting a Traveler would do well to consider where he plans to take the Traveler, places easy or hard, then inspect the IH range of gearing available before he signs on the sales contract dotted line.

In the outback, the Traveler proved itself a crawler that's almost a match for Toyota Land Cruiser and Jeep CJ-5, despite it's too-tall-for-tough-off-road gearing. Power steering and the tilt wheel make it anybody's off-pavement handler. On the freeway, heading home, the Traveler proved itself swift, quiet and comfortable, with more than adequate leg and head space for driver and front bucket passenger, and plenty of space for the third party member to flake out on the rear bench. The driver voiced one complaint that the inside bright molding on the left-hand door nicked his elbow, now and again, and that the armrest hampered steering arm movement, but these seemed minor aggravations.

At the dragstrip, the Traveler proved

ENGINES

Standard . . . . 196-cu-in. in-line Four
Bore x stroke, in. . . . . 4.125 x 3.656
Compression ratio 8.02:1
Net horsepower @ rpm . . . . 86 @ 3800
Net torque @ rpm, lb-ft . . . . 157 @ 2200
Type fuel required . . . . leaded or unleaded

Optional 304-cu-in. V-8 $156
Bore x stroke, in. . . . . 3.875 x 3.218
Compression ratio 8.19:1
Net horsepower @ rpm . . . . 144 @ 3600*
Net torque @ rpm, lb-ft . . . . 247 @ 2400*
Type fuel required . . . . leaded or unleaded
*For Calif., hp rating is 144 @ 3800, torque is
238 @ 2400

Optional 345-cu-in. V-8 $198
Bore x stroke, in. . . . . 3.875 x 3.656
Compression ratio 8.05:1
Net horsepower @ rpm . . . . 163 @ 3600*
Net torque @ rpm, lb-ft . . . . 292 @ 2000*
Type fuel required . . . . leaded or unleaded
*For Calif., hp rating is 146 @ 3600, torque is
275 @ 2000

Optional . . . . 198-cu-in. diesel in-line Six*
Bore x stroke, in. . . . . 3.27 x 3.94
Compression ratio 22:1
Net horsepower @ rpm . . . . 92 @ 4000
Net torque @ rpm, lb-ft . . . . 137.5 @ 2000
Type fuel required . . . . No. 2 diesel
*Diesel engine is available only as a package.
Price of package approximately $2200

DRIVETRAIN

Standard transmission . . . 3-spd manual T-332
Clutch dia., in. 11.0
Transmission ratios: 3rd 1.00:1
2nd 1.55:1
1st 2.99:1
Synchromesh . . . . all forward gears

Optional . . 4-spd wide ratio manual T-427 $155
Transmission ratios: 4th 1.00:1
3rd 1.68:1
2nd 3.09:1
1st 6.32:1
Synchromesh . . . . all forward gears

Optional . . 4-spd close ratio manual T-428 $155
Transmission ratios: 4th 1.00:1
3rd 1.41:1

2nd 2.41:1
1st 4.02:1
Synchromesh . . . . all forward gears

Optional . . . . 3-spd automatic $279*
Transmission ratios: 3rd 1.00:1
2nd 1.45:1
1st 2.45:1
*Not available with 196 Four engine

Rear axle type . . . . semi-floating hypoid
Final drive ratios 3.07:1, 3.54:1, 4.09:1
Overdrive . . . . none
Free-running front hubs . . . . std
Limited slip differential $77
Transfer case . . . . . TC-143 single-speed (std),
TC-145 2-spd (opt)
Transfer case ratios 1.00:1 (TC-143),
2.03:1 & 1.00:1 (TC-145)

CHASSIS & BODY

Body/frame . . . ladder-type frame with separate
steel body
Brakes (std) . . . . front, 11.75-in. dia. disc; rear,
11.03 x 2.25-in. drum
Brake swept area, sq in. 381
Swept area/ton (max load) 123
Power brakes . . . . std
Steering (std) . . . . worm and roller
Steering ratio 24:1
Power steering $178
Power steering ratio . . recirculating ball 17.5:1
Turning circle, ft 38.8
Wheel size (std) . . . . 15 x 6.0JK
Optional wheel sizes . . . . 15 x 7.0JJ
Tire size (std) . . . . H78 x 15B
Optional tire sizes . . . . HR78 x 15B

SUSPENSION

Front suspension . . . . semi-elliptic leaf springs
on live axle and tube shocks
Front axle capacity, lb 3200
Optional . . . . none
Rear suspension . . . . . semi-elliptic leaf springs
on live axle and tube shocks
Rear axle capacity, lb 3500
Optional . . . . none
Additional suspension options . . . HD front and
rear shocks, $12; HD front springs with HD
shocks, $16; HD front and rear springs with
HD shocks, $38

TEST MODEL

Scout Traveler, 345-cu-in. V-8, automatic transmission, 2-spd transfer case, automatic locking
hubs, power steering, tilt steering wheel, AM/FM
radio, electric clock, vinyl side applique, modulated fan, Calif. emission cert., front bucket seats,
custom interior trim pkg, deluxe exterior trim pkg,
air conditioning, door edge guards, storage console, 3.07 axle ratio, HR78 x 15B tires
West Coast list price (includes $466
freight) $8778

ACCELERATION

Time to speed, sec:
0-30 mph 5.0
0-45 mph 8.6
0-60 mph 14.0
0-70 mph 19.7
Standing start, 1/4-mile, sec 19.9
Speed at end, mph 71

SPEED IN GEARS

High range, 3rd (3400 rpm) 90
2nd (4000 rpm) 77
1st (4000 rpm) 46
Low range, 3rd (4000 rpm) 54
2nd (4000 rpm) 39
1st (4000 rpm) 23
Engine rpm @ 55 mph 2150

BRAKE TESTS

Pedal pressure required for 1/2-g deceleration
rate from 60 mph, lb 40
Stopping distance from 60 mph, ft 173
Fade: Percent increase in pedal pressure for
6 stops from 60 mph 105
Overall brake rating . . . . excellent

INTERIOR NOISE

Idle in neutral, dbA 58.5
Maximum during acceleration 78.0
At steady 60 mph cruising speed 75.0

OFF PAVEMENT

Hillclimbing ability . . . . excellent
Maneuverability . . . . very good
Turnaround capability . . . . very good
Driver visibility . . . . excellent
Handling . . . . very good
Ride . . . . very good

ON PAVEMENT

Handling . . . . very good
Ride . . . . very good
Driver comfort . . . . very good
Engine response . . . . good

FUEL CONSUMPTION

City/freeway driving, mpg 14.4
Off pavement 10.0
Range, city/freeway driving, miles 273
Range, off pavement 144

---

itself moderately quick and fast, covering the standing-start quarter-mile in 19.9 sec at a trap speed of 71 mph. The Traveler's 0-60 mph time was 14.0 sec, more than adequate for snaking into fast-flowing freeway traffic.

In braking effectiveness, the Traveler showed itself to be somewhere in the middle of 4wd vehicles, and also in the middle of other '76 Scout vehicles tested earlier, with a straight-line panic stop from 60 mph completed in a distance of 173 ft. The Traveler's disc front/drum rear braking system showed 105 percent fade in six 1/2-g stops from 60 mph, indicating adequate stopping power remaining after excessively hard use.

The Traveler's 345 V-8 delivered 14.4 mpg in city/freeway driving and 10.0 mpg in the off-road situation. These figures reflect neither the epitome of fuel economy nor gas-guzzling. They're about average for engines of this piston displacement class. One note on the Traveler's fuel system is that the fuel gauge is distinctly non-linear in calibration. With the dash panel gauge's needle pointing directly at the half-full mark, the vehicle's

19-gal. tank accepted 12.3 gal. of gasoline. This leaves 6.7 gal. in the other "half" of the tank. Safety is a consideration here because an off-road driver, unaware of the miscalibrated gauge, could easily travel past the point of no return into mountains or desert, counting on a turnaround with more than half fuel showing on his gauge, but less than half fuel actually in his tank. Either knowledge of the gauge or a stout pair of walking boots are indicated here.

The Traveler, as tested, admittedly was the plush unit. But other Travelers are available, starting with a bare-bones model powered by a 196-cu-in. in-line 4-cylinder engine and a 3-speed manual gearbox, and ranging through the 304-cu-in. V-8 and several transmission, transfer case and axle ratio options, up to the 345 V-8, automatic transmission and automatic hubs. Paint, upholstery and trim follow the step-up pattern from spartan to full-house. The point is, the prospective buyer, through his friendly local IH dealer, is able to pick and choose, and order the Traveler that is best suited to his needs, whether they're completely hard core

utilitarian or none other than backroads recreational in nature. Whether it's work or fun, there's a Traveler to suit the program.

It really wasn't all bad that the Traveler got off to a bad start, what with that bad news broken spring. One fluke in manufacture, no fault of IH, but that of the International's spring supplier, simply pointed up the fact that the 1976 Scout Traveler is really the good news. ●

1977
International
Suntanner

by Richard Johnson

Who said going topless isn't an off-road activity? The folks at International Harvester have decided that a flip-top rig is just the thing for off-roading on those sunny days and stary nights. And to demonstrate their belief, they have introduced the new Suntanner, a convertible top 4x4 that is the only vehicle of its kind in America today.

The Suntanner is basically a Scout Terra pickup truck that has been converted to allow a convertible top to be installed. The vehicle is actually a three-way flip-top, providing for the use of a white vinyl top that can be used either up, or removed, and also a fiberglass top that converts the rig into a hard top. Manager of Light Truck Marketing for IH, F. J. Wendling states that "pickups, 4x4 sport utility vehicles, vans, and truck station wagons are now used primarily for personal transportation. We think a convertible pickup, particularly a model that can offer the extra mo-

bility of four-wheel-drive, will be appealing to the general public as well as to ranchers and farmers." So, to check out the opinion of the IH staff, *O.R.V.* decided to do a vehicle test on the new Suntanner and and pass our findings along to you.

The Suntanner is an intermediate sized truck that is smaller and more maneuverable than large full-sized pickups, yet it offers far greater load carrying and towing capacity than the mini trucks. Built on a 118 inch wheelbase, the Suntanner measures 184 inches in length, and 70 inches in width. The turn around diameter is a tight 38' 10" to the outside of the tire, and 40' 5" to clear the bumper. Combining this maneuverability with the 2000 pound cargo capacity gives the owner of one of these vehicles a good mixture of small but heavy-duty.

The Terra pickup is equipped with a six-foot bed/box, and the front seat folds forward for access to 11 cubic-feet of in-cab storage space. Besides all this carrying capacity, the truck can be equipped with a class 1, 2, or 3 towing package. This permits up to 5000 pound towing capability, for a maximum . combined gross weight of 10,000 pounds. So, this is no lightweight truck even though its small size may fool many.

The International Scout Terra truck comes in both two and four-wheel drive, and the difference between the two units is only 180 pounds. The 4x4 can be ordered with either standard locking hubs, or automatic locking hubs for easier selective four-wheeling. We preferred the automatic hubs because it enables us to lock up the front end without getting out in the mud to do so. However, to take advantage of the compression braking, it is necessary to get out and physically lock the hubs. The automatic hubs still give us the option to drive in two wheel any time we wish.

The comfort level of the Suntanner could be improved by installing better seats. The outboard side of the seat has a metal structural member,

where the sitting platform and the back of the seat meet, that catches you right in the upper thigh when entering or exiting. But aside from that, the ride qualities of the truck are very good. It will smooth out a rough road, and keep the passengers from being beat to death. On the highway the ride compares well with most passenger cars. The Suntanner is unique among the Terra line because of its soft top. As with all convertible tops, there is a high degree of noise when cruising down the freeway at 55 mph. It is actually a quieter rig when the top is down. The noise would definitely be a drawback on a long trip across country.

In our economy testing, the Terra pickup truck with the 345 cid V-8 engine and automatic transmission, and 4.09 axle gears gave us an out-

standing 17 mpg on the highway (with the cruise control set at 55 mph), and a solid 13.5 mpg in our off-roading tests. That breaks down to a range of over 300 miles of highway travel, and over 250 for off-road work. The 19 gallon tank will take you a long way, and the engine will work well on regular, low lead, or lead free fuel, so it becomes an economical way to get around.

Handling and maneuverability rates high because of the Integral Power Steering option that we had on the test vehicle. The short hood provides a good view of the ground ahead, and the narrowness of the truck allows the driver to get between bushes and rocks that would stop a wider vehicle. And the tight turning diameter makes it easy to get out of a tight spot. The visibility, with the top

down, cannot be beat. But, with the vinyl top in place, it takes a good look around to see the blind spots. Larger side view mirrors could help out the situation.

The power front disc brakes proved themselves out when we tested the vehicle through deep ponds of water. The brake system sheds water fast allowing the truck to stop even after a thorough drenching.

The test vehicle came with the white vinyl top and separate matching tonneau that covers the pickup bed. We found the removal of the top to be a fast, easy job, and putting it back on was equally simple. It is a pure and simple joy to cruise the back roads with the wind blowing through your hair, smelling the wildflowers, and feeling what off-roading is really all about . . . freedom. ⊙

International Harvester's Scout II is easy to describe but terribly hard to explain. It's strong, stout, sturdy and slabsided. The Scout II is designed for pure function; there are no swoopy body panels and no trim hanging off to be snagged by the underbrush. When a company used to designing farm equipment designs a four wheel drive vehicle, they think practical. The front end is as flat as a bulldog's face. When you are looking at the end of the hood—that's it, that's where the vehicle ends. Same with the rear end; in a Scout the driver knows where the vehicle can fit and not fit just by looking—the Scout's design takes the guesswork (and the dents) out of driving in tight situations.

That describes the tough little Scout II, but how do you explain it? It's one of the overlooked four wheelers; it is often the last vehicle on a four wheeler's dream list. The problem is simply lack of exposure. Once a four wheeler has spent some rough country time in a Scout, a real relationship can grow. The Scout II quickly earns a driver's respect with its agility, power and load carrying capacity.

POWERTRAIN & DRIVELINE

The IH 345-cu. in. V-8 is a proven, reliable workhorse. Power output is 163 horsepower at 3600 RPM, and torque is rated at a healthy 292 lbs.-ft. at 2000 RPM. Regular fuel is all that's needed

for the 8.05:1 compression ratio; the over-6000-lb. GVW eliminates the need for a catalytic converter (for now). The crankshaft is mated to a 3-spd. automatic and it is controlled from the driver's seat by a smooth shifting selector console on the transmission tunnel. The selector is especially useful in off pavement situations when a quick downshift or upshift is needed or a rocking motion from forward to reverse is necessary to get unstuck.

Four wheel motive power is transmitted via a Dana 20, 2-spd. transfer case. A big, solid lever to the right of the transmission selector controls the part-time 4WD mode. Again, as with any new vehicle, the operation of the lever was rather balky and a firm hand (sometimes foot too) was needed to engage 4WD. I personally would rather have a lever that was hard to engage than one that could be knocked into neutral by an accidental bump at the wrong moment.

Freeway and street performance of the Scout II is very good. Even with the 3.07:1 gear ratios, the Scout II has to rank as one of the peppiest 4WD vehicles around. In fact, it's one of the few vehicles left in this emission-controlled automotive world that will actually spin the rear tires on dry pavement. The nimble Scout is a lot of fun in town where you are changing lanes and trying to beat old ladies to the best parking space.

When the pavement ends, the fun

Handsome interior is also functional as well, with gauges and fine transmission selector. Too bad there wasn't a tachometer.

begins. Even though our test Scout was equipped with what are essentially street radials, we had a good time in our off the road bashing. Fortunately it was dry as we doubt the radials would have carried us through the mud. We doubt that the average four wheeler would choose this wheel and tire option however; a more practical wheel and tire option with an aggressive on/off road tread would make more sense. Concensus among the staff was that each of us would raise the ride height and install larger wheels and tires, similar to the modifications made to the Goodrich Tire Test Scouts (February 1977 FOUR WHEELER).

Even in stock condition (barring large logs and deep water) the Scout II is a worthy off road machine. We appre-

SCOUT II RALLYE

A tough little four wheeler with lots of power.
Story by Mike Anson
Photos by lynette mcdonald and Mike Anson

ciated the near-300 lb.-ft. of torque when the going was low and slow. Scout II performance with the 345-cu. in. V-8 engine is impressive.

RIDE, BRAKING AND HANDLING

For a vehicle that rides on four, short leaf spring stacks, the Scout II has a very good ride. A marshmallow Seville it's not, but then how far would a Seville last on the Baja 500 course? The ride is firm and well controlled in all situations. Heavy loads smoothed it out some, but never seemed to slow it down.

Braking is accomplished by a pair of 11.75-in. disc brakes in front and drums at the rear. A huge vacuum brake booster is mounted to the firewall. The reason for mentioning the size of the cylinder is to point out that if the

(Above) Lockable storage console is really handy. It's big enough to be of real value.

(Above Right) Cruise control is especially useful when the watchful eyes of the law are upon you. Set it at the double nickle and just putt-putt along until he is gone.

(Below) Rear seat is O.K. for short trips. With the seat folded forward, more storage room is available.

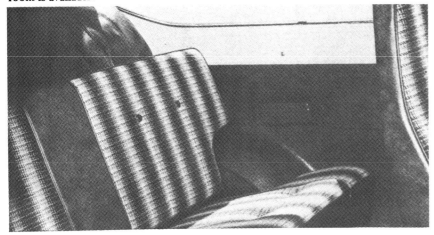

engine, for some reason, is not running, there are still a number of power-assisted stops available. Try stopping a car with disc brakes without a power assist sometime. It can be a real thrill. Disc brakes are linear; the amount of force goes up with the pedal (ultimately, the cylinder) pressure while drum brakes have a self-servo effect—the braking effort is increased without increasing the pedal effort.

All of this translates to fine braking performance for the Scout II. Tires account for a major portion of braking feel and the results with the street radials could be predicted; pavement braking was better than off pavement braking. On loose silt or gravel trails the rears tended to lock up. We used this to our advantage in some situations when we wanted a tight turn. Wow—just like in the movies.

SCOUT II RALLYE
PRICES AND OPTIONS

Base price $5751.00
Locking hubs . . . . $ 72.00
345-cu. in. V-8 with dual exhaust. . $ 220.00
Automatic transmission . . . . $ 306.00
Limited-slip rear end . . . . $ 82.00
Air conditioning. . . . . $ 497.00
Tilt steering . . . . $ 72.00
AM/FM radio . . . . $ 184.00
Electric clock . . . . $ 23.50
Custom interior package (includes vinyl/nylon
  seat trim, wood-grain instrument panel, car-
  pet and cargo mat) . . . . $ 221.00
Deluxe exterior trim (includes bright finish
  grille insert, and moldings) . . . . . $ 60.00
Rallye package (includes tape stripe treatment,
  heavy duty shock absorbers, power steer-
  ing, HR78-15 radial tires, 15x7 chrome
  rims) . . . . $ 648.00
Luggage rack. . . . . $ 92.00

Sliding rear quarter windows . . . . $ 51.00
2-spd. transfer case . . . . $ 67.00

Front bucket seats . . . . $ 101.00
Fuel tank skid plate . . . . $ 39.00

SPECIFICATIONS

Engine . . . . OHV V-8
Bore & Stroke (ins.) . . . . . 3.875 x 3.656
Displacement (cu. in.) 345
HP @ RPM. . . . . .163 @ 3600
Torque: lbs.-ft. @ RPM. . . . . .292 @ 2000
Compression Ratio/Fuel 8.05:1/regular
Carburetion 2V
Transmission. . . . . .3-spd. automatic
Transfer Case . . . . 2-spd.
Final Drive Ratio (axle ratio) 3.07:1
Steering type . . . . recirculating ball;
                                    power assist

Steering Ratio 17.5:1
Turning diameter (ft.) 36.4
Tire Size HR-7815
Brakes . . . . front disc (11.75-in.)/rear drum
Front Suspension . . . . .live axle, leaf springs
Rear Suspension. . . . . .live axle, leaf springs
Wheelbase (ins.) 100.0
Overall length (ins.) 166.2
Width (ins.) 70.0

Height (ins.) 65.7
Front tread width (ins.) 57.1
Rear tread width (ins.) 57.1
Fuel tank capacity (gals.) 19.0
Auxiliary fuel tank capacity (gals.) . . . .N.A.
Engine oil capacity (qts.). 5
Ground clearance,
  front & rear differential (ins.) 7.6/7.6
Approach angle . . . . 49°
Departure angle . . . . 22°
Curb weight (lbs.). 3691

PERFORMANCE RATING

On Road
Acceleration. . . . . .very good
Passing speed . . . . .very good
Steering response . . . . .very good
Maneuverability. . . . . .excellent
Cornering . . . . .very good
Braking. . . . . .very good
Interior noise . . . . .good
Ride . . . . .good
Seating comfort—Front . . . . .good
  Rear . . . . .fair
Accessibility of dash controls . . . . . .good
Accessibility of
  transmission shifter. . . . . excellent
Entry/Exit height to ground. . . . . .very good
Glove Box size . . . . .good
Instrument readability. . . . . .good
Head room. . . . . .good
Seat belt location . . . . .good

Off Road
Traction in soft,
  sandy or muddy oil. . . . . .good
Hillclimbing characteristics . . . . .very good
Rollover angle stability
  (center of gravity). . . . . .very good
Suspension load
  without bottoming . . . . .very good
Turning circle . . . . excellent
Ride . . . . .good
Tire flotation (stock tires) . . . . .fair
Vehicle control . . . . .good
Hi-Range 4WD performance. . . . . excellent
Lo-Range 4WD performance. . . . . excellent
Accessibility of
  transfer case shifter. . . . . .good
Ease of shifting transfer case. . . . . fair-good
Steering response . . . . excellent
Brake, (clutch), accelerator
  pedal location . . . . .good
Roll bar installation. . . . . .N.A.
Occupant seating stability . . . . .good
Close proximity visibility
  over hood . . . . excellent
Sunvisor capability . . . . .good
Headlight illumination for
  off road driving . . . . .good
Storage capacity
  (camping gear etc.) . . . . .very good
Fuel tank filler accessibility
  (for funnels etc.) . . . . .fair
Low gear lugging capability . . . . . . .good
Brakes/Compression
  downhill capability . . . . .good
Ease of access to spare tire. . . . . .very good

Fuel Consumption
On Road . . . . .10.0 mpg.
(Normal driving—highway and surface streets)
Off Road. . . . . 8.2 mpg.

Accessories and Options
Air conditioning effectiveness . . . .very good
Heater/Defroster effectiveness. . . . . .good
Windshield Wiper/
  Washer effectiveness . . . . .good
Wiper area covered . . . . .fair
Horn (loudness) . . . . .good
Dash lighting. . . . . .good
Interior lighting. . . . . .good
Door handles
  (operation and location) . . . . .good
Door locks. . . . . .fair
Hood latch. . . . . .good
Jack/Lug wrench location . . . . .good

IH-built 345-cu. in. V-8 provides good power and excellent torque for the Scout II. Note the size of the power brake booster in the lower right hand corner.

Fade resistance was very good and braking distances on the pavement were also quite good. Off the road it took a bit longer to stop but this was as a result of the street treads and not the braking system.

The Scout handles quite well and is surprisingly nimble. Its small size and good turning circle (36.4-ft.) make for easy going in tight situations. At 70-in. the Scout is narrow enough for most Jeep trails and will carry quite a payload in the rear area. With the rear seat folded forward and the spare tire removed there is a large, usable storage area.

The short wheelbase Scout II, at an even 100.0-in., takes even the big bumps in stride. We found that by accelerating hard just before the washes and bumps we could get through with less wear and tear on the passengers.

COMFORT, CONVENIENCE, OPTIONS

Our fancied-up Rallye (their spelling) version Scout had the full complement of options including cruise control, carpeting, bucket seats, storage console, power steering, air conditioning and vinyl door trim. We traveled about in cool comfort while the choking dust curled around the outside. The seats, while they offer no side support are comfortable and are thick with padding in the lumbar region of the back.

Scouts must have the largest steering wheels in the business. It seems to be everywhere. Fortunately the tilt option allowed us to get it out of the way of the windshield. With the fine power steering, IH could elect to use a smaller, and more stylish (padded, perhaps?) steering wheel in the top line interior.

The hydraulic assists on the rear window are a nice touch and the rubber mat in the rear cargo area looked to be tough and durable. It did, however, have a distinctive odor.

Overall the Scout II remains an impressive four wheeler. The more you drive a Scout the better you like it. It does all the things a larger vehicle does and you can still fit it into the garage. □

International Oiler:
DIESEL TERRA
With a close-ratio 4-speed, this compression ignition 4x4 talks torquey...

Somewhere along the line, someone at International should have spoken up, should have voiced an opinion that, and here's a fancied quote, "The automatic transmission is distinctly second best in our Terra truck and Traveler with the Nissan diesel engines."

PICKUP, VAN & 4WD test crewmen would heartily agree with this non-existent IH spokesman. In 1976, a staff test driver piloted a Nissan diesel-powered IH Terra, with 3-speed automatic, from Fort Wayne to the East Coast, then across the nation to California (PV4, May, '76). This driver's chief complaint with regard to the diesel Terra was that the automatic 3-speed made for sluggish acceleration and abrupt automated upshifts and downshifts when meeting grades.

This year, the same driver was given the assignment to test drive an almost identical IH Scout Terra pickup with the Nissan IN6-33 diesel engine, but with a 4-speed manual gearbox installed instead of the automatic.

Last year's test model with the automatic was equipped with a small diameter torque converter so that the engine would quickly wind up to stall speed at 2000 rpm, the diesel engine's effective torque peak. The effect wasn't so much "dropping the hammer," so to speak, but rather a pause-to-launch, which was sort of an appointment for a mild neck-snapper. Under full acceleration (a phrase that seems not quite right in terms of diesel power), the '76 Terra's automatic upshifted first-to-second at 38 mph and second-to-third at just a shade under 60 mph, unless the transmission's valving was overridden manually by the driver.

Installation of the IH T-428 close-ratio 4-speed gearbox behind the Nissan diesel engine changes all this—for very much the better.

The drivetrain in the test vehicle made the Terra pickup an acceptable 'round-town and turnpike pavement performer, and made very effective use of the diesel's characteristically narrow torque band in a wide variety of off-pavement situations.

The 198-cu-in. Nissan IN6-33 6-cylinder diesel engine produces 92 bhp (net) at 4000 rpm, and delivers 137.5 lb-ft (net) of torque at 2000 rpm, which means the powerplant is most effective and most efficient at 2000 rpm.

The close-ratio T-428 (IH numbers for the Warner T-19A) 4-speed manual transmission provides internal gearing of 4.02:1 in first gear, 2.41:1 in second, 1.41:1 in third and 1.00:1 (direct) in fourth. Reverse is 4.42:1.

Gearing in the 2-speed TC-145 (IH numbers for Dana Model 20) transfer case is 1.00:1 in high range, both in 2wd high and 4wd high modes, and 2.03:1 in 4wd low range.

Dana 44 axles, front and rear (RA-28 Trac-Lok) with optional 4.09:1 final drive gearing were installed in the test diesel Terra.

With respect to operations with a diesel engine that develops its narrow band of peak torque at 2000 rpm, this combination of transmission, transfer and axle ratios, plus limited-slip rear axle capability, and IH (Warn) Lock-O-Matic automatic/locking hubs at the front, proved eminently flexible and useful across a broad spectrum of on- and off-pavement work and recreation situations.

The accompanying table shows calculated (no tach, right?) vehicle speeds in eight forward gears at an engine speed of 2000 rpm.

With the 4-speed and 2-speed transfer box, the trick is to select the proper gear to match that narrow 2000-rpm torque peak to road conditions, altitude and/or the recreational or utilitarian tasks at hand.

For example, in actual driving, the torque/speed relationship was borne out particularly well in terms of the IH

Nissan IN6-33 6-cylinder diesel powerplant produces 92 bhp at 4000 rpm, and 137.5 lb-ft of torque at 2000 rpm. The small diesel's output was made useful in the Terra pickup by the close-ratio 4-speed manual transmission in combination with a 2-speed transfer case and 4.09:1 final drive gears.

DIESEL TERRA

Terra's off-road mountain climbing ability. In 4wd low-range transfer gearing, and third gear selected with the main box, the little diesel pickup snorted lustily up a very steep, rough, cross-grained, sometimes muddy mountain road without effort. The gear selection was exactly right, as a shift up to fourth dropped rpm out of the diesel engine's effective torque band, and a shift down to second caused the engine to border on an over-revving condition. At road speeds of 12 to 17 mph, just about the right rate to make best use of the engine's torque, considering the harshness of the terrain and the pitch of the mountain gradient, that 2000-rpm, low-range, third-gear combination worked like a charm.

Looking at things another way, the gearing combinations available to the diesel Terra driver proved equally as effective in city and freeway driving. Cruise in 2wd direct proved effortless, too, with the diesel engine turning at a fairly relaxed 2800 rpm at 60 mph, just below the revolutions mid-point between torque and horsepower peaks,

and an economical 2570 rpm at 55 mph, closer to the torque peak.

Going through the gears in the stop-light drags, test drivers tried both first-gear and second-gear starts. Ultimately, drivers found themselves always starting out in first gear—pop the clutch, stab the throttle, then upshift immediately at about 20 mph, or about 3800 rpm. The first-gear launch proved best for helping the small displacement diesel to keep up with large-displacement V-8 powered machinery.

The most effective change up to second gear could be made at about 32 mph (again 3800 rpm), and the two-to-three shift was best made at between 45 and 50 mph (in the 3100 to 3400 rpm bracket). And then the Terra could be brought up to freeway cruise of 55 mph (2570 rpm) rather quickly.

At cruise, the Nissan diesel seemed to breathe freely, relax and chuckle along merrily. However, pulling any kind of grade often necessitated a downshift to third gear. And passing on two-lane roads required from one-half to three-quarters of a mile of open road to effect the maneuver. Test drivers who early-on misjudged the diesel's accelerative capabilities in the upper gears at times

thrilled themselves with close observations of oncoming traffic.

Without doubt, at the top end of the Nissan's rpm spectrum, the Terra's acceleration tended to be sluggish in comparison with gasoline-burners. But, the Nissan/4-speed manual/4.09 axle combination in every acceleration respect proved itself superior to the Nissan/3-speed automatic 3.54 axle combination tested last year. The automatic was slushy, truly slow to wind up, whereas the 4-speed permits a knowledgeable driver to make best use of the admittedly slow-to-rev diesel powerplant. What it boils down to is that with the 4-speed, the driver can shift into a gear that will deliver the performance he desires at the moment it's needed, but the automatic does its own thing, whether or not it's appropriate for road or traffic conditions. Maybe diesel Terras should carry a factory-applied bumper sticker that says: "4-Speeds Are Best!"

The test Terra was factory-fitted with a set of optional slotted disc wheels painted white to resemble steel spoke units for the off-road profile. Mounted on these wheels were a complement of Goodyear Tracker A-T 10 x 15LTs in Load Range B (replacing 4-ply rating). The A-Ts are fabricated of four plies of polyester cord in both tread and sidewalls. Maximum load capacity for these aggressive all-terrain tires is 1760 lb at 30 psi cold inflation pressure. What's important about the wheels/tires combination is that the A-Ts present a fairly tall overall diameter, at approximately 30.5 in., and an unladen rolling radius at 14.9 in., which means that the 4.09:1 optional final drive gearing is almost mandatory for the diesel engine's power output. With the large diameter tires, the taller (and standard) 3.54:1 final drive gearing probably would be less effective in acceleration, but likely would prove more economical at 55-mph cruise, with the engine turning at 2425 rpm.

In essence, what's being said here is that buyers of diesel-powered IH Terra pickups probably would do well to opt for the 4.09 gearing when they plan to mount large diameter tires for off-road use, and perhaps should stick with the standard 3.54 gearset when they plan to do most of their cruising on freeways with HR78 x 15s, for example, which show a 2.3-in. shorter rolling radius. A gasoline-engined vehicle offers a broad torque band that is able to accommodate ups and downs in tire sizes, ups and downs in effective axle gearing; a diesel-engined vehicle simply doesn't have the torque range, hence must rely on transmission gearing to match engine to the road. The Nissan/4-speed/4.09 IH Terra pickup *has* the necessary gears.

Outside the $2200 diesel engine op-

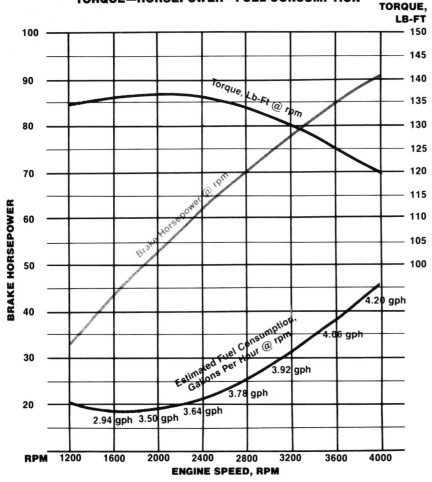

NISSAN IN6-33 DIESEL ENGINE
TORQUE—HORSEPOWER—FUEL CONSUMPTION

Bucket seats, console, air conditioning indicate deluxe treatment, above. Left, thumb on the button lights up the diesel's glowplugs for ignition.

tion, the test vehicle approached the top-of-the-line among Terras, in terms of factory-installed optional equipment.

From a diesel engine option base price of $8205, addition of the 4wd system, 4.09 axles, 2-speed transfer case, hubs, locking differential, heavy-duty front springs, heavy-duty diesel-type electrical system, AM/FM radio, clock, off-road tires and wheels, fuel tank skidplate, interior and exterior deluxe trim packages, carpeting, air conditioning, bucket seats and console, among other items, raised the diesel Terra's list price to $10,349.50, not including $461 in freight charges, Indiana to California.

At 10 grand plus, it's probably a bargain for the buyer/user who plans to run the truck 10 years at 30,000 miles per year. In an area where unleaded gasoline was selling for 71 cents per gallon, No. 2 diesel fuel was going for 51 cents per gallon. Lower cost and extended mileage per gallon of diesel fuel are fairly heavyweight reasons for investing in a $2000-plus Japanese compression ignition powerplant for a domestic midi truck.

The Terra pickup, on the Scout II wheelbase of 118 in., offers a 6200-lb GVWR (Gross Vehicle Weight Rating) with a suspension system comprised of longitudinal semi-elliptical leaf springs, six leaves at the front, four leaves at the rear, and tubular shock absorbers all around.

The test Terra was equipped with vacuum-assisted 11.75-in. disc brakes at

the front, and 11-in. by 2.25-in. drum brakes at the rear. In addition, the vehicle was equipped with Saginaw power steering.

As a highway cruiser and off-road runabout, the diesel Terra proved itself both entertaining and economical. During a three-day test exercise, the truck was driven from sea level to 4000 ft, cruised for a time, then was taken to 5000 ft and cruised, and then was driven up the mountain road to more than 8000 ft above sea level. The return trip was the reverse of the procedure. During this period, the Terra delivered 15.3 mpg. In relatively flat city/freeway running at sea level, the truck produced 20.7 mpg. (Mileage figures are from pump and odometer readings, rather than calibrated with electronic fuel flow equipment, as the diesel engine's high pressure fuel injection system is incompatible with conventional gasoline engine fuel test equipment.)

Back from the three-day tour, the Nissan-powered Terra was put through **PICKUP, VAN & 4WD**'s standard acceleration test cycle at the local dragstrip. A Chevy V-8 the Nissan Six isn't, but nevertheless the small diesel turned in acceleration times of 33.1 sec for the 0-60-mph run, and 24.9 sec at 54 mph for the standing-start quarter-mile. Even though 4-speeds are best, downhill on-ramps for freeways are better.

With Goodyear Trackers, the '77 Scout Terra diesel did not perform as well in braking tests as did the 1976 unit shod with HR78 x 15 Goodyear All Win-

ter Radial tires. The radials offered a solid, tacky bite on test strip asphalt, whereas the aggressive off-road Trackers lost their grip a bit in all-on braking cycles. In the panic stop test from 60 mph to dead halt, the '76 Terra diesel required only 121 ft. This year's diesel pickup took up 167 ft in the 60-0 stop, though the stop was in a straight line with only a bit of lock-up. In the series of 1/2-g stops from 60 mph, the '76 Terra showed 42 percent brake fade; the '77 vehicle showed 84 percent fade. Pedal effort for the six-stop series was varied but little between the two vehicles—35 lb for the '76 model, 34 lb for the '77.

It must be assumed that, aside from minor differences between two vehicles assembled at the same factory, tire treads and compounds play a very significant part in a particular truck's stopping capability. In the case of the two Terras, though pedal effort was almost a constant, the difference in stopping effectiveness between the All Winter Radials and Trackers was 46 ft—about the length of a tandem 18-wheeler.

Drawbacks with regard to the diesel Terra pickup emerged in a variety of subjective opinion on the parts of various test drivers and passengers who rode along on the three-day run.

Chief among the drawbacks was the aforementioned stomach-pit aversion to attempting a passing maneuver on anything but a downslope. Secondary among drawbacks seemed to be engine/drivetrain noise, though the majority of drivers and passengers didn't find the diesel's rumble, together with the Goodyear treads' hum, to be all that objectionable. The noise was there—and it only bugged two of six people who went along on the three-vehicle, three-day evaluation junket. Finally, there was smoke. In making cold starts with the Nissan, exhaust fumes and white smoke from partially consumed No. 2 diesel were wont to swirl around

Tracker A-T 10 x 15LT tires were effective off pavement. With tall tires, choice of 4.09:1 axle is mandatory.

The Engine:
NISSAN ID6-33 DIESEL
Compression ignition, fuel injection and plenty of torque for the IH Scout...

International's venture into diesel power for light trucks and 4wd utility vehicles is based on the Nissan IN6-33 engine. As diesel engines go, this 6-cylinder, fuel-injected, compression-ignition powerplant offers both high rpm capability and a fairly broad torque peak, though the term "broad" is only with respect to diesel power, hence the torque band of this engine may be considered "narrow" in comparison with conventional gasoline-fueled 6-cylinder and V-8 engines now in current use in domestic products.

The IN6-33 delivers its peak horsepower output at a mechanically governored 4000 rpm, producing a maximum of 96 bhp in the flat-out mode. Torque development peaks at 137.5 lb-ft at a moderate 2000 rpm, with strong torque delivery available on either side of the peak, but a shading-away toward the higher end of the rpm spectrum.

The engine is a 4-cycle, water-cooled, normally-aspirated in-line Six. Bore and stroke, respectively, are 3.27 in. and 3.94 in. Total piston displacement is 198 cu. in. The engine's compression ratio, typical of diesel powerplants, is 22:1.

The engine, with accessories, weighs approximately 622 lb.

The 4-cycle diesel engine's operation goes like this: On the intake stroke (piston starting down, intake valve open) air is drawn in through a filter and through the intake manifold. On the compression stroke, the intake valve closes and the air charge is compressed at the 22:1 ratio; as the piston nears the top of the stroke, fuel is injected under high pressure through a nozzle into a swirl (precombustion) chamber adjacent the main combustion chamber; and as the upstroke is completed the atomized, swirl-mixed fuel/air charge is ignited by the heat generated through compression of the intake air. As the burning charge expands, the piston is forced downward in the power stroke. When the piston reaches the bottom, the exhaust valve opens and burned gasses are expelled with the upward stroke of the piston. At the top of the stroke, the exhaust valve closes and the intake valve opens once again to repeat the cycle from induction to exhaust.

The IN6-33's injection pump is mechanical, chain-driven off the forward end of the crankshaft. As the pump shaft turns, cam operated plungers direct jets of fuel in proper firing order to the cylinders. In effect, the diesel injection pump functions as would fuel pump, carbuetor, distributor and ignition advance timing components in a gasoline-burning, spark-ignition engine.

Because of the fairly dirty nature of low-grade petroleum distillates the IN6-33 uses for fuel (No. 2 diesel is recommended, No. 1 is permitted), the injection system is fitted with a large filter. A feed pump drives the fuel oil under pressure through the filter to six injection pumps. The injection pumps, timed by crankshaft rotation, pressurize the fuel still more and deliver it to the cylinders. Pressurized fuel in excess of engine demand from both filter and injectors is collected and directed back to the fuel tank through a return line.

Starting of the IN6-33 in the IH Scout Terra midi pickup and Traveler line is accomplished with a nichrome wire glow plug in each cylinder. When the electrical system key switch on the Scout's steering column is turned to the on position, the glow plugs can be activated by pressing a button under the vehicle's dash to the left of the steering column. In warm weather, the glow plugs raise combustion chamber temperature sufficiently to induce ignition in approximately 20 to 30 sec. In cold weather, the glow plugs must be operated from 60 to 90 sec in order for the engine to fire when the engine is cranked over, using the key switch to actuate the engine's 12-volt starter motor.

Once the engine is running, it is possible to switch off all electricals while the diesel engine continues to function.

To stop the engine in the IH Scout vehicle, a knob adjacent to the glow plug button under the dash is pulled outward. This closes a butterfly stop valve in the engine's induction manifold, hence the engine is starved for air and ceases to fire. ●

INTERNATIONAL SCOUT TERRA DIESEL ROAD SPEEDS IN GEAR AT 2000 RPM
CALCULATED—4.09:1 FINAL DRIVE GEARING—10 x 15LT TRACKER A-T TIRES

GEAR	INTERNAL RATIO	TRANSFER RATIO	MPH AT 2000 RPM
4th	1.00:1 (Direct)	1.00:1	42.8 mph
3rd	1.41:1	1.00:1	30.4 mph
2nd	2.41:1	1.00:1	17.8 mph
1st	4.02:1	1.00:1	10.7 mph
4th	1.00:1 (Low Range)	2.03:1	21.6 mph
3rd	1.41:1	2.03:1	15.0 mph
2nd	2.41:1	2.03:1	9.1 mph
1st	4.02:1	2.03:1	5.2 mph

the vehicle until the engine warmed up a bit, a matter of perhaps two minutes or so. And, in climbing to altitudes above 2500 ft above sea level, the decrease in atmospheric pressure resulted in a richened fuel-to-air ratio and the diesel generated black, sooty smoke—blacker and more sooty all the way to 8000 ft. When the diesel Terra led the three-vehicle caravan up the mountain, drivers and passengers in the other two vehicles trailing behind complained about the smoke and smell. One test crewman went so far as to use the word "stink." However, to the test driver who's **PICKUP, VAN & 4WD**'s resident diesel freak, the aroma of partially burned No. 2 fuel seemed *pleasing*. (Cough! Gasp! Choke!)

Back to the original premise of this article: Now that test crewmen have had the opportunity to drive a diesel-powered Terra with a close-ratio 4-speed, the opinion has been firmed up that automatic transmissions are best installed with gasoline-burners, not diesel powerplants.

Often, editors and test crew personnel are called upon to answer readers' questions by telephone. One frequent question concerns the IH Terra with Nissan diesel powerplant. It goes something like this, "The diesel engine sounds fine to me, but what transmission do you think is best?" Invariably test crew people answer, "The 4-speed, of course." However, the reader usually responds with, "Well, I'd like a 4-speed myself, but my wife needs an automatic, doesn't know how to use a manual."

The IH diesel Terra, then, is for diesel enthusiasts, wives who can shift for themselves and libbers who can take a stick to a gearbox. The automated diesel Terra simply offers a lower level of performance, a level at which neither diesel freaks, manual-shifting spouses of either sex nor liberated women who know how to change gears will be entirely satisfied.

The basic International Terra midi pickup is a tough truck, an off-roader of the first water, which goes without saying. With diesel power and given proper recreation and utilitarian transportation roles to play, the Terra can be both economical to operate over the long haul, and can be a thrifty conservator of energy.

Maybe the opinion that the "automatic transmission is distinctly second best" in IH diesel Terra trucks will filter through to where it counts, Fort Wayne, Ind. With the 4-speed gearbox and some knowledge of how gearing is related to diesel power output, a diesel Terra owner will find this vehicle very satisfying to operate, both on and off the road. ●

1977 INTERNATIONAL SCOUT TERRA DIESEL SPECIFICATIONS AND PERFORMANCE

PRICES

Basic list, FOB, Ft. Wayne, Ind.,
  Scout Terra Diesel $8205

Standard Equipment ....198-cu.-in. diesel in-line Six engine, 4-spd manual transmission, power disc brakes, tilt steering wheel, 85-amp/hr battery, 40-amp alternator, glow plug indicator, diesel stop control, gauges, 2-spd transfer case, folding front bench seat, floor mat, undercoating, tinted glass, 2-spd electric wiper/washer, heater/defroster, chromed front and rear bumpers, H78 x 15B tires

GENERAL

Curb weight, lb (test model) 4200
Weight distribution, %, front/rear 59/41
GVWR (test model) 6200
Optional GVWRs ....none

Wheelbase, in. 118.0
Track, front/rear 57.1/57.1
Overall length 183.8
Overall height 66.0
Overall width 70.0
Overhang, front/rear 22.4/42.5

Approach angle, degrees 39
Departure angle, degrees 21

Ground clearances (test model):
  Front axle 8.0
  Rear axle 8.2
  Oil pan 15.2
  Transfer case 12.8
  Fuel tank 16.3
  Exhaust system (lowest point)............13.4

Fuel tank capacity (U.S. gal.) 19
Auxiliary ....30-gal., dealer installed

ACCOMMODATION

Standard seats ....1/3–2/3 split full-
  width folding bench
Optional seats ....buckets
Headroom, in. 35.4
Accelerator pedal to seatback, max 44.5
Steering wheel to seatback, max 17.1
Seat to ground 34.8
Floor to ground 19.9

Unobstructed load space (length x width
  x height) ....71.5 x 42.1 x 21.6
Tailgate (width x height)...............50.6 x 51.2

INSTRUMENTATION

Instruments ....speedometer, odometer, ammeter, oil pressure, water temperature, fuel gauge
Warning lights.................hazard, seat belts, front axle engaged indicator, glow plugs activated, parking brake
Optional ....none

ENGINES

Standard............198-cu.-in. diesel in-line Six
Bore x stroke, in. ....3.27 x 3.94
Compression ratio 22:1
Net horsepower @ rpm ....92 @ 4000
Net torque @ rpm, lb-ft...........137.5 @ 2000
Type fuel required..................No. 2 Diesel

DRIVETRAIN

Standard transmission ....4-spd manual, close ratio
Clutch dia., in. 11.0
Transmission ratios: 4th 1.00:1
  3rd 1.41:1
  2nd 2.41:1
  1st 4.02:1
Synchromesh ....all forward gears

Optional 4-spd manual, wide ratio ....N/C*
Transmission ratios: 4th 1.00:1

3rd 1.68:1
2nd 3.09:1
1st 6.32:1
Synchromesh ....all forward gears
*No-charge option

Optional 3-spd automatic $141
Transmission ratios: 3rd 1.00:1
  2nd 1.45:1
  1st 2.45:1

Rear axle type ....semi-floating hypoid
Final drive ratios 3.54:1, 4.09:1
Overdrive..none

Free-running front hubs ....automatic, $72
Limited-slip differential $82
Transfer case ....Dana 20, 2-spd
Transfer case ratios 2.03:1, 1.00:1

CHASSIS & BODY

Body/frame ....ladder-type frame with separate steel body
Brakes (std) ....front, 11.75-in. dia. disc; rear, 11.03 x 2.25-in. drum
Brake swept area, sq in. 381
  Swept area/ton (max load) 123
Power brakes ....std

Steering type (std) ....recirculating ball
Steering ratio 24:1
Power steering $189
Power steering ratio 17.5:1
Turning circle, ft 38.8

Wheel size (std).........................15 x 6.0JK
Optional wheel sizes ......15 x 7 styled chrome
Tire size (std) ....H78 x 15B
Optional tire sizes ....HR78 x 15B, 7.00 x 15C, 10 x 15B

SUSPENSION

Front suspension.................semi-elliptical leaf springs on live axle and tube shocks
Front axle capacity, lb 3200
  Optional ....none
Rear suspension..............semi-elliptical leaf springs on live axle and tube shocks
Rear axle capacity, lb 3500
  Optional ....none

Additional suspension options.......heavy-duty front springs, $18.50

TEST MODEL

Scout Terra 4wd, 198-cu.-in. Nissan IN6-33 diesel engine, 4-spd close-ratio transmission, 2-spd transfer case, automatic locking hubs, 4.09:1 axle ratio, heavy-duty front springs, AM/FM radio, electric clock, 10 x 15B tires, steel white spoke wheels, fuel tank skidplate, tiedown rails, bucket seats, custom interior

and exterior trim packages, air conditioning, door edge guards, storage console, body protection package
West Coast list price (not including freight and dealer preparation).....................$10,350

ACCELERATION

Time to speed, sec:
  0–30 mph 7.5
  0–45 mph 16.0
  0–60 mph 33.1
  0–65 mph 48.2
Standing start, ¼-mile, sec. 24.9
  Speed at end, mph 54

SPEED IN GEARS

High range, 4th (2000 rpm) 42.8*
  3rd (2000 rpm)...................................30.4
  2nd (2000 rpm)..................................17.8
  1st (2000 rpm)...................................10.7
Low range, 4th (2000 rpm) 21.6
  3rd (2000 rpm)...................................15.0
  2nd (2000 rpm)....................................9.1
  1st (2000 rpm).....................................5.2
Engine rpm @ 55 mph 2570*
*Calculated

BRAKE TESTS

Pedal pressure required for ½-g deceleration rate from 60 mph, lb 34
Stopping distance from 60 mph, ft 167
Fade: Percent increase in pedal pressure for 6 stops from 60 mph 84
Overall brake rating ....very good

INTERIOR NOISE

Idle in neutral, dbA 60.5
Maximum during acceleration 81.5
At steady 60 mph cruising speed 77.5

OFF PAVEMENT

Hillclimbing ability ....excellent
Maneuverability ....very good
Turnaround capability ....very good
Driver visibility ....fair
Handling ....very good
Ride ....very good

ON PAVEMENT

Handling ....very good
Ride ....good
Driver comfort ....good
Engine response ....fair

FUEL CONSUMPTION

City/freeway driving, mpg 20.7
Off pavement 14.5
Range, city/freeway driving, miles...........393
Range, off pavement.............................275

IH FAMILY CRUISER

PRICES AND OPTIONS

Base price as tested	$6122.00
Automatic locking hubs	72.00
Heavy duty front and rear springs and shocks	41.00
Power steering	189.00
Tilt steering wheel	72.00
AM/FM radio, stainless steel antenna	184.00
Tan Family Cruiser Package	1579.00
Radial tires and wheels	366.00
345 V-8 engine	220.00
Cruise control	80.00
Automatic transmission	306.00
Fuel tank skid plate	39.00
Exterior trim package	60.00
Sliding rear quarter windows	66.00
Luggage rack	92.00
Air conditioning	497.00

SPECIFICATIONS

Engine	90° OHV V-8
Bore & Stroke (ins.)	3.875 x 3.656
Displacement (cu. in.)	345
HP at RPM	163 at 3600
Torque: lbs.-ft. at RPM	292 at 2000
Compression Ratio/Fuel	8.05:1/Regular
Carburetion	2-bbl.
Transmission	3-spd. Automatic
Transfer Case	Single speed/Dash operated
Final Drive Ratio (axle ratio)	3.07:1
Steering type	Power/Recirculating ball
Steering Ratio	17.5:1
Turning diameter (ft.)	38.1

Tire Size	HR78x15 Radial
Brakes	Front disc/Rear drum
Front Suspension	Live axle, Leaf springs
Rear Suspension	Live axle, Leaf springs
Wheelbase (ins.)	118.0

Overall length (ins.)	184.2
Width (ins.)	70.0
Height (ins.)	65.7
Front tread width (ins.)	57.1
Rear tread width (ins.)	57.1
Fuel tank capacity (gals.)	19.0
Auxiliary fuel tank capacity (gals.)	N.A.
Engine oil capacity (qts.)	5.0
Ground clearance, front & rear differential (ins.)	7.6/7.6
Approach angle	49°
Departure angle	22°
Curb weight (lbs.)	3981.0

PERFORMANCE RATING

On Road

Acceleration	Fair
Passing speed	Fair
Steering response	Excellent
Maneuverability	Fair
Cornering	Good
Braking	Excellent
Interior noise	Low
Ride	Smooth
Seating comfort—Front	Excellent
Rear	Excellent
Accessibility of dash controls	Excellent
Accessibility of transmission shifter	Excellent
Entry/Exit height to ground	Low
Glovebox size	Good
Instrument readability	Good
Head room	Good
Seat belt location	Good

Off Road

Traction in soft, sandy or muddy soil	Fair
Hillclimbing characteristics	Good
Rollover angle stability (center of gravity)	Good
Suspension load without bottoming	Good
Turning circle	Fair
Ride	Smooth
Tire flotation (stock tires)	Fair
Vehicle control	Excellent
Hi-Range 4WD performance	Excellent
Lo-Range 4WD performance	N.A.
Accessibility of transfer case shifter	Good
Ease of shifting transfer case	Good
Steering Response	Excellent
Brake, (clutch), accelerator pedal location	Good
Roll bar installation	N.A.
Occupant seating stability	Good
Close proximity visibility over hood	Good
Sun visor capability	Fair
Headlight illumination for off road driving	Good
Storage capacity (camping gear etc.)	Excellent
Fuel tank filler accessibility (for funnels etc.)	Good
Low gear lugging capability	Good
Brakes/Compression downhill capability	Good
Ease of access to spare tire	Excellent

Fuel Consumption

On Road	13.8 to 16.3 mpg.
(Normal driving—highway and surface streets)	
Off Road	11.9 to 14.2 mpg.

Accessories and Options

Air conditioning effectiveness	Good
Heater/Defroster effectiveness	Excellent
Windshield Wiper/Washer effectiveness	Good
Wiper area covered	Good
Horn (loudness)	Fair
Dash lighting	Excellent
Interior lighting	Excellent
Door handles (operation and location)	Good
Door locks	Good
Hood latch	Excellent
Jack/Lug wrench location	Fair

INTERNATIONAL SCOUT TRAVELER "FAMILY CRUISER"

Customized Comfort Directly From The Factory!

Story and photos by Bill Sanders

Ever since the decision was made at International Harvester to go out and compete head to head in the 4x4 market, we've seen one innovation after another. First, IH introduced the Scout Traveler and Terra Pickup. Then they went out and got involved in off road racing. The most recent development has been the "Street Machine" and "ORV" Scout.

Another interesting model, the "Family Cruiser," is an International Scout Traveler with features that make it more comfortable for highway driving.

Road testing the "Family Cruiser" for several thousand miles proves a big point: IH has delivered what they promised. The "Family Cruiser" is certainly family oriented and is certainly comfortable on the highway.

POWERTRAIN AND PERFORMANCE

A fully loaded rig usually also gets the biggest and best in the powertrain department and this unit was no exception. It had the IH 345 cu. in. V-8, automatic tranny, cruise control, heavy duty suspen-

sion and automatic locking hubs. Two items that might seem detrimental to a four wheel drive rig, although we didn't find them so, were a 3.07:1 axle ratio and a dash operated, single speed transfer case. The latter is a feature on IH rigs. It eliminates the transfer case shifter lever on the floor so it looks like you have a 2WD truck. For the occasional four wheeler it is actually an efficient unit, with a dash mounted accessory that simply pulls out, like turning on the lights. This shifts the transfer case, locking in the front end. Even though it is a single speed unit (4-Hi) we had no difficulty making it up the steepest of hills and through soft sand and silt . . . all with street tread radials!

The 3.07 axle also seemed to make little difference off road. The truck rolled up steep hills with ease. However, a lower gear would surely have been essential had we tried more demanding terrain. On the pavement the tall gear was a help. We got up to 16 mpg in some highway driving situations, which ain't all that bad for a four wheel drive box.

The tall gear did have a slight

detrimental effect on performance. Acceleration was a little sluggish in most cases, and passing was something that took plenty of road. All in all, though, performance was a good compromise between acceleration and good mileage.

HANDLING, STEERING, STOPPING

With its 118-in. wheelbase, the Family Cruiser version of the Traveler is certainly a luxurious highway vehicle. The long wheelbase makes for a very comfortable ride on any type road. In addition, the special padded headliner and full carpeting make the Family Cruiser exceptionally quiet, especially for a four wheeler. The low, low noise level is very conducive to highway travel, such as you would expect from a passenger car.

Handling is not sportcarish by any means, but it is firm and precise. Scout uses a rather large steering wheel, larger than most other manufacturers, and this can be detrimental at first, if you are used to one of the smaller wheels. However, with a tilt-wheel steering column, you can actually use the big steering wheel to your own advantage.

Good, flat handling response is accentuated by the addition of power steering. The large diameter steering wheel is used for both manual and power steering, and

Dash is typical IH Scout. Large steering wheel seems cumbersome at first, but helps in driving on long trips. Test rig also had tilt-wheel and cruise control.

(Right) Rear hatchback operates on pneumatic cylinders, lifts completely out of way.

with power assist it is even easier to steer.

The Family Cruiser package is also available on the Scout II, and with its 100-in. wheelbase, obviously handling would be much tighter and quicker.

Brakes too, were excellent and quite capable of stopping the big Traveler with no pulling or fade. Power front disc brakes add a great deal to the stopping ability of this rig. The front discs also help greatly when fording streams or driving in the rain, as they stay drier and don't go away when wet.

COMFORT, CONVENIENCE, OPTIONS

The Family Cruiser is sort of the Cadillac or Lincoln Continental of the IH line, especially when built on the Traveler chassis. You can order a variety of options and convenience items, and our test rig had just about all of them, including automatic locking hubs. These are the type that will lock (and unlock) manually, but will also lock automatically by just shifting the transfer case into four wheel drive.

Probably the biggest feature of the Family Cruiser package is the seating. With front and rear buckets there is room enough to actually move around between

Street tread radials got through soft stuff without too much difficulty. Automatic locking hubs are big help.

the seats, and there is a special third rear seat just for children. The front high back bucket seats swivel and recline, the middle high back bucket seats recline, and the rear bench seat for the kids reclines flat and can be used as a bed for a small child. The entire floor area is covered in matching shag carpeting. All seats are color-keyed to the carpeting and upholstered in a striped tweed fabric that is repeated in the headliner, door panels, rear inner side panels, and hatchback tailgate panel.

SUMMING UP

If you have a family with more than two kids and need seating for six, the Family Cruiser is an ideal four wheeler. It is a great rig for camping trips and long vacations, with its reclining seats. The swivel seats and the versatility of being able to move around inside makes it great for camping.

Smooth, almost effortless driving and extreme interior quietness make it a beautiful family highway rig. It aptly deserves the name "Family Cruiser." □

Factory Off-Roader:
SCOUT SS II
International produces a vehicle that's really ready for the outback...

PV4 TEST The SS II, introduced in the 1977 model year by International, was unique in the industry. Here was a vehicle, right out of the factory, that appeared ready for serious off-roading or heavy competition. For '78, the SS II is continued with only minor changes in paint and trim.

The SS II is derived from the now discontinued Scout II pickup with the 100-in. wheelbase. The Scout II remains available, but only in the Traveltop model. There is, of course, a 118-in. wheelbase pickup called the Terra being produced by International in both two- and four-wheel drive. The SS II is offered in 4wd only.

Basically, the SS II is the pickup without top and doors. The side doors and hardware were completely removed and replaced with a molded plastic insert that covers the exposed door jambs. An optional dealer- or factory-installed vinyl soft top, with removable fabric-covered doors, is also offered. The metal framed doors have snaps at the front edge to help eliminate wind drafts. The soft top can be removed completely, rolled up on the sides and rear, safari style, or folded down like a passenger car convertible top. The vinyl top also can be ordered with a sunroof over the forward compartment.

The SS II carries some equipment as standard that would normally be optional. These features include fuel tank skidplate, 2-speed transfer case, roll bar, padded dash and front sway bar. Heavy-duty options include front and rear shock absorbers and leaf springs, plus brush and grille guards, fender flares, automatic locking front hubs, CB radio, light and heavy-duty electric winches, white spoke wheels with 10 x 15 raised white letter tires, a choice of two 4-speed manual transmissions or 3-speed automatic, locking rear differential and power steering. For special applications, right-hand drive is available.

The interior of a basic SS II is very spartan with only a driver's bucket seat. The inside floor pan is painted metal with drain holes for easy cleaning. A passenger bucket seat is offered, as well as a full-width folding rear bench. No deluxe interior trim packages are

Molded inserts, mounting hardware are part of the soft top SS II package.

available with the SS II. However, a special black-and-gold appliqué trim scheme is offered for the SS II only. Nine colors, ranging from winter white to rallye gold, can be specified. Black front and rear bumpers and a black plastic grille identify the exterior of the SS II.

As usual for International, there are quite a few options in the powertrain department. Standard engine, coupled to a 3-speed manual transmission, is the 196-cu.-in. Four, rated at 86 bhp at 3800 rpm (79 bhp at 3600 rpm for California). The Four (actually one bank of the 392-cu.-in. V-8 now discontinued for light-duty use) can be teamed with either of two 4-speed manuals or 3-speed automatic transmission. The close-ratio 4-speed has a low gear ratio of 4.02, whereas the wide-ratio gearbox is equipped with a 6.32 first gear. All forward gears are synchronized in either gearbox. Standard axle ratio for the Four is 4.09:1 with 3.54 and 3.73 as options.

The next larger optional available engine is a 304-cu.-in. V-8 which delivers 144 bhp at 3600 rpm. This engine is not available in California. The identical transmission selection for the Four is available with the 304 V-8. Standard axle ratio is 3.54 with 3.07 offered along with 3.73 and 4.09. Largest available powerplant is the 345-cu.-in. V-8. Rated at 163 bhp at 3600 rpm for 49 states and 138.5 bhp at 3400 rpm for California, the 345 V-8 is offered with the same transmission/axle ratios as the 304, except the 4.09 cannot be specified. The 6-cylinder IN6-33 diesel engine is not

offered with the SS II. Both V-8s are fitted with dual exhaust and, because of the vehicle's 6200-lb Gross Vehicle Weight Rating (GVWR), do not require use of unleaded fuel. The Four is, of course, fitted with a single exhaust system, and can also use leaded fuel. The SS II is supplied with a 19-gal. fuel tank. As stated previously, the transfer case is the Dana 20 2-speed. The single-speed transfer gearbox is not offered on the SS II.

Both front and rear axles on the International are versions of the Dana Model 44. Axle capacity is 3200 lb for the front, 3500 lb for the rear. Standard axle ratio is 4.09:1, front and rear.

The SS II provided by International for test was picked up in Phoenix, Arizona. The vehicle was factory fresh and sported rallye gold paint with black and gold two-tone appliqué on the side panels. The trick SS II also had a factory-installed Whitco white vinyl top and side doors.

In addition to standard equipment, the SS II was factory-fitted with numerous optional accessories, including 345-cu.-in. V-8, automatic transmission, 3.73:1 axle ratios, locking rear differential, locking front hubs, front tow hooks, rear step bumper, power steering, AM radio, heavy-duty front and rear springs, rubber fender extensions, passenger bucket seat and folding rear bench seat, and 10 x 15 raised white letter Goodyear Tracker A-T tires mounted on white spoke wheels. West Coast list price of the SS II was $8126 which included freight charges of $464.

Some things never change and the dash of an International is one of them. The instrument panel retains the narrow band of gauges with the speedometer to the right of the steering wheel. The radio is in the dead center of the dash with the heater (and air conditioning) controls just below and to the left. The inside hood release is to the right of the heater control. A nice touch and very useful are the covers which snap over the defroster air ducts on top of the dash. The covers prevent dust from gathering in the ducts while driving off pavement. Those who've had occasion to turn on the defroster in a vehicle that has seen extensive duty in dusty terrain know how valuable this little item can be. Nice going Interna

SS II

tional. However, it's too bad the Fort Wayne company doesn't let the engineer who designed the dust covers redesign the Scout steering wheel. The huge steering wheel (17-in. in diameter) would be great on a vehicle of larger proportions and without power steering. But on the Scout, it slows the already slow steering response to a crawl. Most light-duty truck builders equip vehicles that have power steering with a smaller 16-in. wheel. Test crewmen who have driven Scouts over the years believe a 15-in. wheel might not be too small. Word was that International would offer a smaller wheel as an option, but the list of accessories for '78 doesn't show this item.

On the freeway run from Phoenix to the West Coast, the SS II was a pleasure to drive. The vehicle proved very stable and tracked true with few steering corrections. The ride is firm, but very acceptable on concrete road surfaces as well as asphalt. However, as precisely as the vehicle behaved in handling and stability, the noise generated by the vinyl soft top was highly detrimental to the vehicle's overall driver comfort rating. At road speed, the radio cannot be heard above the flapping of the fabric and screeching of the metal framework against the mounting plates. The metal rubbing is akin to running one's fingernails down a chalkboard. A good dose of some WD-40 lubricant at the contact points may alleviate this condition somewhat.

As it was rather warm while crossing the Mojave Desert, the fabric doors were removed. The noise level was only slightly greater with the doors removed and the wide expanse of the door openings seemed to bring the outdoors into the Scout. Travel became much more enjoyable with the flapping and squeaking not quite as audible.

Although the raised mounting for transmission and transfer case shift levers is rather large, it's very convenient to the driver. No useable space is lost with the mounting in conjunction with the bucket seats. There's still room rearward of the raised mounting to fit a storage console.

The bucket seats leave something to be desired for this type of vehicle, however. They are very narrow, with practically no lateral support for hips and back. This becomes even more noticeable with the doors off because driver and passenger get the feeling that if they aren't belted in securely, they could easily slide completely out of the vehicle. Running at speed off pavement necessitated firm cinching of seat belts. Actually, the SS II displays very little body lean when making quick maneuvers, but the lack of seat side support creates the impression that the vehicle is leaning excessively.

The image of the SS II dictates that it's an off-roader's vehicle. Therefore it will probably see a lot of serious back country thrashing. Better seats would make the trip to the outback much more enjoyable—that is to say more secure and much safer.

Speaking of the outback, the SS II was taken to high desert country for a weekend of evaluation. The firm suspension did an excellent job in the rough environment of washboarded roads. The rear end danced around slightly, but directional stability was easily maintained.

The 345 V-8 seems to be stronger than it has been in the past several years. The Scout could be pushed as hard as the driver's nerve would allow—with more horsepower still available. Steep inclines were met and negotiated easily with the 3.73 axle ratio and 10 x 15 tires. Of course, visibility with the doors removed was excellent in the back country. Steering response in the outback would be improved with the

smaller diameter steering wheel, as mentioned earlier. Running at speed required that a maneuver be anticipated and the steering wheel turned earlier than normally would be the case with a vehicle equipped with quicker steering.

Back in the city, the Scout was taken to Orange County International Raceway for performance evaluation. Acceleration runs seemed to indicate that indeed the 345 was developing greater horsepower than in previous years. Several 0-to-60-mph runs averaged out to 11.7 sec. This compares with a '76 Scout 4wd vehicle (PV4, Dec., '76) whose 0-to-60 time was 14 sec flat. The '76 Scout did have a 3.07 axle ratio which would hinder acceleration somewhat. However, the standing-start quarter-mile was also much slower at 19.9 sec at 71 mph for the '76 as compared with 18.6 sec at 74 mph for the '78 SS II.

Along with the improved performance, the SS II was also more economical. The tall axle ratio of the '76 unit should have been an advantage here, but the '78 achieved 14.9 mpg to 14.4 mpg for the '76 vehicle in the city/freeway driving cycle as monitored by electronic fuel flow instruments. The 14.9 mpg is especially significant when compared with the '77 Scout Suntanner tested last year (PV4, June, '77). The Suntanner was powered by a 304-cu-in. V-8, driving through 3.54 axles, but was able to deliver only 12.7 mpg in the identical fuel mileage test.

Braking tests showed the Scout to still be one of the better braking funtrucks around. The panic stop from 60 mph was made in 157 ft with no discernible wheel lockup or slewing from side to side. Brake fade was normal at 62 percent, with only 60 lb pressure required on the sixth and last stop.

International, with the SS II, has certainly created a vehicle that shouts "off-road." This vehicle should have high appeal for enthusiasts who want sporty good looks, along with excellent off-roading characteristics. If International's engineers could only quiet that vinyl top a little, speed up the steering somewhat and put some sideboards on the front buckets, they'd really have a winner. ●

INTERNATIONAL SS II
SPECIFICATIONS AND PERFORMANCE

PRICES

Basic list, F.O.B., Fort Wayne, Ind.
Scout SS II 4wd $5387

Standard Equipment ....196-cu.-in. in-line
Four engine, 3-spd manual transmission, 2-spd transfer case, heater/defroster, 2-spd electric wiper/washers, power front disc brakes, roll bar, tinted windshield, driver's bucket seat, full instrumentation, front anti-sway bar, inside hood release, black front and rear bumpers, H78 x 15B tires

GENERAL

Curb weight, lb (test model) 4020
Weight distribution, %, front/rear 57/43
GVWR (test model) 6200
Optional GVWRs ....none

Wheelbase, in. 100
Track, front/rear 57.1/57.1
Overall length 166.2
Overall height 65.7
Overall width 70.0
Overhang, front/rear 20.5/43.6

Approach angle, degrees 32
Departure angle, degrees 20

Ground clearances (test model):
Front axle 8.4
Rear axle 8.2
Oil pan 14.1
Transfer case 13.0
Fuel tank 15.8
Exhaust system (lowest point) 13.3

Fuel tank capacity (U.S. gal.) 19
Auxiliary ....none

ACCOMMODATION

Standard seats ....driver's bucket seat
Optional seats ....passenger bucket seat, $95; folding full-width rear bench seat, $170
Headroom, in. 35.2
Accelerator pedal to seatback, max 46.0
Steering wheel to seatback, max 18.0
Seat to ground 34.2
Floor to ground 19.2

Unobstructed load space (length x width x height)
With seats in place ....40.5 x 42.1 x 43.7
Rear folded or removed ..69.0 x 42.1 x 43.7
Tailgate (width x height) ....51.0 x 21.2

INSTRUMENTATION

Instruments ....speedometer, odometer, fuel gauge, ammeter, oil pressure, water temperature
Warning lights ....front axle engaged indicator, parking brake warning, hazard warning
Optional ....none

ENGINES

Standard ....196-cu.-in. in-line Four
Bore x stroke, in. ....4.125 x 3.656
Compression ratio 8.02:1
Net horsepower @ rpm ....86 @ 3800*
Net torque @ rpm, lb-ft ....157 @ 2200*
Type fuel required ....leaded or unleaded
*For Calif., bhp rating is 79 @ 3600 and torque 155 @ 2000

Optional 304-cu.-in. V-8 $176*
Bore x stroke, in. ....3.875 x 3.218
Compression ratio 8.19:1
Net horsepower @ rpm ....144 @ 3600
Net torque @ rpm, lb-ft ....247 @ 2400
Type fuel required ....leaded or unleaded
*Not available in Calif.
Optional 345-cu.-in. V-8, $234
Bore x stroke, in. ....3.875 x 3.656

Compression ratio 8.05:1
Net horsepower @ rpm ....163 @ 3600*
Net torque @ rpm, lb-ft ....292 @ 2000*
Type fuel required ....leaded or unleaded
*For Calif., bhp rating is 146 @ 3600 and torque 275 @ 2000

DRIVETRAIN

Standard transmission ....3-spd manual
Clutch dia., in. 11.0
Transmission ratios: 3rd 1.00:1
2nd 1.55:1
1st 2.99:1
Synchromesh ....all forward gears

Optional: 4-spd wide ratio manual
T-427 ....$152
Transmission ratios: 4th 1.00:1
3rd 1.68:1
2nd 3.09:1
1st 6.32:1
Synchromesh ....all forward gears

Optional: 4-spd close ratio manual
T-428 ....$165
Transmission ratios: 4th 1.00:1
3rd 1.41:1
2nd 2.41:1
1st 4.02:1
Synchromesh ....all forward gears

Optional ....3-spd Automatic, $324

Transmission ratios: 3rd 1.00:1
2nd 1.45:1
1st 2.45:1

Rear axle type ....semi-floating hypoid
Final drive ratios 3.07:1, 3.54:1, 3.73:1, 4.09:1
Overdrive ....none

Free-running front hubs ....manual $104
Limited slip differential $87
Transfer case ....Dana 20 2-spd
Transfer case ratios ....2.03:1 and 1.00:1

CHASSIS & BODY

Body/frame ....ladder-type frame and separate steel body
Brakes (std) ....front, 11.75-in. dia. disc; rear, 11.03 x 2.25-in. drum
Brake swept area, sq in. 381
Swept area/ton (max load) 123
Power brakes ....std

Steering type (std) ....worm and roller
Steering ratio 24:1
Power steering $206
Power steering ratio 17.5:1
Turning circle, ft 33.8

Wheel size (std) ....15 x 6.0JK
Optional wheel sizes ....15 x 7.0JJ, 15 x 8.0JJ
Tire size (std) ....H78 x 15B
Optional tire sizes ....HR78 x 15B, 7.00 x 15C, 10 x 15B

SUSPENSION

Front suspension ....semi-elliptical leaf springs on live axle with tube shocks and anti-sway bar

Front axle capacity, lb 3200
Optional ....none
Rear suspension ....semi-elliptical leaf springs on live axle with tube shocks
Rear axle capacity, lb 3500
Optional ....none

Additional suspension options ....HD front and rear shocks, $25; HD front springs (includes HD front shocks), $37; HD rear springs (includes HD rear shocks), $50

TEST MODEL

Scout SS II, 345-cu.-in. V-8, automatic transmission, locking front hubs, AM radio, front tow hooks, HD front and rear springs, power steering, vinyl soft top, rubber fender extensions, two-tone appliqué, passenger bucket seat, folding rear bench seat, spare tire lock, white spoke wheels, 10 x 15 tires, 3.73:1 axle ratio

Note: The soft top can be specially ordered to be installed at the factory when the dealer is not equipped for the installation. Cost is approximately $318
West Coast list price (includes $464 freight) $8126

ACCELERATION

Time to speed, sec:
0–30 mph 3.6
0–45 mph 7.0
0–60 mph 11.7
0–70 mph 16.6
Standing start, ¼-mile, sec. 18.6
Speed at end, mph 74

SPEED IN GEARS

High range, 3rd (3500 rpm) 85
2nd (4000 rpm) 68
1st (4000 rpm) 42
Low range, 3rd (4000 rpm) 48
2nd (4000 rpm) 33
1st (4000 rpm) 20
Engine rpm @ 55 mph 2400

BRAKE TESTS

Pedal pressure required for ½-g deceleration rate from 60 mph, lb 37
Stopping distance from 60 mph, ft 157
Fade: Percent increase in pedal pressure for 6 stops from 60 mph 62
Overall brake rating ....excellent

INTERIOR NOISE

Idle in neutral, dbA 67.5
Maximum during acceleration 79.0
At steady 60 mph cruising speed 85.5

OFF PAVEMENT

Hillclimbing ability ....excellent
Maneuverability ....good*
Turnaround capability ....excellent
Driver visibility ....excellent
Handling ....good*
Ride ....good
*Ratings would have been very good except for slow steering

ON PAVEMENT

Handling ....very good
Ride ....good
Driver comfort ....good
Engine response ....excellent

FUEL CONSUMPTION

City/freeway driving, mpg 14.9
Off pavement 10.4
Range, city/freeway driving, miles 283
Range, off pavement 197

INTERNATIONAL HARVESTER SCOUT II

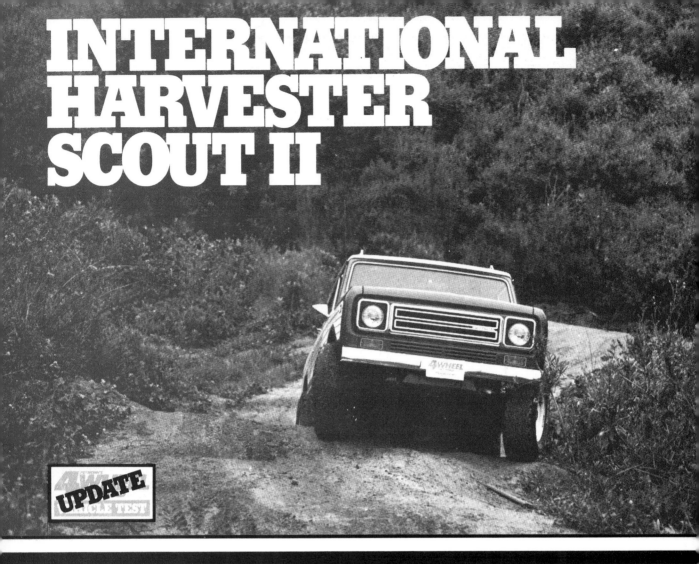

As we pointed out in our April issue, the SSII is a rugged, go-anywhere machine with a Spartan attitude—cloth top, no floor mats and few creature comforts—that was put on the market to compete with the CJ-5 and CJ-7. Well, this same little package with the 100-inch wheelbase has a stylish side, too. In this road test update we look at the SSII's big-city cousin, the Scout II. Although they are built from the same metal stampings and have the same basic shape, it's hard to believe the two are the same vehicle.

The Scout II, with its fiberglass top, air conditioning, carpeting, power steering, power brakes, sliding side windows, tailgate, chrome bumpers, tilt steering wheel, cruise control and deluxe interior trim, cuts a dashing figure—especially when compared with the SSII. This is a country club vehicle, everything the SSII is not. It is warm, dry and comfortable. The only similarity seems to be that they are both tough as nails.

Like the SSII, our Scout II was equipped with the peppy 345-cubic-inch V8 engine that feels like it puts out more than the rated 138 horsepower. The Scout II was not as fast as the SSII because it weighs more and the final drive ratio was 3.54:1 instead of the SSII's 3.73:1. Even so, this little Scout was no slouch when it came to performance, getting up to 30 mph in just 3.9 seconds and 60 mph in exactly 12 seconds.

The base Scout engine is a 196-c.i.d. 4-cylinder, with a 304 V8 as the in-between option. For a fully equipped Scout, such as the one we tested, the 345 V8 seems to be the best all-round engine. The 304, 345 and 390 engines share the same basic design, and even though an aftermarket 4V manifold is hard to find, there is a 4V intake manifold available—right in the dealer's parts book. The 390 version of this engine, used in large International vehicles and not available in the Scout, uses a 4V carburetor. Get one new or used, add a 4V carburetor, and you've increased the horsepower of the Scout II with factory parts.

The automatic transmission (a Chrysler A727) provides three speeds forward and one in reverse. The familiar Dana 20 2-speed transfer case takes care of getting the power to the front axle when it's needed. (The 2-speed transfer case is an option; the base unit is a single-speed.)

The stout, front-drive axle is a Dana 44, fitted with leaf springs rated at 3100 pounds. For an additional $37 you can order the optional heavy-duty spring package that increases the rating another 100 pounds. It may not seem like much on paper, but it makes a surprising difference in the driving; the Scout feels much more stable and firm with the heavy-duty spring package.

The rest of the mechanical details are identical to the balance of the Scout lineup, so we will point out the benefits of the additional creature comforts in this duded-up Scout II.

First of all, the Scout II was much quieter than the SSII, but that's only natural when you consider we had a fiberglass top (upholstered inside), carpeting and another seat to keep out engine and wind noise. It is re-

1. This duded-up version of the 100-inch-wheelbase Scout II proved to be just as tough as the Scout SSII we tested earlier this year, but this time we were riding in air-conditioned comfort with our feet on plush carpeting. Like the SSII, the little Scout II went anywhere.

2. Floor-mounted shift lever is located in a convenient, easy-to-use position. Reverse and Park are locked out for safety; pull the ring up to select those gears.

3. With the rear seat in place there is ample storage space, although relocating the spare outside would be an improvement.

4. The side stripes, made of tape, are available as an extra-cost option. If you plan on running through heavy brush, you might want to pass on this one.

markable how relaxing it can be to drive a quiet vehicle. Noise is great when that's what you want, but for a true dual-purpose four-wheeler, quiet is nice.

The big steering wheel (and we do mean *big)* can be tilted to suit the requirements of most drivers, and the power steering makes it easy to keep things under control. The tight turning radius is another fine Scout II feature whether you are fighting in-town traffic or a narrow canyon in the outback.

Air conditioning is an option we recommend if you have a solid top over your head. Not only does the A/C keep you cool when the weather is hot, but it also acts as a pressurizer that helps keep the dust from creeping in through the windows and doors.

Between the two high-back seats sits a console with lots of storage room. It opens from the front with a pushbutton lock that is hard to see. In fact, one of our drivers never did figure out how to open it.

Every rig has certain little problems and idiosyncrasies that are uniquely

SCOUT II

its own. One of the funniest is the Scout II's hood; it opens from the rear and is hinged at the front. In terms of design it's very good—if the hood latch should pop, then the hood can't fly open. We watched as several people who were unfamiliar with Scouts tried to open the hood.

First, they reached all around the grille trying to find the latch they were certain was hidden there, *somewhere*. Finally, they started searching inside the cab for the hood release, pulling the handbrake release, turning on the lights, but having no luck finding the hood release. Those clever IH people had hidden it in plain sight—right smack dab in the center of the dashboard. Five minutes later they spotted it and thought their search was over. A

quick pull of the knob and the hood would open . . . so they thought. Scout hood releases are famous for being hard to pull, and this one was no exception. Finally, they learned the old put-your-foot-on-the-dashboard-and-tug-like-crazy routine and the hood popped open.

Another Scout legend is its toughness. We confirmed it again and again with this vehicle. The added comfort items cost the Scout II nothing in terms of performance. With the air conditioning humming, we took the same route we had taken with the SSII some months earlier. Our times for the course were just slightly longer than the SSII, and we motored around in comfort at very nearly the same speed.

Overall, the IH Scout line has

shown us lots of performance and off-road ability. They may not be stylish, but this version was certainly comfortable and practical. The optional rear seat could be folded forward when more rear load-carrying space was needed, and it was comfortable enough for those who had to ride in the back seat during short trips. (The rear seat is more suited to children on long trips.)

Nimble in traffic or off the pavement, quiet and comfortable, the Scout II is a fine dual-purpose vehicle. The best thing about Scouts is that they can be tailored to your needs, even for a pickup truck in the Terra model. IH is covering a large part of the four-wheel drive market with one basic vehicle, and it's a good one. ●

4-WHEEL & OFF-ROAD / ROAD TEST SPECIFICATIONS / INTERNATIONAL HARVESTER SCOUT II

GENERAL:
Base List Price $6080
Options .....345 V8 engine, auto trans, power steering, tilt steering, cruise control, deluxe interior trim, air conditioning, 2-sp transfer case
Price As Tested $9782

ENGINE:
Type ....OHV V8
Displacement ....345 cubic inches
Bore & Stroke ....3.875x3.656 inches
Compression Ratio 8.05:1
Net Power ....138 hp @ 3400 rpm
Net Torque ....292 ft/lbs @ 2000 rpm
Carburetion 2V
Recommended Fuel ....Regular
Emissions Control ....California

DRIVETRAIN:
Transmission ....3-speed automatic
Transfer Case ....Dana 20 part-time
Reduction Ratio 2.03:1
Gear Ratios ....Third: 1.00:1; Second: 1.46:1; First: 2.45:1; Reverse: 2.20:1
Final Drive Ratio 3.54:1

CHASSIS:
Body/Frame ....Box frame with steel body
Suspension ....Front: Live axle, leaf springs; Rear: Live axle, leaf springs
Steering ....Integral power (Saginaw)
Brake System ....Front: Power disc; Rear: Power drum
Wheels ....15x8 white spoke
Tires ....10-15LT Goodyear Tracker A/T
Gross Vehicle Weight Rating ....6200 lbs

DIMENSIONS:
Wheelbase ....100 inches
Ground Clearance at Lowest Point ....8.2 inches
Track ....Front: 60 inches; Rear: 59 inches
Length ....166 inches
Width ....70 inches
Height ....65.7 inches
Overhang ....Front: 24 inches; Rear: 41.5 inches
Fuel Capacity ....19 gallons
Cargo Area ....Length: 67 inches; Width: 55 inches
Curb Weight ....3950 lbs

FUEL ECONOMY:
Mileage on 114-Mile Test Loop ....11.7 mpg

OVERALL COMMENTS:
(On a scale of 1-10, 5 is average.)
Exterior Finish Quality 8
Interior Finish Quality 7
Handling 7
Brakes 7
Driver Comfort 8
Dashboard Readability/Accessibility 7
Acceleration In Traffic 9

ACCELERATION:
0-30 mph ....3.9 seconds
0-60 mph ....12.0 seconds

STOPPING DISTANCE:
30-0 mph ....Dirt: 50 feet; Pavement: 37 feet
50-0 mph ....Dirt: 148 feet; Pavement: 110 feet

SPEEDOMETER CALIBRATION:
Indicated 30 40 50 55 60
Actual 33 43 54 59 65

INTERNATIONAL SCOUTS

Fifty New Dealer Options Permit Owners to Tailor Their Scouts To Their Own Requirements

Dual shocks for front axles, suspension kits and a roof-mounted bar for auxiliary lighting are but a few of the new performance and appearance options among the greatly-expanded line of dealer-installed accessories for International Scouts. In all, there are now over 50 items manufactured to International Harvester specifications.

For example, there's a total performance suspension kit that includes heavy-duty springs and a dual-shock package of 4 heavy-duty front shocks and 2 for the rear. These shocks have a special freon cell to keep them cooler than regular shocks under heavy usage.

Among the other accessories: front end guards, available in both the "push-bar" style and full grille brush guard; several styles of aluminum and steel wheels; special competition-type seats of high-back, deep-bucket design (for SS-II models); a wide variety of auxiliary lighting; winches of from 2-8000-lb. capacity; convertible clocks; roll bars; and, tachometers.

What are these accessories used on? On the Scout II, a 100-in. wheelbase model with a full steel top. On the Scout Traveler, a 118-in. wb hatch-back wagon. On the Scout Terra, a pickup with 6-ft. bed on a 118-in. wb. And, on the Scout SS-II, a performance-oriented, open-top model on a 100-in. wheelbase.

DRIVETRAIN

Scout engine choices are: a 196-cid 4, rated at 76.5 hp at 3600 rpm; a 304-cid V8, rated at 122 hp at 3400; a 345-cid V8, rated at 148 hp at 3600;

DIESEL ENGINE is optional in the Scout II (left), Terra and Traveler.

and, a 198-cid, 6-cyl. diesel, rated at 81 at 3800. All gas engines use catalytic mufflers and require unleaded.

The 304 is standard in Travelers; the 196 four with manual is standard in all other models. The diesel engine with manual is optional in the Scout II, Terra and Traveler. For added starting power and to reduce starting time in diesel-engine Scouts, new high-capacity batteries and modified glow plugs are used.

A new auxiliary oil cooler is optional for use with automatic transmissions. It's advised for trailer-towing applications or other driving situations that place high loads on the transmission.

When 4WD Scouts are equipped with optional automatic locking hubs, it's unnecessary to manually twist the front hubs for four-wheel drive. Instead, the front wheels are engaged when the now-standard 2-speed, gear-driven transfer case is shifted into 4WD (indicated by a light on the dash). They are disengaged as easily by shift-

ing to 2WD. Four-wheel drive is now standard on Terra pickups, along with manual hubs.

INTERIOR CHANGES

Among the design and appearance changes in the interiors of Scouts are these:

—The legroom in Scouts using the split 1/3 x 2/3 bench seat has been increased by an added inch of rearward travel.

—Traveler models have new rubber

A VARIETY of optional interior packages are offered on Travelers.

What's the Future?

When International Harvester introduced the Scout in 1961 the only other 4WD vehicle was the Willys Jeep. But as the other Detroit manufacturers followed the first two into the market, competition grew — and so did the market.

In 1970, the market was only 69,000 units, but by 1973 it had jumped to 156,000. Last year, registrations were up to 320,000, with International Harvester now predicting that the market will expand to 350,00 during 1979 and continue to climb to around 500,000 by 1985.

This will be brought about, they say, by a strong consumer demand toward lifestyles that utilize these vehicles. Hunting, fishing, camping, boating and four-wheeling. S/U vehicles are now being substituted for passenger vehicles, or at least, are being added to the family of cars.

As demand grows and the market burgeons, what will buyers expect and what will the industry build? International Harvester's vp and general manager of North American Operations for the Truck Group, Thomas L.

Dougherty, says,

"I look for the product itself to be redesigned to meet safety, emissions and fuel economy standards. (Though the government hasn't set mpg standards beyond 1981, they are expected to.) I believe we will see more efficient engines, lighter weight chassis and bodies, and increased safety designs."

One concept vehicle already developed along those lines on a modified Scout Chassis is built of a composite material so that International Harvester engineers can test the feasibility of such materials for mass production. The body is composed of 7 major parts vs. 116 in a steel-body Scout and I-H engineers believe the principle can be applied to any of their future trucks.

Reaction to the test vehicle during a 6000-mile tour across the country was "unusually favorable to the styling appearance."

snubbers and one-piece latching forks to maintain a tight fit of the hatchback lid.
—Window cranking efforts have been lessened.
—Bright, engine-turned trim is featured on the instrument panel in Deluxe and Custom interiors. It's also on the air conditioning panel and on the automatic transmission shift tower.
—Four new seat trims are offered for the split seats or high-back buckets in Deluxe and Custom interiors.

DELUXE trim on Scouts includes plush seats and panel brightwork.

TERRA with optional pickup cover.

—The optional full-width rear bench seat offered on all models (except Terra) has a higher trim level than previously.
—The optional front seat storage console, available with bucket seats, has a new lid for 2 beverage container holders and 2 change and utility trays.
—A smaller (15-in.) soft rubber rim wheel is offered on all Scouts with power steering.

A Heavy-Duty Hunk:

IH SCOUT TERRA

A serious machine for hard-core off roaders...

PV4 TEST

If there's any one thing that sets the International Scout in any of its versions aside from the rest of the light trucks available in the United States today, it's that in the entire firmament of American truck building, International is the one company that does not also build cars.

The impact—and import—of this is enormous, because it means, among other things, that IH does not have an extensive lineup of automotive parts it can pluck off its parts shelves when it wants to produce light-duty trucks. This is just what the other truck companies do, and as a result one finds that often there are at least as many car parts in most light trucks as there are truck parts—important things like engines, electrical components, transmissions, portions of the steering gear, etc. Additionally, when a company has built cars as well as trucks, the truck division typically benefits from the expertise of the auto exterior and interior stylists so that women—your wives and ours—will be more easily persuaded that driving a truck might not be so bad after all—just *look* at all that plush fabric: looks just like the inside of the family Chevy sedan, right? Thirdly, and perhaps most important, is the fact that when the federal government comes up with a revised set of emissions or safety standards (it doesn't really matter which) which require a great deal of research or engineering, or the expenditure of a great deal of money to find the right answers, those companies that build the most units each year, i.e., those that have their interests spread out over truck lines *and* car lines, are able to spread their costs out over a larger number of units than a smaller manufacturer would be able to. Lastly, the more lines of product a manufacturer is developing, the more standards he

must meet, the more likely it is that he'll come up with a solution to some specific problem which can be applied to other product lines, be they cars, trucks or whatever.

A company which builds only trucks, then, could be at a bit of a disadvantage when it comes to keeping up not only with the demands of the marketplace, but with the demands of the Department of Transportation. That smaller marques like Jeep (owned by American Motors, which builds cars) and Scout (owned by International, which does not) are able not only to survive but to flourish even without the benefits taken for granted by the larger producers of trucks speaks volumes not only about the quality of the company's leadership, but about the product itself.

About the product: it's dead conventional, completely straightforward in its design and execution and that is at once where the Terra's strengths and weaknesses spring from. Our test model was equipped with the 345-cid V-8 engine, the close-ratio 4-speed transmission, 10 x 15 Tracker AT tires, and an interior handsome enough, as far as it went, to make a potential buyer never want to look upon a standard, vinyl-covered bench seat ever again. And something else the Scout was equipped with: more pure—well, for want of a better word—truckiness than anything else we've put a throttle foot to in quite some time.

You doubt that? Well, for starters, just take a look at the thing's shape. About as aerodynamic, as stylish, as a brick, right? Well, think about it: Truck producers have never been *completely* uninterested in style, though Lord knows the average truck stylist's function has been oriented a lot more toward covering all the functional pieces as cleanly as possible than with creating a stylish exterior specifically for the purposes of sales. So what we have here is basically a flat, squarish shape with a few pleas-

antly rounded corners; basically a two box shape. Two-box shape? Right, that means a large box on the bottom, representing the main portion of the truck—its fenders, grille, bed and most of the rest of the sheet metal, and a smaller box sitting on top, representing the space set aside for passenger head and shoulder room, the space covered or this particular truck by the black fiberglass top. Not for International are the fine flourishes, the tender, caring touches aimed at improving either the truck's image or its wind tunnel performance. Which is not to denigrate the efforts of the men responsible for the Scout as it exists today; rather, it's to demonstrate that reality may just be a bit different for a combination car/truck company than it is for a company that has to worry only about trucks, that reality is not a constant. Suffice it to say therefore, that the Scout in none of its guises gets anywhere near as much attention to styling as its competitors get; if you purchase a Scout, chances are you've done so because of what it is and what it can do, not because you suspect that it can supplant your macho image; a nice, straightforward way to do business.

The same thing is true, it would appear, of interior styling; the interior portion of this truck looks just like the interior of a truck. This is particularly true of the dash layout. Which is not to say that the men at International haven't knocked themselves out trying to make the thing look as pretty and as smooth as possible, because they have. The PV4 test rig, which was borrowed from a local IH dealer instead of from the more usual public relations zone office, came to us with a very attractive combination of bucket seats and IH's deluxe interior trim: $121 for the buckets, $154 for the interior trim package, which includes plaid fabric inserts on the high-backed bucket seats. Part of the package is a roomy, locking console be-

TERRA

tween the seats, which we liked a lot, and a tacky, plastic appliqué, supposedly representing an engine-turned finish, applied to the dash around the gauges and to the air conditioner control panel. This we didn't like because, frankly, it just looked cheap. But then, fake plastic junk rarely looks as good as the real item, though Detroit makes giant gains in this direction each new model year. The dash where that appliqué is arranged around has some weak points and some strong points. The weakest of these, in our estimation, is that the speedometer is situated over towards the center section of the dash, not directly in front of the driver, directly above the steering column, where it should be. Thus when you want to quickly check your speed you must not only lower your eyes from their straight-

The Terra's seats (left) were moderately comfy; larger cushions would help.

ahead position, you must also skew them off to the right, a far more complicated procedure than necessary; we'd much prefer a speedo position that would allow a quick glance down to check the speed, one that would require as little movement of the driver's eyes as possible. What *does* the driver see when he glances down to where the speedo ought to be mounted? He sees beautiful, lovely, oh-so-nice-to-see-what's-going-on gauges; actual gauges instead of those hated idiot lights. Engine water temperature, oil pressure, ammeter and fuel level are all monitored by these gauges; at least they're easy to see. A fix, however, would probably take more than just swapping positions of gauges and speedometer; we suspect a rethink of the entire dash is in order. Naturally, this is just the sort of thing any one of the big three could whip right out, but probably IH will have to experience quite a few more Scout sales before it can justify such a change, because such changes are *expensive*. If all you really want is a truck, no excuses, no frills and no substitutions, this probably won't matter much to you. If, on the other hand, you feel flash is more important than substance, well . . . One other aspect of the dash that PV4 test crewmen didn't much care for concerned the glovebox door which was built of extruded plastic.

In the Scout Owner's Survey which appears elsewhere in this issue, we mentioned that owners of Scouts equipped with bench seats complained about a lack of leg room, while owners of Scouts equipped with bucket seats did not. We can vouch for the fact that the bucket-equipped Scout has ample leg room for all but the very tallest drivers. Anyone who drives a Scout over any distance may run into some comfort problems, mind you, but chances are those problems will have little to do with leg room; rather, they'll have to do with bottom seat cushions with minimal amounts of support built in, with wind noise, and with the Scout's pedal layout. First, the cushions, which themselves appear to be adequate in size and thickness. The problem is that the base upon which the seat cushions sit, and from which they get their support, is considerably smaller than the cushion. Hence, unless the driver sits square in the middle in the seat, he's going to feel the base edge through the cushion. In fact, chances are he's going to feel them anyway the first time the forces encountered in stopping or cornering cause his posterior to shift position just a bit on the cushion. As regards the backs, the amount of support delivered from this quarter seems adequate enough so that no back aches were produced. One thing we do wish for, however, is some sort of seatback rake adjustment; the backs of the seats in the PV4 test Terra were laid pretty far back, and while this may be fine for some drivers. it won't be fine for all. One thing about the seats that we do applaud, however, is the considerable amount of storage space found behind them. In most un-pickup truck-like fashion, IH has seen fit to provide enough space behind the seat to stick a couple of suitcases; PV4 test crewmen believe that this makes a great deal of sense.

Then there's the wind noise. International has done a very nice thing for Scout buyers in that it has provided the Terra with a removable fiberglass top. It's held on by seven bolts at the back and by four Phillips-head screws at the front, so removing the thing isn't just a matter of flipping a few catches. Still, if you want to drive topless, you can, and that (at least for us) constitutes a pretty big lure. Unfortunately, the fiberglass top on our test unit did not fit as well as it might have and the result was an uncommon amount of wind noise coming from the areas where the tops of the window frames met the sides of the top itself.

The pedal layout in the Terra was pretty much dead conventional; that is, the clutch was situated on the driver's left, the brake in the middle and the gas on the right. Sounds fairly standard, right? Well, it isn't, because each of those three pedals was (either by adjustment or design or a combination of the two) situated on a different plane than any of the others; each pedal pad occupied a different level, a different distance from the truck's floor boards. This means there was no easy way to slide your foot from the gas pedal to the brake pedal the way you do without thinking in your own car or truck; when the driver wants to slow down he must lift his gas foot and actively hunt around for the brake pedal because it just isn't right smack next to the gas where it ought to be. Surely this is something a driver could get used to, but why should he have to? The result of all this is that the gas pedal is too close to the driver, so his right knee has to execute a pretty serious angle if the foot attached to it is to actuate the gas pedal. Any long-distance drive will find the driver wishing for a way to stretch that leg.

The mechanisms those pedals operate? Well, first there is the clutch pedal, which acts upon a heavy, 11-inch clutch plate. We've driven vehicles with much heavier clutch actions, but we've also driven them with much lighter actions. Suffice it to say these two things: first, here's a clutch that can take considerable abuse, and second, using this clutch is going to do wonders for the muscles in the driver's left leg.

Then there's the brake pedal. Vacuum-assisted, it acts upon huge discs on the front wheels and large drums on the rear. Braking performance is surprisingly good for a truck in this weight class wearing non-radial tires. The

truck displayed stopping distances of 161 feet from 60 mph to earn an excellent rating for its brakes. The kicker to this is that unlike many other pickups, the Terra managed its series of stops with absolutely no drama; it stopped arrow-straight every time, with no evidence of premature rear-wheel lock-up. The rear wheels did lock a bit during the tests, mind you, but they seemed to want to do so at the very end of the run, when the truck was already nearly at a stop. By doing so at this time instead of at higher speeds, the rears had no effect upon the Terra's directional stability when they finally did reach lockup. Really, these have to be some of the better pickup brakes around; we'd have no problem at all trusting them with a heavy load on a steep road.

The gas pedal, of course, is connected to International's 345-cid V-8 but unfortunately, this year's 345 doesn't have the kick that last year's engine of the same displacement did, even though the 1979 engine runs a four-barrel carburetor in place of last year's two-barrel. The reason for all this is one you've heard before—the ever-tightening emissions requirements, which this year demanded that IH add a catalytic converter to the exhaust system of every Scout it builds. The result of that addition is a horsepower rating of 148 for this year vs. 163 horsepower for last year. The last Scout tested by PV4 was a '78 model SSII with the 345 and an automatic transmission; it did zero to 60 mph in 13.7 seconds, the '79 did the same in 14 seconds flat; the '78 did the quarter mile in 19.6 at 70 mph, the '79 did the same in 19.8 and at 69 mph, demonstrating the loss of those 15 horses. But get used to it; this is a situation that will get worse before it gets better. In the engine's favor, it lugged extremely well and pulled like a trooper; the one glitch we noticed was that its throttle response was not as smooth as we would have expected. Particularly noticeable was the bobble experienced every time the carburetor's secondary throats were opened. With the optional 3.73 differential gear set the test Terra carried, those four

carburetor throats and the truck's 4300-odd pounds translated to 12.9 mpg, certainly nothing to celebrate about.

On the other hand, however, what should you expect from a truck? Probably not economy car fuel mileage. What you can expect from this truck is the ability to go nearly anywhere you'd like to go. Equipped as it was with no limited-slip differential, no automatic locking hubs, no full-time 4x4 and none of the rest of the recent accouterments of high-buck fourwheeling; the Terra still proved itself to be a quintessential off roader. Though the close-ratio 4-speed with which our test Terra was equipped might not be the ideal transmission for hard-core fourwheeling, both it and the truck's transfer case proved to be easy to use with relatively light shifting actions, particularly considering the fact that both are extremely heavy-duty units. The Terra seemed at home in the rough country at virtually any speed, its 6200-pound Gross Vehicle Weight Rating (GVWR) suspension working as well to sop up the bumps over a variety of speeds and conditions in the outback as it does to provide a reasonably smooth, relaxed ride out on the highway. We did experience some initial stickiness in the transfer case shifting linkage, but once we used it a few times that cleared up and the case proved quite easy to shift. The tires that came with the truck certainly would not be our first choice for snow tires, but even with these tires, the Terra proved extremely sure footed over ice and snow. We didn't really try as hard as we might have to get the thing stuck; sometimes, however, we do manage to get stuck even without trying; most embarrassing. Needless to say, the Terra did not embarrass us because it was willing to roll over any obstacle we pointed it towards. Which is to say, it might not be real pretty or real quiet, but it's a real off roader and it'll never let its driver forget it. But then chances are he won't want to, not once he's checked the Terra out and recognized it for what it is: A workhorse with a great deal of capacity for play. •

International's plucky 345-inch V-8 is topped this year with a four-barrel carb, but to no avail; power is down over last year's two-barrel version of the same engine. Still, the engine pulls very well, even if the addition of a catalytic converter makes use of unleaded fuel mandatory this year.

INTERNATIONAL SCOUT TERRA
SPECIFICATIONS AND PERFORMANCE

PRICES

Basic list, FOB Detroit
Scout Terra 4wd $6805

Standard Equipment .... 196-cid in-line
Four engine, 3-spd manual transmission, 2-spd transfer case, free-running front hubs, heater/defroster, 2-spd electric wiper/washers, power brakes, full instrumentation, folding front bench seat, tinted glass, inside hood release, painted front and rear bumpers, fiberglass cab top, H78 x 15B tires, 4.09:1 axle ratios

GENERAL

Curb weight, lb (test model) 4430
Weight distribution, %, front/rear 59/47
GVWR (test model) 6200
Optional GVWRs .... none

Wheelbase, in. 118.0
Track, front/rear 58.5/57.6
Overall length 184.2
Overall height 66.0
Overall width 70.0
Overhang, front/rear 24.0/42.2

Approach angle, degrees 44
Departure angle, degrees 22

Ground clearances (test model):
Front axle 7.25
Rear axle 7.6
Oil pan 14
Transfer case 13.25
Fuel tank 16.5
Exhaust system (lowest point) 12.25

Fuel tank capacity (U.S. gal.) 19.0
Auxiliary .... none

ACCOMMODATION

Standard seats .... 1/3–2/3 split bench seat
Optional seats .... bucket seats
Headroom, in. 34.25
Accelerator pedal to seatback, max 42
Steering wheel to seatback, max 13
Seat to ground 35.5
Floor to ground 19

Unobstructed load space (length x width x height) .... 72.0 x 42.0 x 21.3
Tailgate (width x height) .... 54.8 x 21.3

INSTRUMENTATION

Instruments .... speedometer/odometer, fuel gauge, ammeter, oil pressure, water temp
Warning lights ...... front axle engaged indicator, parking brake, hazard, seat belts
Optional .... none

ENGINES

Standard .... 196-cid in-line Four
Bore x stroke, in. .... 4.125 x 3.656
Compression ratio 8.02:1
Net horsepower @ rpm .... 76.5 @ 3600
Net torque @ rpm, lb-ft .... 153.3 @ 2000
Type fuel required .... unleaded

Optional 304-cid V-8, $203
Bore x stroke, in. .... 3.875 x 3.218
Compression ratio 8.19:1
Net horsepower @ rpm .... 122.3 @ 3400
Net torque @ rpm, lb-ft .... 226.3 @ 2000
Type fuel required .... unleaded

Optional 345-cid V-8, $359
Bore x stroke, in. .... 3.875 x 3.656
Compression ratio 8.05:1

Net horsepower @ rpm .... 148 @ 3600
Net torque @ rpm, lb-ft .... 265 @ 2000
Type fuel required .... unleaded

Optional ...... 198-cid in-line diesel Six,* $2589
Bore x stroke, in. .... 3.27 x 3.94
Compression ratio 22:1
Net horsepower @ rpm .... 81 @ 3800
Net torque @ rpm, lb-ft .. 138 @ 1200 to 1600
Type fuel required ....No. 2 diesel
*Includes power brakes

DRIVETRAIN

Standard transmission ...... 3-spd manual T-332
Clutch dia., in. 11.0
Transmission ratios: 3rd 1.00:1
2nd 1.55:1
1st 2.99:1
Synchromesh .... all forward gears

Optional .... 4-spd wide ratio manual*
T-427 .... $162*
Transmission ratios: 4th 1.00:1
3rd 1.68:1
2nd 3.09:1
1st 6.32:1
Synchromesh .... all forward gears
*Standard with diesel engine

Optional .... 4-spd close ratio manual
T-428 .... $203
Transmission ratios: 4th 1.00:1
3rd 1.41:1
2nd 2.41:1
1st 4.02:1
Synchromesh .... all forward gears

Optional .... 3-spd automatic, $392
Transmission ratios: 3rd 1.00:1
2nd 1.45:1
1st 2.45:1

Rear axle type .... semi-floating hypoid
Final drive ratios 3.07:1, 3.54:1, 3.73:1, 4.09:1
Overdrive .... none

Free-running front hubs .... std
Limited slip differential $187
Transfer case .... TC-145 (Dana 20) 2-spd
Transfer case ratios .... 2.03:1 and 1.00:1

CHASSIS & BODY

Body/frame .... ladder-type frame with separate steel body
Brakes (std) .... front, 11.75-in. dia. disc; rear, 11.03 x 2.25-in. drum
Brake swept area, sq in. 381
Swept area/ton (max load) 123
Power brakes .... std

Steering type (std) .... worm and roller
Steering ratio 24:1
Power steering $246
Power steering ratio .... recirculating ball 17.5:1
Turning circle, ft 38.8

Wheel size (std) .... 15 x 6.0JK
Optional wheel sizes .... 15 x 7.0JJ chrome, 15 x 8.0JJ white spoke
Tire size (std) .... H78 x 15B
Optional tire sizes .... P225/75 x 15B, 10 x 15B, 7.00 x 15C

SUSPENSION

Front suspension .... semi-elliptic leaf springs on live axle, anti-sway bar, tube shocks

Front axle capacity, lb 3200
Optional .... none
Rear suspension .... semi-elliptic leaf springs on live axle and tube shocks
Rear axle capacity, lb 3500
Optional .... none

Additional suspension options .... HD front and rear shocks, HD front with rear springs

TEST MODEL

1979 Scout Terra, heavy-duty rear step bumper, heavy-duty front springs, power steering, AM radio, exterior decor side panels, off-road tire and wheel package, 11-in. clutch, 345-cid V-8 engine, Calif. emissions, close ratio 4-spd transmission, 3.73 final drive ratio, bed rails, bucket seats, deluxe exterior trim, deluxe interior trim, air conditioning, storage console
West Coast list price $9788*
*Does not include $495 in freight costs

ACCELERATION

Time to speed, sec:
0–30 mph 4.2
0–45 mph 8.4
0–60 mph 14.0
0–70 mph 21.0
Standing start, ¼-mile, sec. 19.8
Speed at end, mph 69

SPEED IN GEARS

High range, 4th (3300 rpm) 80
3rd (4000 rpm) 71
2nd (4000 rpm) 41
1st (4000 rpm) 24
Low range, 4th (4000 rpm) 48
3rd (4000 rpm) 35
2nd (4000 rpm) 20
1st (4000 rpm) 12
Engine rpm @ 55 mph 2300

BRAKE TESTS

Pedal pressure required for ½-g deceleration rate from 60 mph, lb 34
Stopping distance from 60 mph, ft 161
Fade: Percent increase in pedal pressure for 6 stops from 60 mph 61
Overall brake rating .... excellent

INTERIOR NOISE

Idle in neutral, dbA 59.5
Maximum during acceleration 79.0
At steady 60 mph cruising speed 76.0

OFF PAVEMENT

Hillclimbing ability .... excellent
Maneuverability .... good
Turnaround capability .... good
Driver visibility .... good
Handling .... good
Ride .... very good

ON PAVEMENT

Handling .... fair
Ride .... good
Driver comfort .... fair
Engine response .... fair

FUEL CONSUMPTION

City/freeway driving, mpg 12.9
Off pavement 9.0
Range, city/freeway driving, miles 245
Range, off pavement 171

TOP HEAVY FROM CHICAGO

As befits its 1950s appearance, the Traveltop is International's short back and sides Scout. Did mob rule influence the designers, we wonder?

★ 4·W·D ★
overlander
★ TEST ★

ONE LARGE Sydney motor dealer bills the International Scout as a "luxury 4WD", citing its 5.6L V8 engine, automatic transmission, auto free-wheeling hubs, disc brakes and "incredibly smooth suspension" as the major reasons for his claim.

And by American standards we suppose the Scout *is* luxurious. Unlike the Europeans, who build a small, integrated package (like the BMW cars, or the GTV Alfetta) that is inherently luxurious, the Americans think big. The American dream is an oversized monster with enormous engine, air conditioning, soft and spongy suspension, power steering, and everything that opens and shuts. It's also a disposable item, with a lifespan of only a few years.

The Scout is a typical American motor vehicle. It's big, heavy, cumbersome, thirsty and tinny. Our test Traveltop had a price tag of $14,650, and reminded us of a 1950s Customline. But it is closely comparable in specification to the Range-Rover: same wheelbase (2540 mm), similar kerb mass (1674 kg), similar track (1450 mm), V8 engine, two-door 4WD station wagon.

But a Range-Rover it is not. Its "incredibly smooth" suspension system is good ol' leaf springs all round (the Range-Rover has coils and a self-levelling mechanism). The dashboard resembles a 1960 Chevrolet — plenty of dials and knobs, but badly laid out.

It does have three plus points. Automatic transmission will appeal to certain owners (it's optional on the Traveltop, standard on the LWB Traveler). It's an excellent tow vehicle. And the $14,650 price tag is some $6000 below a locally converted automatic Range-Rover.

International Harvester (Australia) has

been promoting the Traveler (tested OL, Vol 3, No 5) in the press at the expense of the Traveltop. But the 460 mm shorter wheelbase vehicle has several advantages over its stablemate. It's $543 cheaper, is available with a manual gearbox for those who want it, is easier to drive in city traffic, and has a steel hardtop. (Traveler sales have been affected by cracks appearing in its fibreglass top).

The other Scout model is the Terra ute — a drug on the market. At $11,000 tax-free, it's around $3000 more expensive than other 4WDs that will do the same job. Hill and George Pty Ltd, the Bowral (NSW) International dealer which supplied our test Traveltop, has swapped Terra manual gearboxes for Traveler autos, thereby providing a fuller range of Scouts for customers. It still can't sell Terras.

Does the Traveltop represent a viable alternative to the Range-Rover? Is it more suitable for overlanding than its brother, the Traveler?

To find out the answers we scouted our Hill and George Traveltop around in the mountainous country west of Mittagong, NSW. This was terrain that must have seemed impenetrable to the early explorers: soaring ridges, seemingly vertical hillsides, towering eucalypts, all traversed by a maze of Forestry roads and fire trails.

On the road

Cruising down the winding Wombeyan Caves road we soon learnt that the Scout is no ladies' car. Its massively heavy steering demands six turns lock to lock and the Scout suffers from near-terminal understeer.

We would swoop down to a blind bend at a deceptively fast speed, then jam on the power-assisted disc front brakes

Backdrop: Traveltop's fuel consumption varies enormously, depending on road conditions. Farm market has greeted Scouts with only moderate enthusiasm (top, right). Visibility is good, but would be improved by addition of rear window wiper (right).

(thank God for them!), at the last moment changing down to second through the floor-mounted shifter to ensure the Scout did not run away coming out of the corner. It was no task for the faint-hearted, nor the limp-wristed. Wrestling the Scout around that series of bends demanded intense concentration, and a modicum of good luck.

On the highway it was a different story. The Scout is well-suited to freeway cruising at speeds of up to 150 km/h; at 110 km/h it has enormous reserves of power available for overtaking. The three-speed auto box stays in top most of the time but it makes little difference. Compared with even a 302 Ford F100, the International is *gutsy*.

One reason for this is its relative lack of emission controls. Our test vehicle, one of the first of the "New Wave" brought into Australia, complied with no anti-pollution ADRs. Later models comply with ADR 36, a much less stringent regulation than 27 or 27A. Both models still have an EGR system and charcoal canister, but are not smothered by air pumps and spark controls. One significant difference is the use of a single exhaust pipe in later models; our test vehicle had two.

Not even a myopic International dealer could call the Traveltop economical. Average fuel consumption during highway cruising was 15.5L/100 km, rising to 30.8 L/100 km on bush tracks. Mind you, the rough road economy is similar to other big 4WDs. Maximum range from the 72L rear-mounted fuel tank is 460 km — more than adequate for popping up to "the farm".

Not that carrying extra fuel *should* present any problems. The Traveltop has a rated payload of 1140 kg, double that of the Range-Rover — and a GVM of 2.81 tonnes or just over the 2.7 tonne NSW Clean Air Act limit. However, whilst the springs may be tough enough for heavy loads, the standard shock absorbers are not. Our test vehicle was equipped with heavy-duty Rough Country shocks, as recommended by I-H. With a 200 kg load in the back, the suspension still bottomed out in *rough country*.

And what of the much-vaunted luxury? For accommodation, the Scout has two pretty ordinary buckets on runners and a basic rear bench which folds down to give 1.54 m of cargo space — unlike the Traveler, not enough for sleeping. The four seat belts are all lap only.

A flat, padded dash carries a 160 km/h speedo (*sans* tripmeter), water temperature, oil pressure, charge and fuel gauges (not just warning lights) and an efficient heater/demister. Trouble is, the dials cannot be read at a glance. The speedo, in particular, is obscured by the steering wheel. Cheap-looking two-speed wipers (no intermittent control), steering lock, cigarette lighter and a strong heater/demister complete the *luxury* touches.

The between seats bin might qualify, but it is actually only a substitute glovebox.

Our test vehicle had vinyl seats, but the most recent Traveltops feature cloth trim and wall carpet around the cargo decks. The floor mats are rubber. By 4WD standards, cabin noise is minimal.

Full-length protector strips are fitted along the vehicle sides, blending into the factory Go-Faster stripes.

Does all this constitute true luxury? Not as we understand the meaning of the term, although the OED definition: "things desirable but not essential" may come close. What the Traveltop lacks is the feeling of 'class' that we think is also part and parcel of luxury.

The Scout looks like a truck and drives like a truck. No amount of body striping, cloth and carpet can disguise that fact. The 1979 Scout is little more sophisticated than its predecessors of 20 years ago.

In the rough

American 4WD priorities must certainly be different from our own. For the Traveltop automatic has an overall first low of only 17.6:1, compared with the Range-Rover's 47.8:1. Even allowing 50 per cent advantage for the torque converter, it's still only marginally more than half the Rover's ratio. About the only good thing that can be said for the Traveltop is that it has a higher numerical diff ratio (3.54 vs. 3.07) than the Traveller, so performs better in the bush than its brother. The pay-off of course, is increased fuel consumption on the open road.

In gearing specification the Traveltop is very similar to the Holden Overlander (tested Vol 2 No 5). Regular readers will recall that we were highly critical of the Overlander's lack of engine braking in critical situations. While the Traveltop has the benefit of a very big, torquey engine, it still runs away downhill.

Overriding the auto is no real help. We stalled the engine once through over-enthusiastic application of the brakes, and found to our horror that, without power assist, the brakes barely retarded the onward rush. The rear wheels only foot-operated parking brake was of little help. Only a determined right foot on the brake pedal finally brought us to a relieved halt.

International's best bet would be to combine the Traveler's 3.07 diff with, say, a 4:1 transfer box. That way the vehicle would get both a good low gear ratio and improved touring economy. The manual gearbox (which we feel is in many ways superior to the auto) would then make the Traveltop a versatile all-rounder.

Not that the problems end with the gearbox: it's simply the major one. The steering for example, is extremely heavy, despite the fact that the Scout is slightly lighter than the Range-Rover. Six turns lock to lock is quite an effort.

Some omissions from the "things desirable but not essential list" include: a hand

throttle (optional extra — there's a space on the dash for it), protruding front chassis members for bull-bar/winch mounting, offset rear diff, rear window wiper splash-plates and bash-plates. But the Scout does have a PTO facility, Warn auto free-wheeling hubs, a "front axle engaged" light and a strong six-blade steel fan.

Without any requirement to disengage a clutch or fan-belt for creek crossings, and with its high-mounted distributor and disc front brakes, the Scout is an excellent creek crosser, despite its lack of splash-plates (they aren't really needed). We did find, though, that water welled up inside the shift box and trickled inside the vehicle.

Otherwise, the Scout is watertight and relatively dustproof, two features of importance to overlanders.

One surprise was the performance of the standard tyres, H78 x 15 Firestone Snow Biters. In clayey terrain that, following our Traveler test last year, we feared would quickly clog the close tread pattern, the Biters bit. Road noise is not excessive, and wear should be reasonable. The Scout was a safe, sure stopper on the bitumen. The only area the tyres fell down in was over sand. Still, the Scout has the *power*, so improved dune performance is a simple matter of fitting more appropriate tyres.

The heat of the Centre should present no problem. The cooling system has an enormous 20.8L capacity. Even in mid-March, climbing seemingly endless hills, the temperature needle barely reached quarter-way.

And what power there was in abundance for those hill-climbs! The 5.6L V8 is the biggest of five engine options available in the US, including a diesel. I-H Australia evidently thought the large motor would be more saleable. We'd like to see the diesel and four-cylinder motors introduced to Australia.

A criticism levelled at some US 4WDs is that they are too big for Australian conditions. But the overall dimensions of the Traveltop are smaller than the Range-Rover or Land Cruiser wagon. The 10.3 m turning circle is also better than most, always provided there's enough strength in your arms to muscle the wheels round!

But the departure angle (22 degrees with optional draw-bar) is a limiting factor, as are the door-mounted side mirrors, which barely fold back at all. A protruding branch caught the non-spring radio aerial and snapped it in two; the mirrors could well go the same way.

For those who like their creature comforts the Traveltop has a surprisingly good ride on rough tracks and would be a forgiving dirt road handler if it weren't for the understeer. Some advantage may have been accorded it by an optional steering damper.

And consider its virtues for overlanding. The fold-down tailgate is a superb table for food preparation and doubles as a bench seat. If the dash ventilation system proves inadequate you can open the quarter vents and the sliding windows behind the doors. The rear seat folds down in seconds to create a much larger luggage space. The removeable steel top is tough enough to carry roof-bars and a canoe. And there's a cigarette lighter into which you can plug all your electrical appliances, like your 12V hair dryer, insect repeller and electric tooth-brush.

On a more practical note — the seats won't need replacing. They're quite comfortable for long trips and will slide back far enough for long legs. Lateral support is good, with or without the lap belts. Some occupants will distrust the inertia lock reclining mechanism, but it gave us no problems.

For those trips to Fraser Island, it's comforting to know that all Scouts are now Endrusted before sale.

Does all this constitute luxury? In the American idiom, we suppose it does. But we don't think a *luxury* motor vehicle — of any type — should be as poorly finished and *tinny* as the Scout. Sure, the engine and transmission (which are essentially big truck components) should still be going when the last bowser runs dry (something the Scout's advent will hasten), but what of the other components? Here's a list of little things that irked us about our test vehicle:

1. The windscreen wipers would not sit horizontal when stationary. We were assured that this had been fixed in the new models, but when Kevin George tried to demonstrate on a brand-new model, the wipers didn't work at all.

2. The tail-lights, instrument lights and radio didn't work because a fuse had blown for no apparent reason. The fuse box is located underneath the dash where it's darn difficult to reach.

3. The cigarette lighter didn't work.

4. Frustratingly, the storage bin lock was faulty.

5. The transfer case had the worst shift we have ever tried. The transfer box 'crashed' changing from N to 2H with the vehicle stationary. In any case, we didn't like the 4L-N-2H-4H shift pattern.

6. The 4WD warning light malfunctioned, possibly because of the auto free-wheeling hubs.

Little things are usually more important to women than to men, so perhaps our all-male staff should have overlooked these faults. But the vehicle does cost $14,650!

Yet, all things considered, and price aside, we preferred the Scout to Toyota's Land Cruiser Station Wagon, which is $3000 cheaper. In turn, the Scout is $3000 cheaper than the Range-Rover.

The moral is obvious: you gets what you pays for . . .

Engine
Type: International V-345-A ohv V8
Bore x stroke: 94.9 x 89.6mm
displacement: 5653cm³
Compression ratio: 8.28:1
Tested max. power: 80kW at 3500rpm (rear wheels)
Tested max. torque: 212Nm at 1500rpm (rear wheels)

Transmission
Type: T-407 three-speed automatic
Internal ratios: 1st: 2.45; 2nd: 1.45; 3rd: 1.00; Rev: 2.2
High range: 1:1; low range: 2.03:1
Diff ratio: 3.54:1
Gearchange: floor-shifts for gearbox and transfer case

Systems
Fuel: mechanical fuel pump feeding Holley dual-throat carburettor (auto choke) from 72L rear-mounted tank.
Lubrication: mechanical oil pump, bypass oil filter
Cooling: six-blade steel fan; crossflow radiator with integral oil cooler; 20.8L radiator/water jacket capacity
Air filtration: dry elementL Electrical: 37A alternator, 62Ah battery

Running Gear
Wheels and tyres: H-78x15 Firestone Snow Biter M/S tyres on 5-stud 7.00x15 Sunraysia wheels (non-standard)
Brakes (front): vacuum assisted 298mm discs (power-boosted); (rear): 208mm s/s drums; (parking) foot pedal cable to rear drums

Steering
Type: worm and roller, collapsible column
Turning circle: 10.3m
Turns lock to lock: 4.5

Suspension
Front: 6-leaf semi-elliptic springs, stabiliser bar, double-acting shocks
Rear: 4-leaf semi-elliptic springs, double-acting shocks

General
L x W x H: 4220 x 1780 x 1670mm
Kerb mass: 1674kg. Payload: 1136kg
Wheelbase: 2540mm
Ground clearance: 193m (under front diff)
Track (F & R): 1450/1450mm
Fuel consumption: (on-highway) 15.5L/100km (18.2mpg); (off-highway) 30.8L/100km (9.2mpg); (median) 21.9L/100km (12.9mpg)
Range: 460km
Top speed: 150km/h
Base price: $14,650
Optional equipment fitted: Radiomobile radio/cassette; Mark IV air condtitioning ($650); steering damper; Rough Country 505101 shock absorbers; 15x7 Sunraysia spokers; draw-bar ($90); Kordiak aluminium bull-bar ($300).
Options available: power steering, floor carpets, PTO (soon)
Supplier: Hill and George Pty Ltd, Kirkham Rd, Bowral NSW.
Manufacturer: International Harvester Company, Chicago, USA

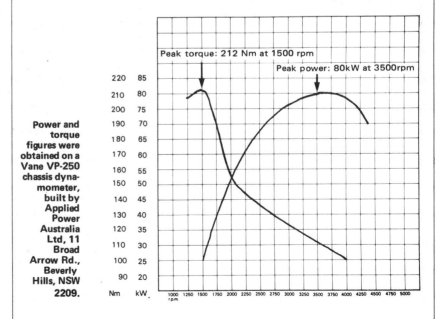

Power and torque figures were obtained on a Vane VP-250 chassis dynamometer, built by Applied Power Australia Ltd, 11 Broad Arrow Rd., Beverly Hills, NSW 2209.

Peak torque: 212 Nm at 1500 rpm

Peak power: 80kW at 3500rpm

SCOUT SS

1. Spartan is the theme and all-business the name of the game for the SS11 interior; easy care, easy access, easy control— everything for the serious off-roader.

2. There is room for gear in the rear! The SS11 has a removable rear seat as well as a standard cargo area. The cloth top affords easy access not found in other off-road wagons.

3. The grille is plastic, the bumper painted, and the windshield and top come off—what more could an avid off-roader ask for?

4. The cloth top on the SS11 just refuses to fit properly. No matter how carefully the door is closed, air and the elements get in to create noise or an uncomfortable climate.

5. There is no worry to crossing streams or running through sand with the SS11. The lack of exterior frills and high-mounted paint trim give you a vehicle that doesn't get damaged and ragged looking.

③

WHY DO YOU THINK THEY CALL IT A UTILITY VEHICLE?

International Harvester's 1979 Scout SSII remains true to its designation as a *utility* vehicle, short on frills but long on features to get deep into the outback.

This year's Scout is essentially the same as the proven model introduced in mid-1977. The slab-sided vehicle is seen by IH as a direct competitor to the Jeep CJ line, and it continues to do well in a head-to-head encounter with its arch nemesis.

The Scout SSII sits on a 100-inch wheelbase (8 inches shorter than its sister Scouts, the Terra and Traveler), but has a 2-foot shorter turning circle than the bobtailed CJ-7. Along with standard rollbar and fuel tank skidplate, the SSII offers a top-of-the-line 345-c.i.d. V8 that cranks out power enough to tackle rough terrain, from sand dunes to mountain switchbacks. Translating the power to the ground, the Scout uses a Dana 44 front drive axle rated at 3100 pounds, significantly stronger and larger than that of its competitors.

Inside, the SSII is all business: no carpet, no windows, and plenty of noise from the soft top (other versions feature a metal top and glass windows), but all the instruments necessary to keep tabs on things are easily read. This year IH expanded the Scout's option list, so the Spartan SSII may now be outfitted with an AM/FM/8-track stereo tape player, various styles and colors of interior trim, a "Rallye" steering wheel, and all-season radial tires as factory options. In addition, several top and door combinations are available. IH has come a long way from being known for its open-air tractors.

All the "new" items in the Scout's 1979 repertoire don't change the most important features of the vehicle, its engine and drivetrain. Those components, the essence of an off-road machine, remain some of the most durable and best designed on the market. And they make the IH Scout SSII one of the top utility vehicles available. ●

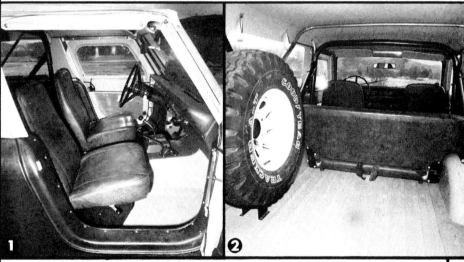

INTERNATIONAL SCOUT
SPECIFICATIONS AND PERFORMANCE

PRICES

Basic list, FOB Detroit
International Scout II ......:................$6604

Standard Equipment ....196-cid four-cylinder engine; 3-spd transmission; 2-spd transfer case; 3100-lb front, 3500-lb rear axles; disc/drum brakes; undercoating; tinted glass; rubber floor mat; 1/3-2/3 front seat; ammeter, water, oil pressure and fuel gauges; inside hood releases; 11-in. clutch; 37-amp alternator; 19-gal. fuel tank; H78 x 15 tires; stainless steel wheel covers; locking hubs

GENERAL

Curb weight, lb (test model)..................4110
Weight distribution, %, front/rear 54/46
GVWR (test model)..................................6200
Optional GVWRs ....NA
Wheelbase, in...100
Track, front/rear 57.1/57.1
Overall length 166.2
Overall height 65.7
Overall width 70
Overhang, front/rear 21.5/42.5
Approach angle, degrees..................................37
Departure angle, degrees.................................23
Ground clearances (test model):
  Front axle 8.25
  Rear axle 8
  Oil pan 13.25
  Transfer case 12.5
  Fuel tank 15
  Exhaust system (lowest point) 15
Fuel tank capacity (U.S. gal.)...........................19
Auxiliary ....NA

ACCOMMODATION

Standard seats ....1/3-2/3 vinyl-covered front, folding rear seat
Optional seats ....individual bucket seats, vinyl or cloth
Headroom, in. 36
Accelerator pedal to seatback, max.......42.25
Steering wheel to seatback, max 16.25
Seat to ground...33.25
Floor to ground..18
Unobstructed load space (length x width)
  With seats in place ....40.5 x 42 x 41
  Rear folded or removed.........58.5 x 42 x 41
Tailgate (width x height) ....51 x 37.5

INSTRUMENTATION

Instruments...............fuel gauge, temp gauge, oil pressure gauge, ammeter, speedometer, odometer
Warning lights ....front axle engaged indicator, parking brake, turn signal, and hazard indicators, seat belts
Optional ....none

ENGINES

Standard ....196-cid Four
Bore x stroke, in........................4.125 x 3.656
Compression ratio 8.02:1
Net horsepower @ rpm............76.5 @ 3600
Net torque @ rpm, lb-ft............153.3 @ 2000
Type fuel required ....unleaded
Optional 304-cid V-8, $203
Bore x stroke, in.........................3.875 x 3.218
Compression ratio 8.19:1
Net horsepower @ rpm............122.3 @ 3400
Net torque @ rpm, lb-ft............226.3 @ 2000
Type fuel required ....unleaded
Optional 345-cid V-8, $359
Bore x stroke, in.........................3.875 x 3.656
Compression ratio 8.05:1

Net horsepower @ rpm ....148 @ 3600
Net torque @ rpm, lb-ft ....265 @ 2000
Type fuel required ....unleaded
Optional ....198-cid diesel Six, $2589*
Bore x stroke, in...........................3.27 x 3.94
Compression ratio 22:1
Net horsepower @ rpm ....81 @ 3800
Net torque @ rpm, lb-ft .....138 @ 1200-1600
Type fuel required ....Diesel No. 2
*Includes power brakes

DRIVETRAIN

Standard transmission ....3-spd manual
Clutch dia., in...11
Transmission ratios: 3rd 1.00:1
  2nd...1.55:1
  1st...2.99:1
Synchromesh ....all forward gears
Optional ....4-spd wide-ratio manual, $162*
Transmission ratios: 4th 1.00:1
  3rd..1.68:1
  2nd..3.09:1
  1st..6.32:1
Synchromesh ....all forward gears
*Standard with diesel engine
Optional ....4-spd close-ratio manual, $203
Transmission ratios: 4th 1.00:1
  3rd..1.41:1
  2nd..2.41:1
  1st..4.02:1
Synchromesh ....all forward gears

Optional ....3-spd automatic, $392*
Transmission ratios: 3rd 1.00:1
  2nd..1.45:1
  1st..2.45:1
*Not available with diesel engine
Rear axle type ....semi-floating hypoid
Final drive ratios 3.07, 3.54, 3.73, 4.09:1
Overdrive ....none
Free-running front hubs....................standard
Limited slip differential $187
Transfer case ....Dana 20 2-spd
Transfer case ratios 2.03:1, 1:1

CHASSIS & BODY

Body/frame.............................ladder frame, separate steel body
Brakes (std) ....11.75-in. front disc/11 1/32 x 2 1/4-in. rear drum
Brake swept area, sq in. 327.8
  Swept area/ton (max load) 105.74
Power brakes ....standard
Steering type (std) ....worm and roller
Steering ratio 24:1
Power steering ....recirculating ball, $246
Power steering ratio 17.5:1
Turning circle, ft...33.8
Wheel size (std) ....15 x 6
Optional wheel sizes ....15 x 7, 15 x 8 spoke
Tire size (std) ....H78 x 15B

Optional tire sizes ....P225/75 x 15B, 10 x 15B, 7.00 x 15C

SUSPENSION

Front suspension..............semi-elliptical leaf springs, beam axle, anti-roll bar, tube shocks
Front axle capacity, lb 3200
  Optional ....none
Rear suspension................semi-elliptical leaf springs, beam axle, tube shocks
Rear axle capacity, lb 3500
  Optional ....none
Additional suspension options ..HD front/rear shocks, HD front/rear springs

TEST MODEL

International Scout II Travel Top, 196-cid engine, power steering, AM radio and antenna, modulated fan, California emissions, close-ratio 4-spd transmission, 3.73 rear axle, insulated cargo area mat, folding rear seat, mud/snow tires, two-tone paint, transportation
West Coast list price...............................$8142

ACCELERATION

Time to speed, sec:
  0-30 mph...6
  0-45 mph...13.4
  0-60 mph...25.5
  0-70 mph..46
Standing start, 1/4-mile, sec...........................23
  Speed at end, mph 59

SPEED IN GEARS

High range, 4th (3200 rpm) 74
  3rd (3500 rpm) 60
  2nd (4000 rpm) 39
  1st (4000 rpm) 23
Low range, 4th (4000 rpm) 45
  3rd (4000 rpm) 34
  2nd (4000 rpm) 19
  1st (4000 rpm) 11
Engine rpm @ 55 mph 2400

BRAKE TESTS

Pedal pressure required for 1/2-g deceleration rate from 60 mph, lb 37
Stopping distance from 60 mph, ft 196
Fade: Percent increase in pedal pressure for 6 stops from 60 mph 34
Overall brake rating ....poor*
*During emergency braking, right rear wheel locked up and caused wild side-to-side slewing and near complete loss of directional control

INTERIOR NOISE

Idle in neutral, dBA 56.5
Maximum during acceleration 82
At steady 60 mph cruising speed 76

OFF PAVEMENT

Hillclimbing ability ....very good
Maneuverability ....excellent
Turnaround capability ....excellent
Driver visibility ....very good
Handling ....excellent
Ride ....very good

ON PAVEMENT

Handling ....good
Ride ....good
Driver comfort............................very good
Engine response ....poor

FUEL CONSUMPTION

City/freeway driving, mpg 18.4
Off pavement 11.9
Range, city/freeway driving, miles 350
Range, off pavement...............................226

Can Less Be More?
INTERNATIONAL SCOUT
Proving that you don't have to spend the maximum to go off road...

Getting by with less is something most of us do only when we have to. Making do with a bare minimum is something most of us don't care to know about, something which most of us will learn about only when we're forced to.

Don't look now, but the Reality of Less may be creeping up on us unannounced; indeed, may well already have crept up on us while we were gorging ourselves on cheap foreign oil, on plentiful electricity, on never-mind-the-cash-buy-it-on-credit acquisitiveness, on the beauty of seemingly endless wilderness, on the apparent fact—borne out by the frontier philosophy—that we don't have to worry about conservation, there's always more where that came from.

Well, we know now that the pioneers were wrong; there isn't necessarily always more of anything, and if we Americans learn anything as this faceless decade shudders its last few spasms of life, it is likely to be that unhappy, unwelcome lesson.

The "there's always more where that came from" philosophy certainly can be mirrored in the kinds of vehicles we've chosen to drive, and a case can be made that it's one of the reasons why stripper, barebones, four-cylinder International Scouts, like the object of this road test, aren't any more plentiful than they are. Nevermind that this particular Scout, equipped with a 4-speed transmission and International's 196-cid four-cylinder engine, pulled down 18.4 mpg during our city/highway driving cycle, and nevermind that its base price, while still representing a whole lot of dough, is well below what it would be if the truck was loaded to the gills with the usual options. It seems, at least to many folks, that form is more important to function. It's lots more fun, don't you know, to use—and to be seen in—a vehicle that

looks, you know, *trick*, a vehicle that will fairly leap whenever its gas pedal is stabbed. And if gas prices are on the rise and crude oil supplies are dwindling, well, that's the Ayatollah's fault, not ours. Maybe, maybe not; in any case, this whole line of reasoning has to be one of the biggest reasons why there aren't any more Scout Fours out there than there are. Consider the sales figures: In 1978 International sold 21,192 V-8-powered Scouts, and 2418 four-cylinder engined Scouts.

There is at least one good reason for this, of course. Not to put too fine a

point on it, it's that the V-8-powered Scouts are rather more pleasant to drive than the four-cylinder version is. For example, the previous Scout tested by this magazine was a 1979 Terra pickup powered by the 345-cid V-8. It weighed 320 pounds more than did this test Scout, but it winged through the quarter mile in 19.8 seconds, 3.2 seconds faster than the Four could manage, with a terminal speed of 69 mph, a full 10 miles per hour faster than the

Four could manage. Now, 69 mph in the quarter mile is not exactly burning up the pavement, and three seconds doesn't sound like much, but a quarter-mile difference of 10 mph? That's significant. What it means is that the Four-powered Scout barely will get out of its own way, and that kind of stodgy performance is not something too many of us would be willing to put up with. On the other hand, the V-8 drank fuel to the tune of 12.9 mpg, while the Four, as mentioned, obtained 18.4 mpg. The tanks on both our test Scouts contained 19 gallons of gas, and that means the V-8 could travel 245 miles between visits to the gas station, while the Four could do 350 miles between fill-ups. As this is being written, we're hearing news reports of three-hour waits in line at gas stations, and 95-cent-per-gallon gasoline. Do you think that maybe, just maybe, all this presages something? We do; we think that while maybe some folks will be willing to put up with the expense and inconvenience of gassing a tricky, monster-motor four wheeler just for the sake of personal pride, some other folks will commence casting about for something more economical in which to go off road. Maybe. The idea that We Are What We Drive is deeply ingrained; will gas prices that sound more like the price of imported perfume help us break that habit? Maybe, maybe no; only time will tell.

Those who do gravitate towards this most economical of Scouts will find, under its very Spartan exterior, the heart and soul of a pedigreed off-road explorer. The aspect of this machine that contributes the least to that aura, and which elicited the largest amount of curiosity, was that odd looking four-cylinder engine. It is odd looking because it is, effectively, International's defunct 392 V-8 minus one of its cylinder banks. So what you see when you open the hood is a bank of cylinders canted over to the right, and a whole lot of crankcase there where the

SCOUT

other bank of four cylinders is supposed to be. It has the same stroke as the 345-inch V-8, but a larger bore than any of the other Scout engines; the bore is 4.1 inches, the stroke 3.6 inches, making for a very smooth engine. This comes as a bit of a surprise because typically, four-cylinder engines of more than two liters or so (122 cid) vibrate like crazy because of what are called unbalanced secondary forces. The bore of the Scout's Four is so much bigger than its stroke, however, that these forces and the vibrations seem held to a minimum and the result is, for a four-cylinder, a fairly smooth, quiet motor. It doesn't make a whole lot of power, however, producing 76½ horsepower at 3600 rpm and 153.3 lbs-ft of torque at 2000 rpm. That of course is the sort of trade-off you have to expect for an engine that will pull a 4110-pound vehicle and get more than 18 mpg while it's

doing it. You'd expect to experience a certain amount of ennui while urging a 76-horsepower, 4100-pound machine up to the speed limit, and, right, you do. Likewise, for all the same reasons, you'd expect to have more than a little trouble keeping the beast on the speed limit once you began encountering headwinds, upward grades or both. The surprise is that because of the engine's generous levels of torque, and because at 55 mph the engine is turning at 2400 rpm, 400 rpm above its torque peak, this is nowhere nearly as big a problem as you would have expected. It *does* take forever to reach cruising speed; merging onto a busy freeway is no joke. Once you've reached the speed you want, however, the little Four has less of a problem than we expected maintaining that speed and in fact, mild grades hardly faze it. Steeper grades will slow it a bit and force the driver to bottom the gas pedal, but even at that, the truck doesn't slow as much as it might. The combination of a steep grade and a

headwind, however, is another story; that's more than the engine can cope with, and when you encounter such a situation, all you can do is sit back and be patient as you watch the speedometer needle slowly sink down from 55 mph to 50, and then to 45, where you might want to think about hitting third gear.

Third gear on our test Scout was delivered courtesy of a Warner T-19A close-ratio 4-speed. This is no light-duty, side-loading automotive transmission pressed into truck duty. Rather, it is a full-blown, top-loading truck transmission, a box with which shifts cannot be hurried, a box which provides solid, heavy detents between gears. It seemed reasonably well suited to the Four's power characteristics, and because of its ratios, a driver could run the vehicle up to 55 mph or so in third, and then shift into fourth, effectively using fourth gear as a sort of overdrive or cruising ratio. This transmission, by the way, though listed as a close-ratio box,

does not have ratios which are all *that* close. They are, in fact, rather nicely spaced so that there are no giant holes between gears, so that each shift seems to come at a point where the engine has the torque necessary to cope with the load it's been asked to pull. But the ratios are not so close that the vehicle is difficult to get rolling from a dead stop. For really hard going, the wide-ratio box, because it has a lower first gear, might be preferable to some drivers; even with the higher ratio first in the close-ratio transmission, however, the Scout never really ran out of low-end grunt no matter where we pointed it; it ran out of traction before that happened.

That brings us to the machine's drive-train, and one of the reasons traction with this particular Scout wasn't as good as it might have been. Equipped as it was with a 4-speed transmission, 2-speed transfer case, and locking hubs, the Scout was pretty much standard issue, and that means it did not possess the virtues of a limited-slip differential. That's too bad, because for the sorts of off roading the PV4 staff does in its evaluations of off-road vehicles, the limited-slip feature sometimes can be the difference between going where you want to go and not going there. This Scout was no exception, in that on exceptionally steep hills covered with loose dirt, if one front wheel and one rear wheel lost traction at the same time, all forward progress halted. Fortunately, limited slip is optional on International Scouts, and it is an option we would recommend. The non-limited-slip differentials in our test vehicle were of the 3.73 ratio, which makes the unit's economy all the more remarkable. Probably a higher gear would mean slightly better economy, but would not, we feel, be worth the loss in performance, which at best already is marginal. We'd also like to mention that our test Scout came to us with H78 x 15 tires. The last Scout we tested also had 3.73 differential gearsets, but had 10 x 15 tires. The difference this made in engine speed was exactly 100 rpm at 55 mph, the smaller tires running the engine at 2400 rpm, the larger tires doing so at 2300 rpm.

What all this means is that the drive-train on this particular Scout was pretty well thought out, and pretty well matched, was probably pretty much the sort of drivetrain you'd want to order up for yourself if this vehicle's economy appeals to you. If it does, please keep in mind that the economy numbers quoted here are for comparison purposes only. Real world usage typically knocks a few mpg from the numbers generated by our electronic testing equipment. We use that equipment so that readers can obtain an accurate comparison of the relative economy of various vehicles tested the same way, driven over the same routes. That being

---

Under the skin of this most economical of Scouts beats the heart and soul of a pedigreed off-road explorer.

SCOUT

the case, the Scout Four still looks pretty good.

There was just one glitch in the vehicle's driveability we should mention. Immediately off idle there was a hesitation in the Scout's engine which, on the street, was merely annoying. Off road, on any sort of grade, it was treacherous. It manifested itself whenever the vehicle's driver was sliding the clutch out, about to launch the vehicle. Stepping on the gas pedal would cause the engine to falter, if it was loaded at the same time. This means that to allow your right foot to jump right from the brake to the gas, and to let the clutch out at the same time, as you'd do when starting up on a grade, was to kill the engine. It happened every time. Could be this problem was exclusive to our test unit. Could be this problem could have been tuned out of the engine, maybe with something as simple as setting the idle speed up. In any case, it was extremely maddening.

Our test Scout may have been Spartan in trim and performance, but that doesn't mean it wasn't comfortable. Indeed, it was far more comfortable, even over relatively long hauls, than we would have guessed. Though that big, wide front bench seat doesn't provide

much lateral support, it does provide good thigh and lower back support, enough so that you're not aching and groaning by the time you reach your destination. Additionally, the Scout's interior is roomy enough so that head room, leg room, and shoulder room are available in copious quantities. And though the Scout's folding back seat does not supply the same comfort levels as the front seat, even it isn't too bad. Indeed, one of the Scout's strong points is that the back seat can, in the best station wagon tradition, be folded up against the back of the front seat to supply additional carrying capacity. The cargo area floor is covered by a serviceable rubber mat, so nothing anyone carries back there is likely to either scar the Scout or become scarred *by* the Scout.

In a continuation of that utilitarian theme, the front floor mats in this most basic of Scouts also are a sturdy rubber, and the seats are covered in a plain but seemingly sturdy vinyl. In fact, probably the Scout's floors could be hosed out when they get really dirty, as long as care was taken not to get the underdash area damp.

So there you are, decked out in your ultra-utilitarian, four-cylinder, sure-ain't - fast - but - sure - is - economical Scout. What you'll notice, as you shuttle along, is that while your econoScout

isn't even as fast as, say, a Land Cruiser, it's a bit more comfortable out on the road. It doesn't have the harshness that a Land Cruiser does; you don't feel every bump, every freeway expansion joint, and this is in spite of a Gross Vehicle Weight Rating (GVWR) of 6200 pounds. Additionally, the Scout's directional stability is of a high order, unlike that of certain other, shorter wheel-based, 4wd vehicles. This seems to be true of all the Scouts, no matter which engine lives in the engine bay. What it means is that when you get the vehicle up to cruising speed, the vehicle doesn't feel twitchy, doesn't feel as though it requires constant correction with the steering wheel. The Scout just goes where it's aimed, with a minimum of effort on the driver's part. It could be that that longer wheelbase might translate to a too-wide turning circle, something that would be a definite drawback in the outback. We did considerable back-country crawling with this Scout, and this never was a problem; we were able to traverse even the narrowest roads, make even the tightest corners, with a minimum of backing and filling.

What little backing and filling we did have to do with the Scout was made

---

With the Scout's tailgate opened and its rear seat folded down, a large amount of cargo capacity appears.

relatively easy by the vehicle's optional power steering, a $246 item. While the system is not up to the standards set by the units in use on General Motors' 4x4 vehicles, standards which include variable ratio and a high degree of sensitivity, the Scout power steering system does at least work well out in the rough. This of course is where this vehicle is most at home, and while the power steering system is too slow and too vague for our tastes when the vehicle is on pavement, its light touch was just what the doctor ordered once out in the rough-and-rocky.

To the everlasting credit of International, when you step into a showroom to buy a Scout, you aren't confronted with the necessity of having to pay extra for a full set of gauges with which to monitor the engine's welfare. Many other companies make the oil pressure gauge and ammeter optional equipment, offering instead, idiot lights as standard equipment. We'll take gauges every time. The way in which those gauges are laid out could perhaps be improved upon, since the gauges and speedometer aren't all instantly visible the way they should be, and the way they are in the best of the contemporary designs. But International builds trucks, and this design is anything but contemporary. For what it is, the Scout's dash works fairly well.

It should be mentioned that the Scout's steel top can be removed. It also should be mentioned that this is not a job we would attempt with anything less than, oh, say, a weekend, a full set of tools and a couple of big, strong helpers. Well, maybe top removal

isn't *quite* that bad, but neither is it a job you're likely to accomplish by yourself in a half hour.

Maybe what all this means is that this particular Scout, equipped with this particular drivetrain, is a compromise vehicle. Maybe what it means is that we off roaders *can* have our full-sized 4x4s and drive them too. Because while this Scout certainly isn't going to add too much to anybody's macho image, while it isn't beautiful enough to make the heads of beautiful women swivel in admiration, it certainly is capable of doing most anything most of the off roaders we know will ask of it, and of getting some pretty good gas economy while doing so. That fact right there has a certain kind of beauty to it. If this Scout doesn't have air conditioning, hydro-pneumatic suspension, wet bar, chrome ball knuckles, and limited-slip status symbols, it does what it is supposed to do, and it does so on a minimum of gasoline. It's the kind of vehicle

---

A peek under the front end of the Scout reveals nothing but heavy-duty metal and plenty of ground clearance (below). Inside (top), the basic Scout is nothing fancy, but provides a readable dash and plenty of comfort all the same.

The Scout's 196-cid Four is really just half of International's 392-cid V-8 big truck engine.

we're all going to have to get used to, the kind many of us have been waiting around for some smart manufacturer to start building. Surprise; International has been building the Scout in this combination for some time. We think, in a time when the Reality of Less seems to be rapidly gaining momentum, that this is a tremendous strike in International's favor, and in the favor of thinking off roaders. •

International Scouts For 1980

Basically unchanged for 1980, the Scout still has some interesting improvements . . .

BY DON E. BROWN

CHANGES FOR 1980 at International are few, but there are a couple of minor surprises—namely the dropping of the two-wheel-drive lineup and the addition of a turbocharger to the diesel engine.

The percent of production of two-wheel-drive Scouts to the four-wheel-drive version was always low and evidently became a non-profitable segment of the Scout lineup. It's a shame really, but probably won't be missed by a large portion of the market. After all, most people think of Scouts and 4wds as one and the same thing.

A quick look at other changes include a new transfer case, taller axle ratios, redesigned air conditioning unit, and larger capacity alternator. Power steering is now standard on all models, as is an automatic transmission on the Traveler. The grille has a new look with rectangular headlights. Standard manual locking hubs have larger finger openings for easier operation. And (finally), the 17-inch steering wheel has been replaced with a styled, 15-inch version. Other minor changes include: six new exterior colors, more corrosion protection, and turbine spoke wheels available with radial tires.

The biggest news, perhaps, is the fitting of a turbocharger to the diesel engine. One of the shortcomings in the aspirated diesel engine tested by PV4 in previous years was the lack of performance. For 1980, the diesel puts out 101 horsepower at 3800 rpm, approximately 20 percent better than last year's powerplant. Throttle response is said to be improved and preliminary tests by International indicate that fuel economy has not suffered and should be in the 21 to 25 mpg range. The diesel is available with one of two 4-speed manual transmissions. The standard axle ratio is a 3.73 with a taller 3.54 optional. The turbo has a preset maximum boost of 6.5 psi which is controlled by the wastegate. A number of internal modifications were made to the engine to accept the additional power supplied by the turbo. These include: an oil jet in each cylinder to help cool the pistons and three oil passages to connect the right and left oil galleries; larger capacity oil pump with an increased oil flow from 11.1 gallons per minute to 12.7; enlarged camshaft journals and cylinder head ports; redesigned crankshaft arms; and a larger air cleaner element.

The new transfer case, a Dana Model 300, has a low gear ratio of 2.62:1 to compensate for the taller axle ratios for slow off-road crawling. A full listing of engines and drivetrain combinations are contained in the accompanying chart.

The year 1980 should be another good year for International and with the taller gears and turbo diesel, the Scout lineup is even more in tune with the needs of the off-pavement enthusiast. •

1980 SCOUT ENGINE SPECIFICATIONS

Engine	Compression Ratio	Horsepower	Torque
196 Four	8.02:1	76.5 @ 3600	153.3 @ 2000
198 Six Diesel	22:1	101 @ 3800	175 @ 2200
304 V-8	8.19:1	122.3 @ 3400	226.3 @ 2000
345 V-8	8.05:1	148 @ 3600	265 @ 2000

POWERTRAIN AVAILABILITY

Engine	Transmission	Std. Axle	Opt. Axle
SCOUT II and TERRA			
196 Four	Manual 3-Spd	3.73	—
	Manual 4-Spd WR	3.73	3.54*
	Manual 4-Spd CR	3.54*	3.73
198 Six Diesel	Manual 4-Spd CR	3.73	3.54*
	Manual 4-Spd WR	3.73	3.54*
304 V-8	Manual 3-Spd	3.31	3.54
	Manual 4-Spd WR	3.31	3.54
	Manual 4-Spd CR	3.31	3.54
	Automatic 3-Spd	2.72**	3.31, 3.54
345 V-8	Manual 3-Spd	3.31	3.54
	Manual 4-Spd WR	3.31	3.54, 3.73***
	Manual 4-Spd CR	2.72**	3.54, 3.73***
	Automatic 3-Spd	2.72**	3.31, 3.54, 3.73***
TRAVELER			
198 Six Diesel	Manual 4-Spd CR	3.73	3.54*
	Manual 4-Spd WR	3.73	3.54*
304 V-8	Manual 4-Spd CR	3.31	3.54
	Automatic 3-Spd	2.72**	3.31, 3.54
345 V-8	Manual 4-Spd CR	2.72**	3.54, 3.73***
	Automatic 3-Spd	2.72**	3.31, 3.54, 3.73***

Engine	Transmission	Std. Axle	Opt. Axle
SS II			
196 Four	Manual 3-Spd	3.73	—
	Manual 4-Spd WR	3.73	3.54*
	Manual 4-Spd CR	3.54*	3.73
304 V-8	Manual 4-Spd WR	3.31	3.54
	Manual 4-Spd CR	3.31	3.54
	Automatic 3-Spd	2.72**	3.31, 3.54
345 V-8	Manual 4-Spd WR	3.31	3.54
	Manual 4-Spd CR	2.72**	3.54
	Automatic 3-Spd	2.72**	3.31, 3.54

* 3.54 ratio with 196 Four and 198 Six Diesel is not available with 10 x 15 tires
** 2.72 ratio with 304 V-8 and 345 V-8 is not available with 10 x 15 tires or tow package
*** 3.73 ratio with 345 V-8 requires tow package
WR—Wide-ratio transmission
CR—Close-ratio transmission
All axle ratios available with locking differential (rear only)

The Scout for 1980 gets a revised grille and a turbocharged diesel engine.

SCOUT
Reviseted

BY TOM MITCHELL

At a time when most manufacturers, especially American, are reviewing their product range with a very self-critical eye, International Harvester must be feeling a little more confident with their Scout models.

While Scout's direct competitors have grown fatter, thirstier and more gimmicky, International have clung to a fairly basic, function-only, design policy — a policy that, naturally enough, has brought some criticism and ridicule over the years from the press, prospective buyers and, of course, the opposition manufacturers. But, with soaring petrol costs becoming a motor vehicle salesman's nightmare, the engineers at GM, Chrysler, Ford and American Motors are scrambling (scalpel in hand) to the design studios and effectively chopping off every petrol guzzling feature possible.

No American car builder can ignore fuel economy as the US Government is enforcing CAFE (Corporate Average Fuel Efficiency) and the penalties for non-compliance are severe.

Here's what has already happened to some makes, and what will shortly apply to all:

(a) Full-time 4WD is axed and will be replaced by part-time. Scout already has a part-time system.

Left to right: Scout Traveler amidst the black Blue Mountains west of Sydney. Light blue interior was cool and pleasant. Note cup holders in console lid and comfy SAAS steering wheel. Rear seat looks thin but is quite comfortable. Big 15 x 10 tyre still leaves a huge amount of room for luggage. Bold SS grille gives Scout a rugged, no-nonsense appearance. Rear of Traveler is clean and uncluttered. Like the roof, the full lift-up rear door is made of a special plastic.

SCOUT REVISITED

(b) Free wheeling hubs will be standard equipment. Scout has automatic free wheeling hubs as standard.

(c) Excessive body panels which add weight and poor aerodynamics to be reduced and redesigned. Scout's body panels are already smooth and uncluttered and do not exaggerate the vehicle's size.

(d) Large block V8 engines and four barrel carburettors will mostly be discontinued. Scout's largest engine is the 345V8 2-barrel that is designed to run on standard grade fuel.

(e) Taller differential ratios will replace "gravedigger" ratios as standard. Scout's ratio (in Australia) is a fairly tall 3.07:1.

So, it can be seen that in the league of BIG four wheel drive vehicles, the "old fashioned" Scout could just be the "ideal" that all the others are striving towards.

BUSHDRIVER carried out a very comprehensive test on the Scout Traveltop back in 1978, and you may remember that we were fairly impressed with the vehicle — especially some of its unique features. Of course, there were defects: the 1978 suspension, for instance, was a mobile disaster area! But the good things that stuck in my mind, like the no-nonsense body panels, the big, quiet, slow-revving engine, the absolutely superb automatic and the excellent off-road manoeuvrability are still the big selling points for International Harvester.

The 1979-80 series of Scouts for Australia are an improvement on the 1978 model we tested some time ago. International have upgraded the springs and shock absorbers, changed the steering geometry, replaced the dual exhaust with a very "throaty"-sounding single system, improved the sealing around the rear windows and back doors, and have all vehicles Endrusted before they leave the warehouse.

BUSHDRIVER was fortunate to have the use of two Scouts, a 100" WB Traveltop and a 118" WB Traveler, over an extended period of time. Both vehicles were provided by Suzuki-Jeep-Scout dealer Pete Geoghegan at Haberfield, Sydney. The Traveltop was used as everyday transport in and around the city, several runs to country towns and a special economy type run to Canberra and back. Non-standard equipment on the Traveltop included radial tyres, chrome spoke wheels, velour upholstery, air conditioning, carpet, radio stereo, SS grille, bull bar and Dura-torque tow bar.

With its subtle decals, the pale yellow Scout Traveltop was quite an eye catcher. However, the thing that impressed me most was the steering. Geoghegans had had the renowned C & E Steering of Ashfield in Sydney alter the steering geometry, and the results were amazing. In our last Scout the heavy understeer and vagueness had been a major disappointment, but, in this vehicle, the improvement was very noticeable. Even though there are still too many turns lock to lock and, like many other 4WD's they can be heavy to park, the Scout was really pleasant to wheel around.

Because of the growing emphasis on fuel saving, our main test of the Traveltop concentrated on economy. Our run from Sydney to Canberra, with four people on board, was paced to use as little throttle as possible. In other words, we were careful not to exceed the speed limit and to try to anticipate stops and overtaking situations long before they occurred, so that slow, gentle throttle openings were possible. The result of this particular run was a fairly impressive 16.5 l/100 km (17 mpg): nowhere near Suzuki economy, of course, but remember this is a 5.6 litre vehicle weighing in at nearly two tonnes unladen, and that four people and their luggage can't sit in a Zook anyway!

The run to Canberra impressed us, but the trip back to Sydney amazed me. For comparison's sake, we decided to come home "in a hurry". In other words, to drive without any regard for economy. We also ran the AMC air conditioning non-stop, and although we didn't purposely exceed the speed limit, I must admit that here and there I fudged where it was perfectly safe to do so. The result? The fastest time I have ever recorded in a Canberra-to-Sydney run, and a staggeringly low 18.6 l/100 km (15 mpg) fuel consumption! If you don't believe that figure to be good, try the same test with a Toyota or Nissan or even with four people crammed into a Daihatsu. Don't forget to leave the Daihatsu's air conditioner on too!

Shortly after this test I was interested to read in Time magazine that US aircraft companies support the theory that air conditioners in cars can *save* fuel. They have run tests to show that the improved aerodynamics of having the windows closed, more than makes up for the small power-robbing effects of the air conditioning equipment. Naturally, this applies only to open-road motoring and not when you are sitting in peak hour traffic jams.

All in all, the Scout Traveltop was a pleasure to use. The average consumption over a period of suburban running was 4.89 l/100 km (14 mpg) and we had no mechanical problems apart from the right rear wheel which kept locking up under hard braking. I would still have preferred heavier shock absorbers, especially on the rear, and I would also recommend replacing the headlights with something a little brighter.

Following our acquaintance with the Traveltop, we stepped straight into its big sister, the 118" wheelbase Traveler. I suppose you could say that the most unique thing about the Traveler is that it has big insides. The amount of room available for five people and their gear is amazing. Bear in mind that this model is no wider or longer than a Toyota Landcruiser station wagon and is, in fact, several inches lower. The flat floor, huge opening back door and relatively "thin" rear seat give the Traveler a very positive advantage over the carrying capacity of the Toyota/Jeep Cherokee/Range Rover opposition.

Our particular Traveler test vehicle was equipped with power steering, SAAS steering wheel, white spoke-wheels and Goodyear Tracker tyres.

The power steering is interesting in that it is a conversion carried out by Ian Hand of Off Road Equipment at Taren Point in Sydney. Ian utilised all genuine I.H. parts and even the steering box is from an American left-hand-drive Scout. The conversion, at around $1400, is expensive, but it does make it easy for the lady of the house to wiggle the vehicle in and out of car parks etc. In fact, I would have to say that the steering is possibly too light. But, naturally, that depends on what you have been used to driving previously.

We used the Traveler to tour some of the trails in the Blue Mountains west of Sydney. This area was chosen as, a few weeks before, thousands of acres had been completely burnt out in major bushfires. In fact, in many places, the bright blue Scout was the only sign of colour on the ground. My wife thought it looked like a colour transparency superimposed on a giant black and brown negative.

The Traveler handled the off-road situations quite well, although selecting low range took a little practice until I acquired the knack. We certainly didn't attempt any hard core situations, but the Scout always showed a willingness to push on regardless. Once again, I was disappointed with the rear shocks. Where they had been acceptable in the short Traveltop, they were inadequate in the longer and heavier Traveler. Bumps and corrugations had the rear wheels dancing all over the place. I think it is about time International pulled their fingers out on this problem: no other 4WD sold in Australia has such an obvious flaw, so why should a vehicle distributed by Australia's leading truck

Left to right: Traveltop beside the 195-metre high Telecom tower atop Black Mountain, ACT. Short "bobtail" styling of Traveltop makes parking and off road manoeuvres a breeze. Alongside Canberra's War Memorial. Note good approach and departure angles. A visit to 2001. The ultra-modern shopping and commercial centre of Belconnen City, ACT.

organisation?

While the power steering made off-road driving easy, I wasn't too impressed by the tyres. I think the standard Goodyear Town & Country version would have done everything the wider Goodyear Trackers did. To my mind, money spent on a "cosmetic" tyre like the Tracker is a waste of money. If you need large tyres, there are far superior types available.

Over a period of two days that combined good, sealed road and mild off-road travel, the Scout averaged 21.4 l/100 km (13 mpg).

The long wheelbase Traveler hasn't got the "chuckability" of the shorter Traveltop, and surprisingly, the extra 18 inches of wheelbase doesn't make a vast difference in ride quality — not that the Scout has poor ride anyway.

Although I preferred the cosier atmosphere of the Traveltop, the Traveler would, obviously, be near perfect for a long trip or for hauling a big boat or caravan. With the exception of the shock absorbers, the Scout gives a definite impression of indestructibility. Sure, it's not fancy like the Cherokee or stylish like the Range Rover, and the instrument panel is a mess, but the overall impression is of a "comfortable truck". And, to many people, the advantages of owning an International truck with their genuine reliability, vast spares and service network, and no-nonsense design, far outweigh the style and sometimes pseudo comfort of other brands. 🚜

International Scout II Turbo Diesel

A closet Conestoga that breaks the 20-mpg barrier.

• Today's Bronco is a hobbyhorse, the Blazer has all but given up the trail for life on asphalt, and the Ramcharger's been dehorned. Manufacturers have wethered most of the hard-boned crankiness from their trucks to make them attractive to the vast throngs that love the macho look as long as it's comfy. So if it's a genuine, solid-axle, strong-like-dirt *truck* you're after, your choices are limited. AMC's still in the business with its basic Jeep products. And there's International Harvester, the one and only light-truck builder that has no car division to cloud its thinking and hone down hard edges. IH's Scout II is a truck the way they used to build them, which is in no small part due to the fact that, even though the original has sired a junior, the II's been screwed together pretty much the same way for more than nine years. It's noisy, crude at times, never luxurious in any sense of the word, but very good at being a truck.

Which is *not* to say that progress has passed the Scout by. Right here on these pages we have International's two-pronged stab at a future of federally required fuel efficiency. It packs the two hottest buzzwords of the business under its hood: turbocharging and diesel. The two work hand in hand to boost the Scout's trucky character right up to Peterbilt status, producing 20-mpg fuel economy in the process.

International has offered a diesel option in the Scout for three years now, and 1980's 6-33T version is a logical extension of the program. The engine is basically the same Nissan 3.3-liter (198 cubic inch) six-cylinder diesel available since 1976 in normally aspirated form, but now it has an AiResearch TO3 turbocharger to pack intake air to a 6.5-pound pressure. The turbo-diesel makes 101 hp at 3800 rpm, and 175 pounds-feet of torque at 2200 rpm, which is roughly 25 percent more oomph than last year's diesel. There's also a larger oil pump with 14 percent more flow capacity, an oil-jet system plumbed into the block to cool the pistons, and a larger oil cooler to reject more heat to the atmosphere. The crankshaft and piston rings are beefier, the camshaft journals are larger, and both the cylinder head's intake ports and the air filter have been enlarged to handle more airflow with the turbocharger.

The Nissan 6-33 was a truck engine from its inception, and it will never, ever, let you forget that fact. The starting ritual involves pushing a very stiffly sprung glow-plug button and waiting a while before cranking. Twisting the key initiates what sounds like jackhammer warfare under the hood, while the tailpipe starts spewing a milky-white smoke screen dense enough to cover a whole invasion force. After a minute or so, the exhaust fog turns into a fine black mist, the din subsides to a dull clatter, and you're ready to thunder about town on not very much diesel fuel. To shut it down, you pull what looks and operates like a choke knob.

The particular Scout we tested had a close-ratio four-speed gearbox, which means that first is almost as useful for driving as for stump extracting. It's one of those high-effort, long-stick transmissions with so much detent action that ladies around the office tend to grab the eight-ball-sized shift knob with both hands. You use the accelerator pedal like a go/no-go switch, and shifts are best snapped off smartly, as with a ten-speed RoadRanger, because the engine is happiest on the high plateau of its torque curve, which is between 1600 and 2200 rpm. Just like a real eighteen-wheeler.

Unlike turbo cars, the Scout offers no thrill of boost swelling up under the hood, in fact no clue at all that turbine wheels are spinning to speed you along your way. Nor is there a boost gauge or a tach to suggest what's really happening in the powerhouse. Though former diesel Scouts were downright poky, the new turbo truck does a good job of keeping pace with traffic. Its acceleration times are a close match to the VW Rabbit Diesel's, although wind resistance keeps the Scout from breaking the 83-mph barrier.

All of which is quite tolerable because this is a truck with plenty of true truck grit for entertainment in lieu of breakneck speed. It comes together en route to the secret fishing hole when you shift the transfer case into low range, effectively multiplying the diesel's torque curve by a factor of 2.62. All four wheels pull reassuringly when twisted by the big gear, but the transfer case does have its evil side as well. It buzzes unmercifully on-road, and whines like a siren off-road.

The ride and handling won't scotch the

Vehicle type: front-engine, 4-wheel-drive, 5-passenger, 2-door truck
Price as tested: $12,638 (base price: $9861)
Engine type: turbocharged diesel, 6-in-line, water-cooled, cast-iron block and head, fuel injection
Displacement . . . . .198.5 cu in, 3253cc
Power (SAE net) . . . . .101 bhp @ 3800 rpm
Transmission . . . . .4-speed, with 2-speed transfer case
Wheelbase . . . . .100.0 in
Length . . . . .166.2 in
Curb weight . . . . .4300 lbs
Acceleration, 0–60 mph . . . . .18.2 sec
Standing ¼-mile .21.0 sec @ 64 mph
Braking, 70–0 mph . . . . .264 ft
Top speed . . . . .83 mph
EPA estimated fuel economy .20 mpg

fun of it all *if* you stay with a conservatively equipped Scout, as we did. Our test truck started with a 100-inch wheelbase (118-inch versions are called Terra in pickup form and Traveler in a wagon body style; all Scouts have 4wd). What we had in mind was optimum on-road/moderate off-road use, so the package was shod with Goodyear Tiempo radial tires and fitted with base springs and heavy-duty shock absorbers. Not what you'd Scout the Amazon with, but quite happy at casual off-road excursions and surprisingly content on the way home on pavement. Power steering is standard in all Scouts this year to make them manageable without that queasy, out-of-control feeling that used to be an essential part of the truck experience during fast driving.

International went further by dressing up our tester in fake allen-head screws (in the steering-wheel hub), fake turbine blades (in the fake aluminum wheels), and real air conditioning, none of which altered the Scout's essence a bit. It was still a pure, unadulterated truck. Which is a nice thing to have around if you really need one. —*Don Sherman*

Intl Scout Terra

IH merges the diesel's seeming indestructibility and economy with the turbocharger's power boost...

International Harvester has some good news for you, and some bad news. The good news is that its 1980 Scout, powered by a turbocharged diesel, will get in excess of 18 mpg in everyday, real-world driving and still provide adequate performance. The bad news is that the thing is as noisy as a steel mill, and that it isn't as easy or pleasant to drive as even a similarly equipped gas-powered Scout.

Better than 18 mpg in everyday driving, you say? Right, it's true. This new Scout, powered by Nissan's six-cylinder, in-line, turbocharged 198-cid diesel, averaged 18.3 mpg while being flogged through PV4's usual road testing procedure, with a low of 15.3 and a high of 20.9 mpg. And those figures, friends, were generated by real-world means, not by our gasoline flow-meter which we use, on gas-powered rigs, to generate fuel economy comparison figures. We don't know about you, but we'd call any standard-sized 4x4 capable of that kind of economy genuine Good News.

There is other good news, as well, and it has to do with the fact that this diesel actually will get out of its own way, actually is capable of something which will pass for mild performance. That's what we'd call a breakthrough, nevermind that the thing isn't as plush, quiet, or smooth as some other vehicles.

The basic vehicle for this test was, as you can see from the accompanying pictures, a Scout Terra pickup. That's the long-wheelbase version of the Scout, the same basic chassis upon which the Scout Traveler is built. You should note that its wheelbase is long only by comparison: At 118 inches, the wheelbase is just slightly more than an inch longer than that of the short-wheelbase Ford pickup, and just a half-inch shorter than Chevy's short-wheel base 4x4 pickup. This basic Terra was pretty much loaded, despite its plain looks. Most obvious are the stripe package and the 10x15 off-road tire and wheel package. Also included were air conditioning, AM/FM/stereo radio, automatic locking hubs, heavy-duty front springs, and other items. This vehicle also was equipped with the turbocharged diesel engine and that is the item most folks are curious about.

The engine is the Nissan 6-33 which, under natural aspiration, develops 81 horsepower at 3800 rpm. Now, 81 horsepower really isn't enough to provide the amounts of power most folks demand so the canny folks at IH have added a turbocharger to the package. Actually what they've done involves more than merely bolting a turbo onto the engine, and we'll get to that in a minute. First, a disclaimer: to many buyers and manufacturers alike, the word "turbocharger" is magic, kind of like Abbra-Ka-Dabbra. Wave the magic turbocharger technology at an engine, so popular belief has it, and you turn a mundane economotor into an instant fire-breathing beast capable of launching a vehicle into the 14-second quarter-mile bracket. Well, maybe that's true in some cases, but it isn't necessarily true in this case. Because what the addition of the AiResearch TO-3 turbo unit to

the Nissan diesel does is raise its level of performance from nearly unacceptable to more-or-less acceptable. With the turbo and its 6.5 pounds of manifold pressure, the engine grinds out 101 hp at 3800 rpm, and 178 lb-ft of torque at 2200 rpm, an increase of 37 lb-ft. This idea of using a turbocharger to fatten up the torque curve and add just a bit more horsepower is exactly the way turbochargers have been used on diesel truck, boat and industrial engines for years now and it works very well on the Scout's diesel.

When you add a turbocharger to an engine, you quite naturally increase the loads the engine's pistons, rods and bearings will have to accept. Not recognizing this, or recognizing this and failing to do anything about it, can result in an engine's early demise, particularly if the driver enjoys the boot a turbo gives to acceleration and uses that boot with any frequency. Happily, the engineers at IH did recognize this, and have stressed the Nissan engine in a number of ways. To reduce the likelihood of pistons melted by the additional heat generated by a boosted engine, a cooling jet of oil is sprayed onto the tops of each of the pistons each cycle. To provide for this increased oil demand, and to provide for lubrication of the turbo unit itself, the engine's oil pump capacity has been increased, and its drive spindle strengthened. Additional camshaft bearing surface has been added, the crankshaft arms have been redesigned for increased strength, the cylinder head ports have been enlarged a bit, the oil engine cooler capacity has been increased, and a larger air cleaner element has been added. International says that these changes insure that the turbocharged engine will last every bit as long as the naturally aspirated version of the same engine and while we see no real reason not to believe that, we'd still not recommend retreat from your usual skepticism of manufacturers' claims.

So we've got a turbocharged diesel engine pulling around a Scout.

TERRA

How can we quantify its performance levels? As usual, we do this at the drag strip, where the diesel Scout toured the quarter-mile in 22.9 seconds at a speed of 59 mph. Not exactly eyeball-flattening acceleration, eh? By way of comparison, we'll note that a '77 Scout diesel did the quarter in 24.9 seconds at 54 mph; a '78 Dodge W-150 powered by a diesel did the quarter in 24.9 seconds at 58 mph; and a '79 Scout powered by the 196-cid Four did the quarter in 23 seconds at 59 mph. The '77 Scout diesel, by the way, averaged 20.6 mpg while the Scout Four obtained 18.4 mpg. The numbers by themselves indicate that the performance levels of the Four- and diesel-powered Scouts are nearly identical, but there really is considerable difference in the way the diesel responds to throttle inputs at traffic speeds. The little Four gets the Scout

The 1980 Terra is basically unchanged from its form of years past. It does sport a re-designed grille (left) and interesting side stripes (above).

away from stops a bit more briskly than the diesel, but the diesel seemed far more capable of passing traffic and pulling grades than the Four was, possessing a firm acceleratory surge when the throttle is banged open and the turbocharger awakened.

Another area we quantify is that of noise. Using a decibel meter, we check to see how much noise each vehicle we test produces. As you can see from the figures in the accompanying data panel, the Scout makes lots of noise. Much of that is your standard diesel engine racket, in quantities that'll make you think you've got a front-row seat in a boiler factory, or maybe at a train wreck. Some of it also comes from a very rattley transfer case shift lever. Each source by itself is enough to give driver and passenger

alike a case of mild nervous craziness, but both together are enough to make driver and passenger absolutely nutso. There is some insulation, a low-rise layer of foam directly under the Scout's rubber floor covering, but a good spray application of insulation on the underside of the Scout's hood and on its firewall probably would help a great deal. There would seem to be little one can do about the transfer case shifter's rattle, except to strap it to the regular shift lever with a nice, fat rubber band, or constantly lean one's hand or foot against it.

The '80 diesel Scout is available in two drivetrain packages: one uses a close-ratio 4-speed transmission and the other uses a wide-ratio 4-speed. Axle ratios of 3.54 and 3.73 are available as well. Given the '80 Scout's low-range transfer case ratio of 2.62:1, and given first gear ratios of 4.02:1 on the close-ratio box and 6.32:1 on the wide-ratio box, this means an ultimate, low-gear-low-range gear ratio of 39.16:1 with

The most interesting feature of our test Scout undoubtedly was its turbocharged diesel engine. To start it, the glowplug button is held down until the red light right next to it winks out. Then the key is twisted until the starter is engaged and the diesel stutters into smokey life.

the close-ratio transmission and 58.6:1 with the wide-ratio trans. It was our experience that with the close-ratio box and the 3.73 gears, with which our test Scout was equipped, even in low-low we found it difficult to throttle back enough to go suitably slowly over really rough areas. The alternate axle ratio/transmission choice surely would solve that problem. For folks who really like to do back-country rock crawling, or who use their Scouts for heavy farm chores, the alternate axle/transmission option of wide ratio trans and 3.73 gear sets might be the way to go. Be advised that the trailer towing package is not available with this package.

You Scout fans probably are aware that the '80 Scouts use the new Dana 300 transfer case instead of the older Dana 20 case. The 300 case has a lower low-range ratio than the 20 (2.62:1 vs. 2.02:1), it is lighter, weighing 77 pounds, has a revised shifting design, and uses helical-cut gears to reduce noise. The lower low-range ratio is welcome, and so would be easier shifting. We found, however, that while the 300 transfer in our test Terra seemed a bit easier to shift than the older 20s in past test vehicles, shifting it still occasionally required considerable effort. Additionally, when cruising along in low range and in the upper transmission gears, gear howl still is quite evident.

Our test Scout came to us wearing the optional Warn automatic locking hubs. Whichever transmission/differential option you choose, we can suggest that this is an option you should consider. It may well be that you'll decide, as we have, that automatic hubs are every bit as handy as full-time four-wheel drive. Certainly they're different, and certainly they take some getting used to. The idea, of course, is that automatic hubs are—automatic. You can climb out of your vehicle and dial them into locked position, but you don't necessarily have to, particularly when you're not going to be involved in prolonged amounts of off-road running. All you have to do to use them is shift your vehicle's transfer case into 4x4; when the front axle begins to drive, the hubs engage and stay engaged until you either shift back into 4x2 or until you lift off the gas pedal.

This business of the hubs disengaging when the driver lifts is the part which, for us, took some getting used to. This was most noticeable, in the test Terra, when clawing our way down steep inclines under engine compression. This is the sort of thing which naturally disengages the hubs; so we'd aim the Scout's nose over a brink, proceed downward a few feet, hear a muted sort of mechanical clank from the front axle, and then accelerate downhill quite rapidly. Why accelerate? Because the front wheels were carrying most of the Terra's weight, and doing most of the work. When the hubs disengaged, the vehicle went automatically back into two-wheel drive, and the very light rear end did not possess enough weight to provide sufficient traction for the rear wheels. Thus the rears would start sliding, without causing the engine to turn any faster, and the Scout would pick up downhill speed.

The fix for this of course is either to dial the hubs into lock, or to ride the brakes down the hill. Which course you choose depends upon your level of laziness.

This lock/unlock behavior was really the only drawback (if you really can call it a drawback) we could find with the auto-hubs. Considering full-time 4x4's biggest drawback (the expense of operating a vehicle so equipped), we'll take automatic hubs any day.

A couple of interesting points about this particular test vehicle have to do with what happened when we began climbing hills with it. First of all, when we got it pointed up an incline that was just a bit too steep, it would puke engine oil out of its dipstick tube. Not just a little oil, either; rather, lots of oil exited the crankcase, enough to give us an idea of what a leak in the Alaskan pipeline might look like. We lost two quarts from the diesel's 9.2-quart crankcase in no time at all. Secondly, while the diesel engine will run happily at nearly any incline angle as long as it is given a bit of throttle, it refused to idle on even a slight incline. Once it died it would always restart easily, and run happily at just a few rpm above idle, but any attempt to

allow a standard idle while on anything but flat ground resulted in a dead engine. An IH spokesman told us these problems have not been found in other '80 diesel-powered Scouts, and probably can be tuned out of our test vehicle.

We also discovered while climbing the Scout that at least with these particular tires (10 x 15 Goodyear Tracker A/Ts) once a certain amount of steepness was encountered, the vehicle would bog down. Plenty of engine left, but not enough traction for our preferred method of slowly crawling over every obstacle, no matter how steep, without a spin of a wheel. When this happened, our only recourse was to bomb the steep area, take it as fast (or as slow) as seemed prudent. Probably a really good set of off-road radial tires would help in this department.

Indeed, with those exceptions, the Terra literally went everywhere we pointed it, and often did so with greater ease than we would have expected, all the while burning hardly any fuel. Working that diesel engine does take some getting used to, though. For instance, the thing is so torquey that it is possible to fall into the trap of relying on low-rpm torque when there really isn't any left. Re-

Nissan, the builder of Datsun cars, also is the builder of the Scout's diesel. The engine has received the full turbo treatment. Oil injection to the piston tops, improved crankshaft strength, and other changes, including greater oil pump strength and capacity, ought to insure the engine's longevity.

ally, the bottom several hundred rpm can't be expected to pull the Terra, even when shifted into low range. Again, here was the sort of situation where we found ourselves wishing for a first gear of really low ratio so we could keep speed over rough country down and engine rpm up just a bit. Every other situation, tight turns, bumps, long pulls, the whole bit—was met by the Scout's fierce ability to plow ahead like the piece of heavy-duty equipment it is.

Alas, this heavy-duty aspect of the Scout's personality means that out on the highway it is not a particularly pleasant vehicle to drive. The 4-speed transmission's shifter is stiff, the truck's acceleration is—well, stately, and its ride, while being rela-

With the exception of a new, smaller-diameter steering wheel, the Scout's interior basically is unchanged for '80.

tively smooth and controlled, still leaves a bit to be desired. The vehicle's handling can't be faulted; corners are taken at a near level attitude, the pavement handling showed us a bit of understeer, while dirt handling showed us a bit of oversteer, which could be provoked with a bit of throttle. Indeed, some of the most fun we had with the Scout involved play-racing it down a curvy, suitably deserted, dirt mountain road where, thanks to its excellent Saginaw power steering, it felt very secure and predictable, never bottoming and never riding so harshly its occupants felt the need for kidney belts.

Getting the Terra rolling and shutting it down at the end of a trip proved to require unorthodox methodology. Hot starts are no problem; you just twist the steering column-mounted key and go. Cold starts, on the other hand, require a few more steps than gas-powered trucks call for. First step is to turn the ignition key on; second step is to push in a rubber-covered button below and to the left of the steering column. Third step is to hold that button down until the red glow plug light next to it is extinguished. Fourth step is to turn the key into starter mode and get the engine cranking over. Fifth step is, once the diesel coughs into life, to keep it

The Scout's optional 10 x 15 tires were Goodyear Tracker A-Ts. We suspect an off-road radial is a better choice.

turning, not always easy. Sixth step is to drive away as quickly as the cold diesel engine will allow so as to escape the huge cloud of grey white exhaust smoke which billows out in the Terra's stern during the earliest phases of cold-start diesel combustion.

Shutting the Terra's diesel down is nowhere nearly that complicated. You just turn the key off and pull the strangler, a knob below and to the right of the steering column, which closes the engine's air intake. The interesting part about this is that with this system, it is possible to shut off the ignition switch, remove the key, lock the vehicle up and walk away from it with the engine still running.

Our test truck was equipped with the optional cloth seat trim package, and the bench seats covered with a plaid fabric were attractive as well as comfortable. The new-for-this-year, small-diameter, padded sports-type steering wheel is a welcome and long-overdue addition, and visibility is good, though for off roading, the Terra's hood line remains high enough so that when cresting steep brows at the top of climbs, it's a good idea to dismount to make sure which way the road goes. One item of interest concerning our test Terra was the way its doors and windows fit. With the windows rolled partially down, the doors could be shut quite

easily, but with them fully closed, the top part of the metal window frame contacted a portion of the white fiberglass top, interfering with the closing action to the extent that white scrape marks from the top remained on the black window rims. At the same time, this particular Terra came to us with rather fewer air leaks around the doors and windows than past Scouts/Terras have had, so we're lead to suspect that there may a good deal of manufacturing variation in the way these fiberglass tops fit.

The story concerning the rest of the Terra's interior is unchanged since our last Terra road test (February, 1979). The dash layout, with its full complement of gauges and off-center, awkwardly placed speedometer remain as before, as do all the rest of the controls. As in the past Scouts, the hood latch is inside the vehicle, and as before, this particular Terra's hood did not fit tightly, shaking violently at its rear corners when the vehicle was underway.

What we've tried to describe for you here is what we think is a fairly crude vehicle, crude at least by the increasingly automotive-oriented comfort levels of the rest of the light-truck industry. But then that isn't exactly right either, because we remain impressed, as we always have been, by the vehicle's toughness, its proven off-road capabilities, and its truly exceptional economy. We wouldn't suggest for a moment that this particular Terra represents the ultimate refinement of the 4wd vehicle, or that it is a machine with universal appeal, but we would suggest that its presence in the off-road world indicates that International remains hard at work—and is making considerable progress—on the problem of producing sturdy, efficient off-road vehicles. We would also suggest that there is a small but solid market out there in off-road-land for a character vehicle just like this one. •

With a GVWR of 6200 pounds, the Terra is capable of hauling substantial loads in its deep double-wall cargo bed, though the spare tire mount intrudes upon available space (left). The optional bed rails on the test Terra were equipped with sliding tie-downs (above).

INTERNATIONAL SCOUT TERRA
Specifications And Performance

PRICES

Basic list, FOB Fort Wayne, Ind.

Scout Terra Diesel	$10,145
Scout Traveler	$8783
Scout II	$7748
Scout Terra (gas)	$7649

Standard Equipment . .198-cid, turbocharged diesel engine, 4-spd transmission, four-wheel drive, power steering, manual locking hubs, 3200-lb-ft axle, 3500-lb rear axle, power brakes, white fiberglass top, left and right air intake vents, heater / defroster, bed-mounted spare tire carrier, windshield-mounted rear-view mirror, 11-inch clutch, 625-amp battery, 40-amp alternator, glow-plug indicator, cargo area light

GENERAL

Curb weight, lb (test model)	4030
Weight distribution, %, front / rear	61 / 39
GVWR (test model)	6200
Optional GVWRs	NA
Wheelbase, in. (test model)	118
Track, front / rear	57.1 / 57.1
Overall length	183
Overall height	66
Overall width	70
Overhang, front / rear	21.5 x 42.25
Approach angle, degrees	36
Departure angle, degrees	25

Ground clearances (test model):

Front axle	9.25
Rear axle	9.25
Oil pan	15
Transfer case	13
Fuel tank	15.25
Exhaust system (lowest point)	15.75
Fuel tank capacity (U.S. gal.)	19
Auxiliary	NA

ACCOMMODATION

Standard seats	vinyl-covered bench
Optional seats	cloth bench seats, vinyl bucket seats, cloth bucket seats
Headroom, in.	35.5
Accelerator pedal to seatback, max	41
Steering wheel to seatback, max	16
Seat to ground	34
Floor to ground	18.5

Unobstructed load space (length x width x height) . . . . .71.5 x 39.25* x 21.25
Tailgate (width x height) . . . . .50.75 x 21.25
*Limited by spare tire mount

INSTRUMENTATION

Instruments . . . . .speedometer, odometer, fuel gauge, temp gauge, oil pressure gauge, ammeter
Warning lights . . . . . .front axle engaged, high beam, turn signals
Optional . . . . .NA

ENGINES

Standard	196-cid Four
Bore x stroke	4.12 x 3.65
Compression ratio	8.02:1
Net horsepower @ rpm	76.5 @ 3600
Net torque @ rpm, lb-ft	153.3 @ 2000
Type fuel required	unleaded

Optional	198-cid Diesel Six, $2496*
Bore x stroke, in.	3.27 x 3.94
Compression ratio	22:1
Net horsepower @ rpm	101 @ 3800
Net torque @ rpm, lb-ft	175 @ 2200
Type fuel required	diesel no. 2

*Includes large battery, tilt wheel, power steering

Optional	304-cid V-8, $368
Bore x stroke, in.	3.875 x 3.218

Compression ratio	8.19:1
Net horsepower @ rpm	122.3 @ 3400
Net torque @ rpm, lb-ft	226.3 @ 2000
Type fuel required	unleaded

Optional	345-cid V-8, $499
Bore x stroke, in.	3.875 x 3.656
Compression ratio	8.05:1
Net horsepower @ rpm	150 @ 3600
Net torque @ rpm, lb-ft	265 @ 2000
Type fuel required	unleaded

DRIVETRAIN

Standard transmission	3-spd manual
Clutch dia., in.	11-inch
Transmission ratios: 3rd	1:1
2nd	1.55:1
1st	2.997:1
Synchromesh	all forward

Optional	4-spd manual, close-ratio, $216*
Transmission ratios: 1st	4.02:1
2nd	2.41:1
3rd	1.41:1
4th	1:1
Synchromesh	all forward

*Standard with diesel, wide-ratio 4-spd available with diesel at no extra cost

Optional	4-spd manual, wide-ratio, $172
Transmission ratios: 1st	6.32:1
2nd	3.09:1
3rd	1.68:1
4th	1:1
Synchromesh	all forward

Rear axle type	semi-floating hypoid
Final drive ratios	2.72, 3.31, 3.54, 3.73
Overdrive	NA
Free-running front hubs	standard
Limited slip differential	yes, $199
Transfer case	Dana 300 2-spd
Transfer case ration	high-1:1, low-2.62:1

CHASSIS & BODY

Body / frame	welded steel / ladder frame
Brakes (std)	power disc / drum
Brake swept area, sq in.	327.8
Swept area / ton (max load)	105.74
Power brakes	standard
Steering type (std)	recirculating ball
Power steering	standard*
Power steering ratio	17.5:1
Turning circle, ft	38 feet 10 inches (33 feet 10 inches on Scout II
*Standard with diesel engine	
Wheel size (std)	15 x 6

Optional wheel sizes	15 x 7, 15 x 8
Tire size (std)	H78 x 15
Optional tire sizes	P225 / 75R x 15, 10 x 15

SUSPENSION

Front suspension	beam axle, leaf springs, tube shocks
Front axle capacity, lb	3200
Optional	none
Rear suspension	beam axle, leaf springs, tube shocks
Rear axle capacity, lb	3500
Optional	none

Additional suspension options . . . . .heavy-duty shocks, heavy duty front springs / shocks

TEST MODEL

Scout Terra Turbo Diesel, 3.73 axle ratio, locko-matic hubs, heavy-duty front springs, AM / FM / stereo radio, emission labels, spare tire lock, spear appliqué, off road 10 x 15 tire / rim package, heavy-duty clutch, fuel tank skidplate, tie-down rails, interior trim package, air conditioning

West Coast list price $12,280

ACCELERATION

Time to speed, sec:

0–30 mph	6.5
0–45 mph	13.0
0–60 mph	23.1
0–70 mph	36.9
Standing start, ¼-mile, sec.	22.9
Speed at end, mph	59

SPEED IN GEARS

High range, 4th (3400 rpm)	81
3rd (4000 rpm)	68
2nd (4000 rpm)	39
1st (4000 rpm)	23
Low range, 4th (4000 rpm)	36
3rd (4000 rpm)	26
2nd (4000 rpm)	15
1st (4000 rpm)	9
Engine rpm @ 55 mph	2300

BRAKE TESTS

Pedal pressure required for ½-g deceleration rate from 60 mph, lb	31
Stopping distance from 60 mph, ft	161
Fade: Percent increase in pedal pressure for 6 stops from 60 mph	45
Overall brake rating	excellent

INTERIOR NOISE

Idle in neutral, dBA	63
Maximum during acceleration	79
At steady 60 mph cruising speed	77

OFF PAVEMENT

Hillclimbing ability	very good
Maneuverability	very good
Turnaround capability	very good
Driver visibility	good
Handling	excellent
Ride	good

ON PAVEMENT

Handling	good
Ride	poor
Driver comfort	poor*
Engine response	poor

*High noise levels make riding any distance in the diesel Terra very tiring

FUEL CONSUMPTION

City / freeway driving, mpg	18.3
Off pavement	11 mpg
Range, city / freeway driving, miles	348
Range, off pavement	209

SCOUTING THE TURBO DIESEL

Turbo! The word conjures up visions of a high-powered, low-slung sports car screaming through backroads, turbocharger whining, the twisty mountain course yielding to the little two-seater—certainly an awesome concept.

Diesel! Another potent concept that produces images of 18-wheelers flashing down the turnpikes, rumbling brute power and the crackle of the CB radio.

It would seem that the mating of two such concepts in one four-wheel drive vehicle would spawn *the* dream vehicle—a sensual, turbocharged sportster with the raw power of the big rig diesel hauler—the best of both worlds. Unfortunately, reality and dreams are seldom the same, and the end product usually is a compromise vehicle. The 1980 International Harvester Turbo Diesel Scout is just such a compromise, a mixture of the potential power of a turbocharged engine and the rugged individuality of the diesel mill.

Upon first entering the Turbo Diesel, you are struck by the ordinariness of the interior; there are no clusters of gauges or lights to indicate that this Scout is anything but a Scout. There are no operating room sensors to tell you how much boost the engine is receiving, how hot the diesel fuel is at combustion; only a kill switch and a glow plug button indicate that this is not your average Scout. It is about as sexy inside as it is on the outside, and that's not sexy at all. Nothing about the Turbo Diesel Scout leads you to believe that this is the offspring of two such dynamic ideas.

Starting and stopping the IH Turbo Diesel requires one of the few throwbacks to the big rig diesels, the "diesel drill." To start, you push in the engine kill switch, turn the key and then depress the glow plug button. At this point, you might as well sit back and relax until the glow plug light comes on—then you can turn the key to start. If you are the impatient type and try to start the engine before the light comes on, the engine will sputter, but won't fire.

When the 101hp Nissan diesel engine awakens, there will be no doubt in your mind that you are seated behind the wheel of a diesel; the rattle associated with these engines will din in your ears and the air will fill with the characteristic scent of diesel. The diesel six idles very roughly for the first few minutes, but cleans itself out quickly once warm to become a crisp-sounding mill. However, the rattle still persists,

The underside of the Turbo Diesel is typical all-business International Harvester. The diesel power is transmitted through a Borg-Warner T-19 4-speed gearbox and 2-speed Model 20 Spicer transfer case.

A good combination of spring rates allows for complete travel on the suspension while crawling across rough areas.

The Nissan 6-cylinder diesel powerplant puts out 101 (flywheel) horsepower. Its injection pump is located on the right side of the vehicle, and the turbo is tucked away beneath the air cleaner on the left.

if at somewhat lesser intensity, and the odor of diesel is ever-present.

Operating the Turbo Diesel is something less than a dramatic experience; nothing about this diesel 4x4 really separates it from any other standard transmissioned Scout. Shifting the 4-speed Scout is smooth, but not slick. The clutch action and gas pedal are similar to other truck driveline operations, but shifting in the lower gears requires a tad more effort than should be necessary, which could make the novice driver feel as if he or she has just taken command of a Peterbilt, not a Scout. A narrow power band on the other

SCOUTING THE TURBO DIESEL

The interior of the turbo diesel-powered Scout is almost identical to gasoline-powered models. The only noticeable difference is the glow plug button on the left of the steering column and the engine stop knob on the right.

Soft sand and mud are no problem for the Goodyear A/T Tracker-equipped Turbo Diesel. Front end weight, however, caused the vehicle to sink noticeably in soft ground.

Cavernous is the best way to describe the cargo area. Actually, the Scout Traveler we tested will hold 103 cubic feet of cargo or sleep two comfortably.

end of the pedal, though, may cause concern for those used to the action of a gasoline-engined vehicle. This narrow band is characteristic of a slow-winding diesel engine, so the time required to produce speed from each progressive shift should not be a cause for concern. Accelerating through the gears produces engine clatter that overwhelms what little turbine whine there might be. In fact, there is little or no perceptible effect of the turbine, though a seasoned hand may feel a slight boost in available power; it does enhance the

mid-range to top-end performance.

Out on the highway, two diesel-related concerns immediately come to mind. First off, where do you find fuel for this beast, and second, who is going to fix it if something goes amiss? We discovered that diesel fuel was readily available, but not at the usual places. To find that elusive No. 2 diesel pump, you have to start thinking like a truck driver, knowing that all manner of trucks, tractors, welders and so on run on the same stuff the Scout does. After a quick tour of the areas where we most often saw those types of vehicles, we had no trouble finding fuel. As for repairs, we were told the local International dealership could handle them, but also were recommended to find several independent garages specializing in diesel engine work.

Cruising the highways, the diesel Scout is not much different than its gasoline-engined brother. All the interior features were common to most Scout vehicles, with functions much the same. The only real differences were the necessity of cranking up the radio a bit louder to cover engine clatter and the ever-present smell of diesel exhaust.

Off the road, the diesel was capable of churning over just about anything that offered decent traction; there was no noticeable difference in lugging power between the gasoline- or diesel-engine Scout. One deficiency in its off-road performance we did not care for at all was the tendency to bog and stall during erratic maneuvers, but this was more a problem with the vehicle, not the engine.

In handling, the extra weight of the diesel engine was noticeable, as the front of the vehicle tended to bottom out easily, and the body lean in cornering was quite pronounced. While the front tires stayed put during side-loading action, the suspension flex gave drivers a feeling of instability.

Overall, the International Harvester Turbo Diesel Scout is a very capable four-wheel drive vehicle that leads us down two separate paths. The first path seeks the practicality of low maintenance and the cheaper fuel that come part and parcel with the diesel engine. But, the second path leads us to want a zippier performance from the turbocharger and less noise and hassles in finding fuel. In the end, the Turbo Diesel Scout is a viable alternative to the gasoline problems currently plaguing the 4x4 market, but driving a compromise vehicle like the Turbo Diesel from place to place on a daily basis definitely takes some getting used to. ●

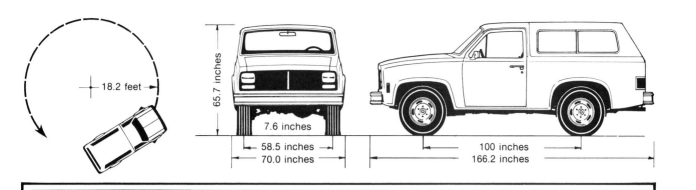

18.2 feet	65.7 inches	7.6 inches		
	58.5 inches	70.0 inches	100 inches	166.2 inches

4-WHEEL & OFF-ROAD / ROAD TEST SPECIFICATIONS
INTERNATIONAL HARVESTER SCOUT TRAVELER TURBO DIESEL

GENERAL:
Vehicle .... IH Scout
Model .... Traveler Turbo Diesel
Base Price $10,378
Options ...... Locking hubs, heavy-duty suspension, power steering, AM/FM stereo, spare tire lock, air conditioning, dual mirrors, exterior group, interior group, sliding quarter-window, luggage rack, folding rear seat.
Price As Tested $13,351

ENGINE:
Type .... 6-cyl. turbocharged inline diesel
Displacement .... 198 cubic inches
Bore & Stroke .... 3.27x3.94 inches
Carburetion .... Mechanical fuel injection
Fuel Requirement .... No. 2 diesel
Fuel Capacity .... 19 gallons
Oil Capacity .... 11 quarts
Radiator Capacity .... 12.5 quarts

TRANSMISSION:
Type .... 4-speed Warner T-19A
Ratios .... First: 4.02:1; Second: 2.41:1; Third: 1.41:1; Fourth: 1.1:1; Reverse: 4.42:1

TRANSFER CASE:
Type .... TC 146 2-speed geardrive
Ratios .... High range: 1.1:1; Low range: 2.62:1

AXLE RATIOS:
Front 3.73
Rear 3.73

TEST RESULTS:
Rear Wheel Horsepower .... 96 hp
Rear Wheel Torque .... N/A
Horsepower To Weight Ratio .... .02 hp per lb.

WEIGHT BALANCE:
Curb Weight .... 4438 lbs.
Front .... 2672 lbs.
Rear .... 1766 lbs.
Advertised GVW .... 6200 lbs.

BODY & FRAME:
Chassis .... Ladder frame
Body .... Cab with detachable fenders
Cargo Area .... Length: 60.8 inches; Width: 54.8 inches; Height: 43 inches

SUSPENSION:
Front .... Multi-leaf with hydraulic shock absorbers
Rear .... Multi-leaf with hydraulic shock absorbers

STEERING:
Type .... Power
Turns Lock-To-Lock 5

BRAKE SYSTEM:
Front .... Power-assist disc
Rear .... Drum
Parking .... Expanding rear

WHEELS:
Type .... White spoke
Size 15x8

TIRES:
Type .... Mud and snow
Size 10-15LT

MILEAGE:
EPA Estimate .... City: 22 mpg; Highway: 24 mpg
Actual .... City: 17 mpg; Highway: 23 mpg

PERFORMANCE:
0-30 .... 12 seconds
0-60 .... 36 seconds

STOPPING DISTANCE:
30-0 .... Pavement: 40 feet
50-0 .... Pavement: 130 feet

SPEEDOMETER CALIBRATION:

Indicated	20	30	40	50	60	70
Actual	21	31	42	52	62	—

OPTIONS:

ITEM	DESCRIPTION/PRICE
Automatic Transmission	N/A
Power Steering	$87
Power Brakes	Std.
Air Conditioning	$607
FM Radio	$167
Engine Performance Package	Std.
CB Radio	N/A
Extra Fuel Tanks (32 gallons)	$185
Locking Hubs	Std.
Posi-Trac/Ltd. Slip	Std.
Skidplates	$67
Rollbar	N/A
Heavy-Duty Suspension	$58
Tire Option (Radial)	$270
Wheel & Tire Combination Option	$505
Exterior Group	$198, $213
Interior Group	$337, $161
Cruise Control	$117
Grille Guard Combination	$144
Winch (8000 lb.)	$585

VEHICLE: 1980 IH Scout Terra Pickup

PRICE —

   BASE: $10,020.00   AS TESTED: $12,516.25

   OPTIONS, TEST CAR: Automatic Locking Front Hubs, Heavy Duty. Springs AM Pushbutton Radio, Off-Road Tire & Trim Package, Custom Interior, Airconditioning, and Storage Box Console.

WARRANTY: 5 years or 100,000 miles on engine

   12 months or 12,000 miles on vehicle

ENGINE

TYPE: Turbo Diesel Six in-line   HEAD: Cast Iron

VALVES: OHV

BORE: 3.27-ins.   STROKE: 3.94-ins.

DISPLACEMENT: 198 CID (3.24 liters)

COMP. RATIO: 22:1

SAE NET HP (RATED): 101 @ 3800 rpm

SAE NET TORQUE (RATED): 175 lbs./ft. @ 2200 rpm

INDUCTION: Turbocharged

EXHAUST: Single

FUEL REQUIRED: Wide cut diesel

ELECTRICAL SYSTEM: 12-Volt

MAX RECOMMENDED RPM: 4150

DRIVETRAIN

CLUTCH: 11-inch angle link, 2000 plate pressure

TRANS TYPE: 4-speed manual syncromesh

RATIOS: 1st/6.32:1   2nd/3.09:1   3rd/1.68:1   4th/1.00:1 REV: 6.96:1

   TRANS CASE REDUCTION: 4H 1..:1   4L 2.62:1

DIFFERENTIAL(S): Dana model 44   L.S.: Optional

STEERING

TYPE: Power

TURNS L TO L STD: 4½   POWER: Standard

TURNING CIRCLE: 38' 10"

BRAKES

TYPE: Dual operating hydraulic with warning lights Disc Front, Drum Rear

DIA. FRONT DISC: 11.75 ins.,   DRUM: 111/32 ins.,   width drum; 2¼ ins.

SWEPT AREA: 226 front sq. ins.   OPT. ASSIST: power

BRAKING — PAVEMENT: Good   DIRT: Good   SAND: Good

CRUISING SPEED: Highway 55+ MPH

ACCELERATION: PAVEMENT: 0-30 5(sec.)   0-45 9 (sec.)   0-55 19 (sec.)

ACCELERATION: LEVEL SAND OR DIRT: 0-20 4 (sec.)   0-30 6.7 (sec.)

   0-40 10.2 (sec.)

PASSING ACCEL: 30-55: 12 Sec.

CHASSIS

FRAME: Steel Box Section

RAIL DEPTH: 4x3x.012

BODY: Separate

FRONT SUSPENSION: Leaf Under Live Axle

REAR SUSPENSION: Lear Under Live Axle

SWAY BARS: N/A

STEERING DAMPENER: N/A

SHOCK ABSORBERS:

   TYPE: Hydraulic Tube   NUMBER: 4

SPRING RATE:

   FRONT: 3200   REAR: 3500

AXLE MAKE: Dana Front Locking Hubs   TYPE: 44

WHEELS STD: 8.00 JJ

   OPTIONAL: Various

TIRES STD: 10-15 Goodyear LT   LOAD CAP: 1760 @ 30 P.S.I. lbs.

   OPTIONAL: Various

GVWR: 6200 lbs. lbs.

DIMENSIONS

WHEEL BASE: 118-ins.

TRACK FR: 48.6 ins.   REAR: 48.6 ins.

GROUND CLEARANCE: 7.6 ins.   LOW POINT: Rear Differential

HEIGHT: 66-ins.

WIDTH: 70-ins. O.A.

LENGTH O.A.: 184.2 ins.

OVERHANG FR: 24 ins.   REAR 42.2 ins.

APPROACH ANGLE: 44 Deg.

DEPARTURE ANGLE: 26 Deg.

ADV WEIGHT: 4117 lbs.

WEIGHT TO H.P.: 40.7 lbs. H.P.

FUEL CAPACITY: 19 gals.   OIL: 11 qts.

PERFORMANCE

FUEL CONSUMPTION: 18.3 MPG Average

NEW TURBO DIESEL SCOUT

Article by Jerry Vonne   Photos by Jim Matthews and Jerry Vonne

The Terra pickup has a six-foot bed and is the only pickup offered in the US with an optional, factory installed turbo- charged diesel engine.

Square headlights accent the front of the 1980 Terra. Measuring in a 7.6 inches, the Terra has ample ground clearance.

Instrumentation is adequate and is in good position for driver viewing. The lack of a boost gauge and/or tach is a real oversight, especially with the turbocharger.

The turbocharged Nissan diesel took to the hills with ease. Excellent fuel mileage plus low upkeep costs and long engine life are important bonuses.

4x4s TESTS

Back in 1976, International Harvester introduced the 3.3-liter (198 cubic inch) six-cylinder Nissan diesel engine to their Scout lineup. The then, relative to gasoline, cheaper fuel costs combined with outstanding mileage, about 19 mpg in our '78 road test, gave reason for the consumer to overlook lackluster street performance. Another factor the diesel has going for it is bullet proof realiability combined with low maintenance and a life span of some 200,000 miles. In fact, for 1980 IH is offering a five year/ 100,000 miles warranty for engine durability and resistance to corrosion. But we're getting ahead of ourselves.

The big news is that IH has added an AiResearch turbocharger to their diesel package this year. However, if you're one of those individuals who equate the word turbocharger with blinding acceleration, then you're in for a disappointment. 6.5 pounds of boost notwithstanding, the Terra turbo is definitely not in the same league with Porsche — hell, it isn't even in the same ball game. To be fair, we must remember IH has asked the little 198 cubic-inch diesel to haul around a vehicle with a curb weight of 4117 pounds. Since the engine develops 101 horses at 3800 rpm that's 40.76 pounds per horse. Not too shabby for 198 cubes.

The first morning we had the Terra we trundled ourselves into the plaid Tartan Blue interior and looked around. We had comfortable bucket seats with a convenient console between them. There's no headliner as such, only a sprayed roof in dull black. The fifteen inch "turbo" steering wheel is leather wrapped and with the tilt steering mechanism it may easily be adapted to a variety of driving styles. In the interests of the macho look, they've even added simulated Allen bolts to hold down the steering wheel. The instruments were more than adequate, including the speedometer with a top speed of 85 mph. These 85 mph speedos have been standard on every '80 model vehicle we've tested thus far, and we suspect it's an EPA ploy to make more palatable the 55 limit. If 85 is tops, then 55 doesn't look so bad on the dial — at least not as bad as it did with 120 mph speedos.

The one thing we can't understand, especially with a turbocharger, is the absence of a tachometer with the four speed manual transmission. For the $2500 extra they charge for the turbo diesel they could have included a tach and/or boost gauge.

Our Terra with Goodyear A-T's had no trouble matching any terrain we put it up against. Neither heavily rutted roads nor streambeds proved to be any problem.

A turbocharged diesel Terra at work during the Baja, we're not surprised it finished. Trackside Photo

On chilly mornings you simply turn on the ignition, depress the glow plug button until the light goes out, (about 20 seconds), and turn the key to start. Your next thought runs something along the line of, "Who the hell drained the crankcase last night?" It clanks, rattles, and in general protests waking up. White smoke billows forth from the tailpipe as if the Sioux Nation were attempting to signal peace with the cavalry. After a minute or so the metal to metal sounds diminish to mere clicking and you're ready to get underway.

The close-ratio four-speed engages first without problem and with a few added rev's you're off. In two-wheel high top speed in first is about 12 miles an hour. The throws to second and third, however, are not so easy when the engine is cold. The gears don't want to engage, especially third. This problem all but disappears when the engine warms up, however, and within a few miles you begin to appreciate the short-throw wide-ratio gear box. With the Terra empty you can take off in second gear, but the engine isn't comfortable doing so and it takes longer to get up to speed. And as with its big brother 18-wheelers, you're advised to snap off the shifts smartly and keep the rev's up to around 2000 rpm where we guess the boost comes on. (Remember no tach and/or boost gauge).

Around town the heavy-duty 11-inch angle-link clutch with a 2200 pound pressure plate is a little hard on the legs, but you get used to it. At one point we became entangled in an infamous Southern California freeway snafu and discovered that the Terra could creep along at about 2 mph in low gear without disengaging the clutch every fifty feet . . . a definite advantage.

For 1980 IH has increased corrosion protection for their 4x4 vehicles. They now use zinc-rich primers and wax heated to 325 degrees is sprayed onto selected non-visible inner body surfaces. Extensive use is also made of galvanized steel. One thing they apparently forgot were the bolts securing the front chrome bumper. During their short little life these bolts have already rusted.

Another interesting feature on this Terra was the gas pedal. It's sort of a poor man's cruise control. Once depressed, almost no effort is required to keep it at its original setting.

There was one aspect of this 1980 Terra we found particularly distressing. The damn fuel gauge is about an eighth of a tank optimistic. We discovered this when the truck came to a sputtering halt on the freeway. Fortunately it was a short hike to the off ramp and a call to the troops at the office had us more diesel fuel and we were on our way again. We're here to tell you the absolute maximum range on the Terra is 375.6 miles, and that we averaged 18.38 mpg city/highway/off road.

And off road is where this truck takes the prizes. What it lacks on the street in the way of performance, it more than makes up for in the dirt. In fact, the IH folks told us that our test vehicle was one of the support trucks used in the Baja 1000 last year. We went to our almost local test area and proceeded to put the Terra through its paces. The one thing you must remember is to keep the rev's up. Lugging this truck in the dirt means absolutely no power. But when you punch the transfer case into 4H with the wide-ratio four-speed transmission you have a low gear ratio of 6.32 to one. And in 4L the first gear ratio is 16.55 to one. That's enough to climb Mount Everest! On our little grade of about 45 degrees the Terra pulled to the top after a running start in 4H without complaint. With a standing start, however, 4L was required. With the engine screaming we climbed the hill at about three mph. You can believe it when we say there isn't much that's going to stop this truck.

The Terra picked its way over bolders and other obstructions with fine agility and even the shocks held up well on rutted trails. The power brakes require a little getting used to, but they worked well enough in the dirt and after fording a stream. We give the transfer case a "C" grade because half the time it worked easily and the other half of the time it was back-up-and-try-again. Same goes for the locking hubs — they were a little sticky. We should point out, however, that the hubs were brand new having been replaced shortly after we picked up the rig. It appeared somebody had run the hubs on the highway in the locked position for some distance and when we picked up the truck they were making some strange noises.

All things considered, the new turbo Terra is a hell of a truck off road. On the street, it's another story. It will get you where you're going, but not in a hurry. The Terra will be a tough sell for the wife, but it's all 4x4 and if we worked off road, we'd buy it in a minute. ●